M·I·L·K

HONEY

~~~~~~~~~~~~~~~ AND

MONEY

Smithsonian Series in Ethnographic Inquiry

Ivan Karp and William L. Merrill, Series Editors

Ethnography as fieldwork, analysis, and literary form is the distinguishing feature of modern anthropology. Guided by the assumption that anthropological theory and ethnography are inextricably linked, this series is devoted to exploring the ethnographic enterprise.

ADVISORY BOARD

Richard Bauman (*Indiana University*), Gerald Berreman (*University of California, Berkeley*), James Boon (*Princeton University*), Stephen Gudeman (*University of Minnesota*), Shirley Lindenbaum (*New School for Social Research*), George Marcus (*Rice University*), David Parkin (*University of London*), Roy Rappaport (*University of Michigan*), Renato Rosaldo (*Stanford University*), Annette Weiner (*New York University*), Norman Whitten (*University of Illinois*), and Eric Wolf (*City University of New York*).

M·I·L·K
HONEY
AND
MONEY

CHANGING CONCEPTS IN RWANDAN HEALING

CHRISTOPHER C. TAYLOR

Smithsonian Institution Press
Washington and London

Editor: Jack Kirshbaum
Designer: Kathleen Sims

Library of Congress Cataloging-in-Publication Data
Taylor, Christopher Charles.
    Milk, honey, and money : changing concepts in
    Rwandan healing / Christopher Charles Taylor.
        p.   cm.—(Smithsonian series in ethnographic
        inquiry)
    Includes bibliographical references.
    ISBN 1-56098-104-0
    1. Folk medicine—Rwanda.   2.   Economic anthro-
    pology—Rwanda.
3. Hutu (African people)—Medicine.   4.   Rwanda—
Economic conditions.
5. Hutu (African people)—Economic conditions.   I. Title.
II. Series.
GN659.R85T39   1992
615.8'82'0967571—dc20   91-12885 CIP

British Library Cataloging-in-Publication data available

Manufactured in the United States of America
96 95 94 93 92   5 4 3 2 1

In Memory of My Father

CONTENTS

A Note on Transcription

I have followed the transcription method used by Irené Jacob in his three-volume abridged version of the Institut National du Recherche Scientifique (INRS) dictionary of Kinyarwanda. Tonality and vowel length are therefore provided for all Rwandan words used in this book that appear in the dictionary. Those few words that do not appear in Jacob's work I have transcribed without indicating vowel length and tonality. Nouns are given with their augmentative and classificatory prefixes. For example, the word for "relative" appears as *umubyéeyi*, which consists of

u-	the augmentative prefix, which reiterates the vowel of the classifier;
-mu-	the classifier, which identifies the word as belonging to one of the ten Kinyarwanda noun classes (in this case, the singular for persons);
-byéeyi	the root, which is often derived from a verb (in this case, it is *kubyáara*, meaning "to engender").

Acknowledgments

From the outset of this project to its completion, I have benefited from the help, suggestions, and assistance of many friends and colleagues. I would especially like to thank Fred Damon, Edie Turner, Roy Wagner, Joe Miller, Emmanuel Habimana, Michelle Wagner, Richard Handler, David Sapir, Chris Crocker, Marcel d'Hertefelt, André Coupez, Telesphore Kayinamura, Marilyn Strathern, Richard Werbner, Jan Vansina, Jack Kirshbaum, Jean Comaroff, John Comaroff, Daniel Wolk, Andrew Apter, Ray Fogelson, Eytan Bercovitch, Mark Nichter, and Doug Feldman. I am also grateful to the people associated with the Université Nationale du Rwanda, the Institut National du Recherche Scientifique, and the Centre Universitaire de Recherches sur la Pharmacopée et la Médecine Traditionelle for facilitating my research in Rwanda.

My fieldwork was made possible by financial support from the Social Science Research Council, the National Science Foundation, the Institute for Intercultural Studies, and the Carter G. Woodson Institute. I was fortunate to have been associated with the Woodson Institute as a predoctoral fellow for two years.

I owe the largest debt to the Rwandan popular healers and their patients, whose names I have changed in the pages that follow. With several of them I transformed slowly from an annoyance to a friend, although with others I probably remained an annoyance. I look forward to the day when we will meet again.

September 1991
University of Alabama at Birmingham

M·I·L·K
HONEY
~~~~~~~~~ AND ~~~~~~~~~
MONEY

Most Rwandans do not live in villages. Instead, they live in dispersed settlements that house a single extended family, like this one in central Rwanda. In part of northern Rwanda, however, Belgian colonial authorities attempted, with some success, to "villagize" the population.

Introduction

Anthropologists who do fieldwork today in non-Western societies almost inevitably find themselves confronted with the problem of transformation. Although there may be a few areas of the globe left completely untouched by colonialism and the world economy, such areas are few and far between. Today's researcher usually has to deal with a field situation more influenced by the cognitive categories of his own society and culture than the classic monographs of his profession would lead him to believe or prepare him for. Instead of "animists," he finds converts to Christianity and Islam. Instead of indigenous handicrafts, he finds Coleman lanterns, Panasonic radios, and hand tools made in China. Instead of clans and lineages, he finds only their vestiges. Furthermore, he often discovers that the anthropological models he has learned in the course of his training have lost their patina as well, revealing the shaky foundation of ahistoricity upon which they were constructed.

My purpose here is to make sense of historical transformation as this is manifest in Rwandan popular medicine. Integrating a historical methodology into the analysis of healing is necessary, because today new forms of treating affliction are being practiced in Rwanda. These new therapies coexist with older modes of therapy, but innovations in popular healing

3

do not simply reflect matters of fad and fashion. They also reflect the profound social and cultural changes that have accompanied Rwanda's increasing involvement in the global economy. Like many other peoples in the developing world, Rwandans are attempting to reconcile the symbols and meanings that once defined their lives with those that derive from world capitalist culture. One privileged locus of this synthetic attempt is the realm of healing. In this study I examine the plight of individuals caught in the clash of two different "socio-logics" (Augé 1984) by paying attention to the symbolic language of sufferers' bodily symptoms and healers' therapeutic interventions. In order to analyze the two systems in which symptom and cure are embedded, I must reconstruct one system from its vestiges and describe the other from patterns whose outlines are not yet completely clear.

Models that deal with the problem of transformation are not lacking in anthropology. Henry Maine portrayed change as a transition from social relations based on "status" to relations based on "contract" (Maine 1874); Emile Durkheim saw it as a shift from "mechanical" to "organic solidarity" (1902); and Louis Dumont described change as the passage from "holism" and "hierarchy" to "individualism" and "egalitarianism" (1965). Whereas these writers' works have all served as more or less conscious models for the present study, I am not dealing with institutions, social groups, nor types of authority as much as with problems that are situated within the minds and bodies of individual social actors. For this reason I employ an analytical approach that can move gracefully between the "micro" level of the individual and the "macro" level of world trends. The most fundamental change that I perceive as influencing the cognition of the self and body in misfortune is a social, individual, and historical one. I describe this change, extrapolating from Chris Gregory (1982), as the impingement of "commodity logic" upon "gift logic."

FROM GIFTS TO COMMODITIES

In employing this distinction, I contrast two ideal types of political economy. In a gift economy persons and things are perceived as relatively inseparable; in a commodity economy persons and things are divisible. People in a gift economy are linked by ties of reciprocal dependence as they exchange relatively inalienable things. People in a commodity economy, however, are in a state of mutual independence in which the transactors exchange alienable things, the most alienable of which is money (Gregory 1982, 120).

Although Rwanda is coming under the influence of world capitalist culture, the transition is not complete. Commodity notions take their place alongside persisting notions of the gift, which are evident in core Rwandan concepts. For example, the term for "man" in Kinyarwanda, *umugabo*, is derived from the verb *kugaba*, which means "to give" (Jacob 1984, 308).[1] Gift giving and reciprocity are central to the Rwandan ideal of manhood. *Ubugabo*, or "manliness," is primarily a social quality, "generosity," though it is more frequently translated as "virility" or "courage," connotations that the term encompasses but to which it is not limited. It is thus justified to talk about a Rwandan gift economy and to investigate what becomes of concepts concerning the body when the commodity begins to become the society's master trope.

Gregory's discussion of gift economies builds upon the theoretical insights of Karl Marx (1867), Marcel Mauss (1925), and Claude Lévi-Strauss (1947). For our purposes it has the advantage of situating production and exchange within an encompassing system of collective representations. To Mauss the gift combines what Westerners would call religious, political, and economic representations (1925, 1). The gift binds transactors in social relations that obligate the participants to give, to receive, and to reciprocate. These ties are expected to endure and are not directly motivated by the desire for profit, although utilitarian trade between persons or groups is often a concomitant of gift relations (71). Most important, the gift is a repository of social meaning; it embodies "spiritual power" (8–10). This power connects the thing given to its giver and receiver, and it could be construed as representative of non-alienated human productive activity, for each hand the gift passes through augments and ramifies its power. Persons united by gift relations embody aspects of each other: Mauss observes that "to give something is to give a part of oneself" (10); to receive something is to incorporate aspects of the other within the self.

This latter aspect is manifest in Rwandan ideas related to food. For example, after the period of seclusion (*ikilili*) that follows the birth of a new child, people bring food and other gifts to the new mother. The wife's parents bring a quantity of sorghum porridge (*igikoma*). Since this beverage is thought to stimulate the production of breast milk, the wife's parents can be said to aid their daughter's lactation through their gift. Furthermore, they indirectly participate in the development of the baby's body, for maternal milk is its principal source of sustenance. This custom is indicative of what Gregory finds to be a central characteristic of gift economies: an emphasis on consumption.

Reproducing social relations in a gift economy is contingent upon control over the means of consumption; people produce each other through the gift of things that they consume. Gregory, following Marx, refers to this process as "consumptive production" (1982, 71, 101). In a gift economy, food is both substance and symbol, nourishment as well as a meaningful gift. It is thus not surprising to find food employed as a central symbol in issues related to social and biological reproduction. In Rwanda, liquid foods are especially privileged symbolic vehicles. Myths that explain the origin of the social hierarchy of the Tutsi, Hutu, and Twa ethnic groups focus upon milk (see chapter 1). Rwandan customs related to sexuality and reproduction also involve liquid aliments as important symbols (see chapter 3). Although the symbolic elaboration of consumption is not entirely absent in a commodity economy, it is much less pronounced.

Commodities differ from gifts in other respects. As Marx emphasizes, the commodity is an alienable object, that is, separable from its producer and its exchanger (1867). Once it is bought or sold, no aspect of its producer clings to it as a "spiritual power," no social bond necessarily results from its role in exchange (178–79). Those who buy or sell commodities enter the transaction independently of one another and they exit the transaction in the same social state. Moreover, commodities seem to operate independently of human agency, since their exchange does not depend on the perpetuation of personalized relations. The apparent activity of commodities independent of human agency gives them the aspect of animate capacity. In speaking about commodities as if they were imbued with animate powers, we "fetishize" them.[2] Whereas gifts are perceived as linked to specific human agents, commodities are not. Visible hands manipulate gifts; an "invisible hand" (A. Smith 1776)— the market—manipulates money and commodities.

But whereas market exchange conceals the nature of social relations that underlie commodity production (Marx 1867, 168), gift exchange makes social relations evident. Every gift makes a statement about the giver and the receiver. Gifts are qualitatively and hierarchically differentiated; commodities are not. In Rwanda, the gift of a cow is more significant than the gift of alcoholic beverages, which in turn are more significant than the gift of solid foodstuffs. Commodities do not follow this logic; instead, they are qualitatively identical in the sense that all are the products of human labor. Each differs, however, in just how much labor it represents. Money provides the basis whereby this difference can be marked. Commodities are not ranked according to an exchange order, but according to their exchange values. The relation among commodities appears as a relation among material objects; the fact that commodity production and exchange are predicated upon a relation among social classes is obscured (169).

In a gift economy, things are perceived as connected to, and take on the properties of, the people who exchange them. Gift exchange establishes a social connection that is often hierarchical in nature. The giver of a gift may become superior to the receiver, unless the latter reciprocates with a more significant gift (Mauss 1925, 72). In some instances, as in Rwanda, marked hierarchical inequality may result from gift giving. Mauss recognized this dual nature of gifts, for while he underlines the integrative function of the gift, he also shows that the gift may engender social asymmetry.

One example of an asymmetrical gift relation in precolonial and colonial Rwanda was *ubuhake* (abolished in 1954; see chapter 2). In *ubuhake,* a Tutsi cattle patron (*umushéebuja*) gave a cow to a Hutu client (*umugarágu*) in exchange for prestations of beer, agricultural goods, occasional labor, and loyalty in warfare (Maquet 1954). The Tutsi patron protected his Hutu client, usually from the exactions of other Tutsi. The client possessed usufruct rights in the cow's milk and its male offspring, but the female offspring of the cow had to be returned to the Tutsi patron. In central Rwanda, the king was linked to important Tutsi vassals through *ubuhake,* they in turn to other, less important Tutsi, and so on down to Hutu cultivators. While the means of consuming cattle products moved downward in this system, the means of reproducing cattle moved upward. Before the arrival of Europeans, *ubuhake* was most prevalent in central Rwanda. In other parts of Rwanda, alternative gift arrangements existed between pastoralists and agriculturalists, which were often less one-sided (cf. Newbury 1988).

Despite frequent asymmetry, the accumulation of wealth for its own sake is deemphasized in a gift economy. Instead, wealth tends to be transformed into social relations between persons and groups through its conversion into dependents—wives, clients, and children. Ascendancy takes the form of "personal domination" (Barnett and Silverman 1979, 55), a relation of indebtedness such as that of Hutu clients to Tutsi patrons.

Overall, debt is positive in a gift economy in that it is a source of social cohesion. Debts rarely revert to "zero" since indebtedness between exchange partners is seldom fully acquitted. In many instances, it is impossible to repay the original gift in full, even though exchange continues between the two partners. In such a case the receiver is subordinated for life. There is no necessary emphasis on continuity in a commodity economy. On the contrary, it is characterized by the appearance of discontinuity among apparently isolated acts of production, exchange, and consumption. Debt does not have the same social significance as it does in a gift economy, where it implies social relation that is expected to endure. In a commodity economy, one should acquit one's debts according to notions of mathematical equivalence.

Gift economies are characterized by notions and practices of reciprocity and redistribution. Ideally, persons and things are exchanged in relatively continuous patterns. In Rwanda, this ideal of continuity is expressed through the exchange of liquid aliments (and bodily fluids). As we shall see in chapters 3–5, such liquids both embody and represent the quality of continuity; they are "symbols that stand for themselves" (Wagner 1986). For example, the Kinyarwanda verb used politely for "to eat," *gufuungura*, otherwise means "to dilute a drink so that more people may partake of it" (A. Coupez and S. Bizimana, pers. comm.; Jacob 1984, 301). Eating solid food, in other words, is seen as a modest substitute for the commensality and redistribution associated with drinking (see Appendix B).

Finally, in a commodity economy the notion of private property is developed to a higher degree than in a gift economy. It is extended to human labor, which is treated as an alienable commodity and exchanged for a wage. People act in exchange not so much according to the dictates of kinship or patronage, but as independent transactors seeking to maximize their utility.[3] Rather than the "personal domination" of the gift economy, commodity economies are characterized by "abstracted domination" (Barnett and Silverman 1979, 42–55), which is based on attributes separable from the person, and whose most common form is class domination. This abstracted domination, moreover, depends upon private property of a particular sort: that which concerns the means of production.

These two different "socio-logics" are opposing poles of a spectrum. In actual social life and depending upon the context, people's behavior may oscillate between the poles. Furthermore, commodities can often be changed into gifts, and gifts may sometimes be converted into commodities.

The awareness that there exists a spectrum of possibilities between the gift and the commodity has led some authors to question the received wisdom concerning the distinction. Ian Morris (1986) criticizes Gregory's evolutionist bias in correlating gift economies with simple clan-based societies. Morris shows that the concept of gift economy can also be applied to complex class-based states, such as archaic Greece. Furthermore, he demonstrates that gift relations can engender and reinforce hierarchy—a possibility that Mauss was quite aware of, but which Gregory tends to deemphasize.

A more fundamental criticism has been raised by J. Comaroff and J. L. Comaroff (1990), who, following Arjun Appadurai (1986), maintain that the gift commodity opposition is misleading. Among the Tswana, cattle were used both in the highest spheres of gift exchange and in ways that resembled money, the most archetypal commodity. However, although these authors dispute the validity of such dichotomies as use value/exchange value and gift-commodity, some of their own analytical categories are dichotomous. When they distinguish between a "moral economy of persons" and a "material economy of things" (J. Comaroff & J. L. Comaroff, 195), they merely substitute one dichotomy for another. Furthermore, their ethnographic evidence shows that the Tswana today see the ownership of livestock as a way of staving off the anomie of the cash and commodity world. Clearly the Tswana perceive something akin to the gift/commodity distinction, even though they use cattle in both types of transaction. The authors' major point is well taken; one should not insist upon an unbridgeable gulf between gifts and commodities. Still, one should also be aware that the primary advantage of the distinction lies in its ability to describe difference in a way that approximates indigenous discrimination.

THE "FLOW/BLOCKAGE" DIALECTIC IN RWANDAN SYMBOLIC THOUGHT

Rwandan "gift logic" possesses culturally specific modalities of operation and expression. Fluid substances are the raw materials from which a "science of the concrete" embodying this logic is edified (Lévi-Strauss 1962). These substances are of interest for their movement; fluids may circulate in an orderly fashion or they may be excessive or insufficient. In the simplest form of expression, substances are perceived to operate according to a dialectic of "flow" versus "blockage." As I will show in chapter 1, this dialectic was dramatized in precolonial myth and ritual, and it was manifest in notions concerning the body and fertility. Fluid imagery suffuses the rituals of divine kingship once performed by the Rwandan king (*umwaámi*) and his ritual specialists (*abíiru*). Today the flow/blockage dialectic continues to serve as an organizing metaphor in various forms of Rwandan popular therapy, though it is never explicitly verbalized by Rwandans themselves. Quite recently, new therapies have arisen that depart from the flow/blockage model.

The assertion that this implicit structure is part of Rwandan indigenous concepts is supported by linguistic evidence. The noun for a "flow" in Kinyarwanda, *isibo*, designates (1) a group of cattle rushing toward a watering trough, a flow of cattle; (2) (in war poetry) a flow of living beings, a swarming multitude; and (3) force, élan, flight, impetuosity, as in *guca isibo* (especially when speaking of the *intoóre* [Tutsi warriors] dances), which literally means "to cut the flow," that is, to jump very high while dancing (Jacob 1985, 3:169). But the verb from which *isibo* is derived, *gusiba*, means (1) to plug, to fill up, to obstruct, to fill a hollow or empty space; (2) (neologism) to clean, to erase; (3) to decimate, to eliminate, to make something disappear; (4) to hoe the earth without taking care to remove weeds; (5) to reduce an adversary to silence by irrefutable argument; (6) (when speaking of mammary glands) to be obstructed; and (7) (when speaking of a path) to become covered over with plants (167). Other usages include *gusiba inkarú*, to do grave harm to someone; and *gusiba inzira* (literally, "to block the path"), to lose one's unmarried daughter through death.

Notice, then, that the noun *isibo* and the verb *gusiba* encompass two apparently contradictory meanings: the idea of living beings in movement and the idea of blockage and loss. A single verbal concept in Kinyarwanda thus encapsulates the image of "flow" and its paradigmatic opposite, "blockage." Furthermore, in this second instance, the notion of "blockage" is related to the idea of doing harm to someone (as in *gusiba inkarú*) as well as to the idea of losing one's unmarried daughter (as in *gusiba inzira*). In the phrase *gusiba inzira*, an analogy is drawn between "blocking a path" and "losing one's daughter." In effect, when one loses a daughter, death blocks the "path" between one's own family and that of another family; that is, the alliance relation, which could have resulted from the gift of one's daughter to another man, is preemptively extinguished. *Gusiba inkarú* suggests an analogy between the action of blocking and the action of doing serious harm to someone, an idea that comes very close to Rwandan notions of witchcraft and sorcery (as we shall see in subsequent chapters.)

This apparent antinomy between the fields of meaning denoted and connoted in the words *isibo* and *gusiba* might appear illogical to someone situated outside the context of Rwandan social action. Within this context, the contradiction is nothing less than an ineluctable corollary to the workings of social life itself, its internal dialectic. Just as social relations can "flow" or be "blocked," just as the sky can yield its fertilizing liquid in the right measure or not, so the body can be "open" and mobile in life or "closed" and static in death. The words *isibo* and *gusiba* exemplify the recognition that one state implies the other.

In the domain of political economy, this dialectic receives expression in the alternatives of relatively continuous and "open" exchange (not confined to a small group) and interrupted, aborted, or relatively "closed-circuit" exchange (restricted to a small group). "Flow" implies openness and relative continuity; "blockage" implies interruption or closure. Ordinarily, the option of flow takes social precedence over blockage; that is, flow is positively valued, and blockage is considered negative. People are encouraged to give, receive, and reciprocate in almost fluid fashion. This ideal receives concrete expression in the form of liquid gifts, such as milk, honey, the various types of Rwandan beer, and sorghum porridge, all of which are imbued with particular significance. They are important consumption items and gifts in hospitality and matrimonial transactions, but they also embody the ideal of motility in reciprocal relations (see chapter 3).

Similar symbolic structures based on the opposition of "open" and "closed" have been noted among other central African Bantu peoples by Victor Turner (1967), Luc de Heusch (1972), Renaat Devisch (1984), and Wauthier de Mahieu (1985). De Heusch demonstrates the importance of this opposition in the mythical conceptualization of Luba and Lunda kingship. He concludes that kingly legitimacy derives in part from the ability to control the closure of bodily and natural apertures (de Heusch 1972, 33–36). De Mahieu, basing his conclusions on firsthand observation, shows that the "open/closed" dialectic is the most fundamental opposition in the ritual practices associated with male circumcision among the Komo of Zaire (1985, 132). Devisch, also from fieldwork evidence, shows that the Yaka of Zaire use the opposition of "open" and "closed" to conceptualize female fertility problems and that metaphors involving terrestrial waters sometimes participate in these symbolic conceptualizations (1972, 26). De Mahieu's observations bear somewhat closer resemblance to my own concerning Rwanda when he shows that substance movement is also an important Komo concern: an obstructed penis is an infertile one, a closed hunting trap is an unproductive one (1985, 49, 133).

Where my observations differ from those of de Heusch, Devisch, and de Mahieu is in placing primary emphasis on the substances that pass through points of opening and secondary emphasis on the apertures themselves. Reminiscent of Victor Turner (1967, 61–66), I am more concerned with the "rivers" of life than with the narrows through which they pass. By taking this tack, I hope to achieve a dynamic view of Rwandan symbolic process and simultaneously to avert the algebraic hermeticism of some structuralist studies and the cavalier disregard for underlying logic shown by some processual studies.

Perhaps the fluid substance of most concern in early Rwanda was rain. It was the Rwandan king's responsibility to control rainfall ritually and to protect the kingdom from drought or inundation (see chapter 1). Then, as now, the Rwandan year consisted of two rainy seasons and two dry seasons, but these tended to be irregular. Rwandan agriculture was perennially at the mercy of occasional drought, flooding, and rains that arrived at the wrong time.

Another of the king's responsibilities was to eliminate beings who lacked the capacity to "flow." Two such persons were girls who had reached childbearing age and lacked breasts (impenébeere) and girls who had reached childbearing age and had not yet menstruated (impa) (d'Hertefelt and Coupez 1964, 286). In both cases, these girls were put to death for the inability to produce fertility fluid: milk or blood. Such girls, "blocked" in their capacity to reproduce, were thought to be potential sources of misfortune to the entire kingdom, for their aridity could cause the sky to refuse to yield its fertilizing rain. The ideal of "flow" was thus an important metaphor in precolonial Rwandan notions of production and reproduction.

Today the dialectic of flow/blockage persists in some realms of Rwandan symbolic thought. Rwandan abarozi (witches or poisoners) subvert the flow process. They are people who breach the morality of gift logic or who divert production, exchange, and fertility. Moreover, what they do to social relations is analogous to what they do to their victims' bodies. Rwandan witches are "blocking beings" who make women sterile and men impotent by stopping their flow of generative fluids. Or, they are vampirish, anthropophagic beings who parasitically suck away the vital fluids of others. There are thus two basic expressions to pathology in this model: "blocked flow" and "hemorrhagic flow."

COMMODITY LOGIC AND FLOW

I maintain that commodification alters the relationship between flow and blockage. In order to accumulate commodity wealth, one must block certain avenues of gift exchange, in particular, those avenues that do not bring personal profit. Where gift logic prevails, blockage is ordinarily perceived as socially negative; where commodity logic prevails, blockage is an almost inevitable corollary to the imperative of retaining one's capital. In many respects the two systems are contradictory. Often, what is positive in one system is negative in the other; the commodity system's maximizing individualist is the gift system's witch.

Nevertheless, many societies incorporate aspects of both gift logic and commodity logic to varying degrees. One cannot say that commodity logic characterizes all production and exchange in industrialized societies. Some studies have shown the significant degree to which gifts remain important mediators of social relations in such societies (see, e.g., T. Caplow 1982, 225–45). In Western societies, however, conflict between gift logic and commodity logic is no longer problematic. It could be argued, though, that during the witchcraft craze of the sixteenth and seventeenth centuries—a period that coincides with the efflorescence of capitalism in Europe (Wallerstein 1976)—this conflict was indeed a problem. In peasant societies today conflict between precolonial ideology and capitalist ideology remains problematic (cf. Taussig 1977, 1980a). As the commodification of peasant economies has proceeded with the progressive absorption of postcolonial states into the world economy, the tension between gift logic and commodity logic has been exacerbated.

With both gifts and commodities present in a society, social actors often must clearly discern when gift logic or commodity logic is operative. People are placed in ambivalent situations where they may offend others who are not relating according to the same logic. For example, if a

Rwandan has brewed beer in order to sell it, he cannot allow relatives, friends, and neighbors to drink it as a gift. Without risking impoverishment, salaried Rwandans cannot feed, shelter, and clothe every relative who shows up on their doorstep. In refusing hospitality to those who appeal to gift logic, however, a Rwandan runs the risk of being considered ungenerous or, worse, of being considered a witch. These are simple examples, but they reflect the dilemma of having to choose between gift logic and commodity logic. Making this selection often entails either jeopardizing a social relationship, because one has failed to heed reciprocity notions, or losing money, because one has heeded them. Being unable to choose, however, is probably the worst predicament of all, for it means that the dilemma is never resolved either in the mind of the individual or in his or her social conduct. Unresolved conflicts of this sort can lead to personal crisis and to illness.

In Rwanda, where the process of commodification has altered peasant production patterns, patterns of consumption, land use, land distribution (cf. Freedman 1979), and social stratification (cf. Sylvestre 1974; Freedman 1979), these changes have made themselves felt in therapeutic practices. I contend that just as there are two basic models of production and exchange operative in Rwanda, so there are two underlying models for social relations reflected in the healing context. These two models have collided. It is no longer possible to comprehend Rwanda and the malaise of sufferers who frequent popular healers uniquely through the lens of an ahistorical model.

RWANDAN SOCIAL ORGANIZATION

In delving into Rwandan history, we find a society that consisted of an integrated polity (smaller in area than present-day Rwanda) composed of three ethnic groups: the Tutsi, the Hutu, and the Twa. Although the Tutsi are said to have been the region's most recent immigrants, they came to dominate the other two groups. A small Tutsi kingdom emerged and then slowly expanded to become Rwanda proper.[4] It is probable, however, that Hutu kingdoms existed before the Tutsi one (d'Hertefelt 1971, 32). Some scholars believe that Tutsi emigrated to Rwanda from Ethiopia and Somalia, bringing large herds of long-horned Ankole cattle with them. Hutu, whose major subsistence activity was cultivation, already possessed short-horned cattle in small numbers. Eventually, all three groups came to speak a single Bantu language, Kinyarwanda, although there were regional and ethnic variations. The Twa, whose physical characteristics suggest relatedness to central African short-statured forest dwellers, originally practiced hunting and gathering; today they constitute 1 percent or less of the total population, in comparison to Hutu, 85 percent, and Tutsi, about 15 percent. Twa occupation of Rwanda predates both that of Hutu and Tutsi, coinciding with a time when Rwanda was largely forest.

As early ironworkers and agriculturalists cut away the forests (cf. Van Noten and Raymaekers 1988), many Twa began to specialize in pottery making; others became entertainers, executioners, subchiefs, and police for powerful Tutsi cattle lords and the Rwandan king (*umwaámi*). About 1900 central Rwandan society was a tripartite hierarchy with the Tutsi at the top, the Hutu in the middle, and the Twa at the bottom (Vansina 1962). Northern Rwanda was not characterized by this hierarchy. Each group in central Rwanda tended to be economically specialized and endogamous, traits that have led some authors to consider them as quasi castes (cf. de Heusch 1966). In 1960, after decades of Western influence, the Hutu revolted and overturned Tutsi domination. The position of the Twa did not change appreciably (Kagabo and Mudandagizi 1974).

Rwandans were once divided into separate clans (*ubwóoko, amóoko*) of Hutu and Tutsi origin (cf. d'Hertefelt 1971), but eventually these groups amalgamated into fifteen interethnic clans (cf. D. Newbury 1981 for comments on this process). Clanic social functions were extremely limited, however, and may have concerned matrimonial prohibitions alone, rather than group identity (de Heusch 1966). Today many urban and even some rural Rwandans, particularly in the south, claim not to know their clanic affiliation.

Three of Rwanda's fifteen clans, the Zigaba, the Gesera, and the Singa, were termed *abasaangwabutaka* ("those who were found upon the earth"). These autochthonous, originally Hutu, clans had a special relation to the earth (d'Hertefelt 1971, 45). Whereas *abasaangwabutaka* could directly contact the earth without risk of ritual pollution, this action was believed dangerous for nonautochthones (d'Hertefelt 1971, 5). *Abasaangwabutaka* maintained a ceremonial relationship, *ubuse*, with other Rwandan clans. When other Rwandans wished to establish a dwelling, bury their dead, or recommence agricultural activity after mourning (activities of transition involving the earth), the *abasaangwabutaka* accomplished the necessary ritual actions for their *abase* (those

Although the subsistence activities of the Tutsi and Hutu do not differ appreciably today, most Twa remain potters. Here a Twa potter stands beside several unfinished pots that he, his wife, and his daughters have formed. These pots, fashioned without a wheel, are ready to be fired. In 1984, a finished pot sold for the Rwandan equivalent of about fifty U.S. cents.

to whom they were linked through the *ubuse* relation). *Abasaangwabutaka* also maintained relations of easy familiarity and cooperation ("joking relations") with their *abase*.

Rwandan clans did not unite socially or economically. The *umuryaango*, a patrilineal segment consisting of all the descendants of a man for some six generations, constitutes something closer to the anthropological idea of a "corporate group." Today this unit continues to function. The oldest or most influential male in the *umuryaango*, the *umutware w'umuryaango*, presides over decisions affecting the *umuryaango* as a whole, including land distribution. The *umuryaango* retains importance in "traditional" religious practices (ancestor propitiation, Nyabingi ceremonial activities in the north, and *kubaandwa* in the south), in matrimonial transactions, and in regulating disputes over land inheritance. Its significance, however, appears to be waning in favor of bureaucratic administrative structures erected during the colonial era. The smallest named patrilineal segment within an *umuryaango* is called *inzu*, or "house," which consists of all the descendants of a man for three generations. Sometimes, though, *inzu* is simply used to mean "household."

Land in rural Rwanda is usually bestowed through patrilineal links, but on occasion a man may inherit land from matrilateral kin. Inheritance is called *umunaáni* ("eight"). A man divides his belongings and land among his male children or tries to find land for them. Occasionally a woman, especially one who remains unmarried or returns home after divorce, may acquire land from her father. Some lands belong to the *umuryaango* as a whole and are exploited for the common benefit of it or are later allocated as the *umuryaango* sees fit. Land is scarce in Rwanda and many areas of the countryside are overexploited. Pasture lands have tended to disappear, often being replaced by "paysannats"—newly established portions of arable land where land-poor peasants from various parts of Rwanda have been encouraged to settle and begin cultivation. Despite the diminution of pasture land, cattle remain important both economically and as a sign of status; they graze where they can. No longer do Tutsi own more cattle than Hutu; today members of both ethnic groups cultivate the land and own cattle when possible. Principal subsistence crops include sorghum, bananas, beans, sweet potatoes, potatoes, manioc, maize, and peas. Livestock includes cattle, sheep, goats, and sometimes pigs. Cash cropping of coffee and tea is more prevalent in central and southern Rwanda because of its earlier introduction there and more favorable growing conditions.

Cash cropping, wage labor, and biomedicine—all core artifacts of Western commodity culture—have had an effect upon the way sickness is experienced in Rwanda today. Dovetailing with this shift in political economy, religious changes have taken place as well. Rwanda has undergone an intensive process of missionization. Today close to 50 percent of Rwanda's population has received Catholic baptism (Maindron 1984, 22). In addition, there are numerous Protestant sects, including Episcopalians, Seventh-day Adventists, Methodists, Baptists, and Pentecostals,

Close to 100 percent of Rwanda's arable land is already under cultivation. Most of the land resembles the hilly topography shown here, although often the slopes that Rwandans must farm are even more steep.

who have been successful in gaining sizable followings. Missionaries have altered the character of Rwandan spiritual life, but they have also changed the character of Rwandan temporal life (see chapter 2).

METHOD OF ANALYSIS AND PRESENTATION

In order to integrate individual, social, and historical dimensions in this study, I follow the methodological approach advocated by Marc Augé (1984, 57). He proposes the consideration of three interrelated logical domains: (1) the logic of differences, that is, the equivalencies, oppositions, analogies, and homologies that characterize symbolic phenomena and that constitute their intellectual armature; (2) the logic of references, that is, the relation between the oppositions, etc., of level 1 and the empirically observable social order; and (3) the logic of events, that is, the relations of sense that obtain between the first two levels and that are subject to historical forces. Augé's methodological schema has the advantage of incorporating a historical perspective into the analysis of misfortune. It means that we need to consider the internal logic of the symbolic system mobilized by social actors in any illness occurrence, the conflicts in which the sufferer and significant others are embroiled, and the historical circumstances in which the symbolism and the social conflicts are embedded.

This method is applicable to Rwanda, for the particularistic actions of individual sufferers have been conditioned by the symbolic patterns of the past, even though the society has been changing rapidly since 1900. Rwandan history has been characterized by major transformations: the transition from a polity based on the absolute powers of a divine king to a modern nation headed by a military government and a single political party; the transformation of a quasi-feudal political structure, where the cattle-owning Tutsi dominated the agricultural Hutu majority and the aboriginal Twa, into a modern bureaucratic nation-state that espouses egalitarianism and the values of economic development.

In other sub-Saharan ethnographic areas, the general problem of changing world view in response to incorporation has been discussed in relation to religious innovation. New religions of Christian inspiration have sprung up in virtually all parts of missionized postcolonial Africa (cf. Jules-Rosette 1979). These new religions have had to come to grips with a number of problems, including changing concepts of misfortune, changing views of the individual in relation to society, and acceptance or rejection of the postcolonial social and economic order. In most of these movements, attempts have been made to redefine the nature and causation of misfortune. New religions have proven to be especially fertile arenas in which people attempt to synthesize old concepts and new ones. Moreover, these religions demonstrate that Africans have responded to the challenge of incorporation in a variety of ways (cf. Fabian 1971; Augé 1975; Walker 1979; Kileff and Kileff 1979; van Binsbergen 1979; Beidelman 1982; MacGaffey 1983; Comaroff 1985). In some cases new religions have tended to affirm the postcolonial economic and social order (cf. Augé 1975; Walker 1979); in other cases they have challenged it (cf. van Binsbergen 1979; Comaroff 1985).

In Rwanda aspects of the clash between older and newer modes of conceptualization have surfaced in popular healing. In order to demonstrate that Rwandan views of the self and body have transformed, I must convey some idea of what these views were before the influence of Western commodity culture. Although there is no Rwandan material of precolonial origin that deals specifically with the self and body, in chapter 1

I draw inferences from another source. Virtually the only window of access into precolonial Rwandan symbolic forms are the rituals once performed by the divine king, *umwaámi,* and his college of ritual specialists, *abíiru.* The texts of these rituals were transmitted orally from one generation of *abíru* to another, with each ritualist memorizing portions of text. Periodically, the king asked a ritualist to recite his allotted portion. If he faltered, he might be subject to execution. Kept secret from Europeans until the 1960s, the texts of the rituals were first transcribed in the 1940s and 1950s by Alexis Kagame, a Rwandan priest (cf. 1947). Shortly after a referendum in 1961 brought an end to the monarchy in Rwanda, the texts found their way to Marcel d'Hertefelt. He and André Coupez translated the texts into French, added crucial linguistic and ethnographic clarifications, and published them in *La royauté sacrée de l'ancien Rwanda* (1964). These rituals, as well as legends and myths taken from other sources, provide the basis for chapter 1. From these sources I attempt to show the importance of flow/blockage symbolism in precolonial Rwanda.

Although the forces associated with colonialism and world capitalism have operated in Rwanda as in other parts of sub-Saharan Africa, new religions have not developed to any appreciable extent. In chapter 2, I show that the reason for the absence of syncretism in Rwanda has to do with the especially privileged position that the Catholic Church has been able to maintain. Chapter 2 examines the profound influence of the Rwandan Catholic Church upon the country's political and economic evolution. It also illustrates that Church influence varied between northern and southern Rwanda. The most fervent and long-lived resistance to missionization and colonialism took place in northern Rwanda and was spearheaded by leaders of the Nyabingi cult. The chapter ends with an assessment of "new religions" in other sub-Saharan areas and their experimentation with different perceptions of the self and body.

Whereas the second chapter focuses on "macro" forces emanating from colonialism and world capitalism—"evenemential history" according to Sahlins' (1985) paraphrase of Lévi-Strauss—in chapter 3, I redirect my attention to "micro" phenomena and to the issue of structure as this is manifest in present-day Rwandan healing practices. Using observations gathered through conversations with healers and patients during twenty-one months of fieldwork in Rwanda, I focus attention upon a popular therapy practiced by healers in the northern Rwandan commune of Butaro. Considered something of an enclave by central Rwandans, Butaro is characterized by its sociocultural conservatism, its predominantly

Hutu population, and the continued activity of the Nyabingi cult. Even though Butaro was never well integrated into the precolonial Rwandan polity, it is probably the area where the representations discussed in chapter 1 have been the most well preserved. Healers here commonly rely on a technique of witchcraft detection termed *kuraguza amaheémbe* (to divine with horns). Illness is often seen as a perturbation in the movement of one or more bodily humors, a movement whose cause comes from outside the self—from witches and spirits. Butaro healers attempt to identify the person(s) within one's social nexus who is responsible for one's misfortune, and then they neutralize the spell, either by fortifying the patient or by counter-aggressing the witch.

In chapter 4, I examine the case of two women from central Rwanda afflicted with spirit possession illnesses. This case is of interest because it demonstrates the multiple levels at which the older metaphors of Rwandan culture interact with those of today. First of all, the two female patients sought treatment at a new kind of healing establishment in Rwanda, one that has all the trappings of a biomedical dispensary, but where the professional staff consists of popular healers, each with his or her own consulting room. Until quite recently, the head of the dispensary was a Rwandan Catholic priest who spoke excellent French and was schooled in the oral traditions of popular Rwandan healing. Whereas most of the males involved in this case participated in the commodity economy—either through small-scale entrepreneurship or wage labor—all of the women were more directly involved in the rural economy of domestic production. Finally, the case is of interest for its contrast with the predominantly accusatory mode of the northern Rwanda healers; the therapy here combined aspects of both confession and accusation.

Chapter 5 is a discussion of the practices of healers who work in southern Rwanda. Here the symbolism of flow/blockage is also present, although in certain instances, the imagery is less pronounced than in northern Rwanda. Central and southern Rwanda were touched by colonialism and missionization at an earlier date than northern Rwanda and they have been more profoundly affected by these forces. Today people in these regions participate more extensively in the cash economy, and they are more likely to be practicing Christians. In regard to healing techniques, the popular therapies in southern Rwanda often integrate aspects of both confession and accusation.

One southern Rwandan popular therapy that is exclusively confessional is *Nanga y'ivuza*. In chapter 6, I examine the healer and his method. In this therapy, flow/blockage imagery differs from that seen in the more conservative techniques. Furthermore, the healer is an unabashed apologist of the commodity ethic. He is an ardent defender of progress, individual enterprise, and personal independence. Besides treating patients, he gains his livelihood from various small business affairs and from the raising of cash crops.

By employing an interpretive approach that integrates a structural view of symbolism with a politico-economic view of history, I attempt to make sense of particular instances of sickness and social conflict against the background of changing Rwandan society. I rely heavily on the case history method of exposition and attempt to provide sufficient details about the cases so that the reader can formulate his or her own judgments about them. In the conclusion, I summarize my findings on popular medicine in Rwanda and consider them in relation to the general problem of symbolic systems and historical transformation.

CHAPTER 1

The Dynamics of Flow

~~~~~~

One cannot step twice into the same river, nor can one grasp any mortal substance in a stable condition, but it scatters and again gathers; it forms and dissolves, and approaches and departs.

HERACLITUS

Le symbolisme culturel rwandais ne renvoie à aucun code explicite, à aucun système de correspondances établi. Le Rwanda traditionnel n'avait pas d'art figuratif, ni de lieux de culte fixes, ni de cycle de fêtes fixes, ni de capitale fixe, ni de village malgré une des plus fortes densités de l'Afrique; on a affaire ici à une culture où le symbolisme à l'image de l'habitat, est omniprésent mais diffus et mouvant. Une chose n'est practiquement jamais là pour en representer une autre de façon permanente ou automatique; tout au plus peut-on dire qu'elle la rappelle, ou la suggère, ou l'évoque de façon habituelle dans certains contextes.

PIERRE SMITH[1]

THE RWANDAN KING

One of the major difficulties in the study of Rwandan cultural symbolism is determining an avenue of access into it. Smith expresses this problem very cogently, when he emphasizes the apparently amorphous aspect of Rwandan spatio-temporal organization and settlement pattern. Nevertheless, it would be wrong to take this amorphousness as the fundamental nature of Rwandan cultural symbolism. This symbolic expression, as I will show, is highly structured and characterized by recurrent patterns.

My claim is that one finds this patterning in areas of representation that best express the qualities of diffuseness and motion—in things that flow. Liquids are the clearest expression of this; they embody the amorphousness that Smith speaks of. You cannot sculpt them, you cannot depict them as they are. They are neither solid nor ethereal, but instead move between realms, between tangibility and intangibility, between being and nonbeing. You cannot grasp them, yet they can be contained and directed. You can acquire them, but their power lies as much in their capacity to be given away as in their appropriation, in their capacity to transform social relations, and in their capacity to mediate between disparate realms of being. By focusing on things that flow and their use as symbols, we may perceive structure as well as process; we may see that there is form to Rwandan symbolic thought even in its diffuseness and mobility.

In this chapter I construct a model of Rwandan symbolic expression before its exposure to Catholic and colonialist influence. Although it is impossible to reconstruct in full the precolonial Rwandan gift economy and its cultural notions, I will show that Rwandan gift logic was predicated upon relative continuity in the production and exchange of various substances. Most important, these substances included liquids involved in human and natural fertility, as well as liquids involved in social interaction. I use evidence gleaned from a study of Rwandan myth, legend, and kingship rituals. From this evidence I advance the hypothesis that precolonial Rwandan notions of pathology were based upon the openness or closure of the body (see introduction), and the flow or blockage of substances into, within, or from the body. This dialectical structure was never directly verbalized; instead, it was a form of implicit knowledge.

Ritual and myth were two different contexts in which Rwandans enacted and experimented with flow/blockage imagery, but without rendering it explicit. Such imagery resided partly beyond language in metaphor and partly beneath language in the body; it was neither wholly abstract nor purely ideational. On the contrary, it seemed constantly to require a focal point, a means of concretizing itself in something. This usually implied a human vehicle in whose body its potentialities could be encapsulated (M. Strathern, pers. comm.). In precolonial Rwanda, the primary human vehicle was the king.

For example, many of the connotations associated with flow/blockage imagery inhere in the meanings of the Kinyarwanda verb *kwáama* and the Kirundi verb *kwâma,* from which the noun for king, *umwaámi,* is derived (Kinyarwanda and Kirundi are dialects of a single language; Vansina, pers. comm.; DeLacger 1959, 83; Rodegem 1970, 6). In Kinyarwanda, *kwáama* means "to be famous, to be known by everyone; to have done something for a long time and to continue to do it, to have a certain habitual comportment; to be prosperous or to live a long time" (Jacob 1983, 23). In Kirundi, *kwâma* means "to bear fruit, to fructify, to be fertile; to always be; to make or do something without stopping" (Rodegem 1970, 5–6). According to Francis Rodegem, the noun *umwaámi* is derived from the verb *kwâmira* (6). *Kwâma* and *kwâmira* have the same root (*-âma*) and mean essentially the same thing. Their only difference is the infix *-ir-*, which is employed in Kinyarwanda and Kirundi whenever the beneficiary or aim of an action is specified.

According to Jan Vansina, *kwâma* also had a popular meaning: "to lactate" (pers. comm.). Another verb in Kinyarwanda and Kirundi, *gukáma,* means "to milk." In several interlacustrine regions, the terms *umukama* (from *gukáma*) and *umwaámi* (from *kwáama* or *kwâmira*) were used as synonyms (Rodegem 1970, 209). In the nearby kingdom of Bunyoro, the king was called "Mukama" (the Kinyoro language also uses the term *gukáma* for "to milk"). When the Bunyoro "Mukama" died, a man would ascend a ladder, pour milk onto the ground and say, "The milk is spilt; the king has been taken away!" (Beatty 1960, 28).

The terms *umwaámi* and *umukama* encompass several notions that are central to Rwandan symbolic thought: continuity, productivity, fertility, prosperity, and their metaphorization in the popular imagination as a flowing process, lactation. Another meaning of *gukáma* in Kirundi and Kinyarwanda gives a hint that embedded within these representations is their contrary, for it can also mean "to dry up" (Rodegem 1970, 209). In other words, one cannot "milk" one's environment without running the risk of depleting it. One cannot have flow without blockage.

IMÁANA

Another important concept in precolonial Rwandan cosmological thought was *imáana*, the primary embodiment of motile force in Rwandan culture. According to Marcel d'Hertefelt and André Coupez, this term referred to:

> Une qualité puissante, principe dynamique de vie et de fécondité, que les anciens Rwanda cherchaient à s'approprier par des techniques rituelles. Dans certains récits cosmogoniques, cette même force est pensée sous la forme d'une entité consciente et d'une volonté qu'on pourrait appeler Divinité. Mais aucun culte ne s'adresse à cette hypostase anthropomorphique précisément parce que le terme imaana ne désigne pas avant tout un être personnel qu'il faudrait honorer et implorer, mais un fluide diffus qu'il convient de capter.... La qualité d'imaana s'attache à une vaste catégorie de personnes et d'objets par le truchement desquels les anciens Rwanda pensaient pouvoir jouir de ses effets. (1964, 460)[2]

Imáana was thought to invest certain trees and plants, royal residences and tombs, animals and objects used in divination, and protective talismans. Diviners, ritual specialists, and ancestral spirits were also believed to embody *imáana*. "Mais, selon les conceptions des Rwanda, c'est le souverain qui est le suprême détenteur du fluide fécondant imaana; le rituel royal n'est autre chose que la description des techniques qui permettent d'en diriger les effets bénéfiques sur le pays entier" (1964, 460).[3]

One could object that in following Alexis Kagame, the Rwandan Catholic priest who first transcribed the royal rituals, d'Hertefelt and Coupez erred in describing *imáana* as a "diffuse, fecundating fluid" and that Kagame's depiction shows evidence of Christian influences. From other Rwandan sources, though, it is clear that there is a strong association between *imáana* and fertility fluids. For example, the following poem, composed by a Rwandan named Munyanganzo, was recited to King Rwabugiri in 1875, twenty-five years before the first mission settlement in Rwanda:

Ntawashobora Igihugu Nk'umwami

Abami nimwe mutwemera rubanda.
Ni amaganga y'lmana iduhaye
Muhanyi wa Rusaza arayivubisha.

(Muzungu 1974, 155)

(No One Can Lead the Country Like the King

Kings you aid the masses.
It is the urine of Imáana you give us
Friend of Rusaza you make it rain.)

The poem equates rain with the urine of *imáana,* and in chapter 3 I will show that Rwandans consider urine to be important in human sexuality. For now, though, what is important is that the poem establishes a connection between human, terrestrial, and bovine fertility and *imáana.* Furthermore, it demonstrates that the king was the one who mediated the process of *imáana*'s descent. The royal rituals thus become the basis for reconstructing some of the workings of *imáana* in its various guises and avatars, as these were lived in pre-Christian Rwanda.

Other than the kingship rituals, which clearly expressed the pastoralist bias of the dominant Tutsi, there is relatively little documentary evidence about whether the dominated Hutu majority and the Twa made alternative use of flow/blockage symbolism. Such evidence that does exist, however, suggests that the Tutsi became more acculturated to preexisting Hutu cultural forms than did the Hutu to Tutsi cultural forms. Hutu kings were called *abaámi* (sing. *umwaámi*) in southwestern Rwanda—the same term used later by the Tutsi king of Rwanda—and *abahiínza* (sing. *umuhiínza*) in other parts of Rwanda (Linden 1977, 11). These Hutu kings were present in Rwanda before the arrival of the Tutsi. The rituals that they performed (e.g., in rainmaking) resemble those performed by the Nyiginya Tutsi kings (d'Hertefelt 1971, 32).

From the royal rituals, it is readily apparent that the precolonial representation of *imáana* differed from that of the Judeo-Christian God. Today the two images tend to be conflated by many Rwandans—the direct result of missionization. The term *imáana* is used in Christian contexts and in the Kinyarwanda Bible as a direct equivalent to the

Judeo-Christian concept of God. The term *God* is translated into Kinyarwanda as *Imáana* and conversely, the term *imáana* is usually translated into Western languages as "God." When Rwandans are asked to explain *imáana*, even those who do not regularly practice Christianity almost always provide an explanation that has been permeated by the Christian idea of God.

Nevertheless, the precolonial image of *imáana* was not associated with ideas about judgment, punishment, or election (Habimana 1988, 42), all of which suffuse the Judeo-Christian representation of God. Instead, *imáana* was linked to ideas concerning destiny and fertility. Liquids were especially favored vehicles of *imáana;* these emerged in divination and in notions regarding human and agricultural fertility. Such liquids included water, primarily in the form of rain, but also secondarily in the form of rivers and springs; blood; semen; saliva; milk; honey; and beer. These substances were the primary media of flow.

In a less direct, more conceptual, but no less important way, cattle were also a medium of flow. They produced precolonial Rwanda's most cherished aliment, milk, and they mediated the transfer of human reproductive potential from one group to another by serving as the most important valuable in bridewealth exchange. Cattle incorporated both the static aspect of wealth and the active aspect of its transformational possibility in the spheres of production and exchange. Milk and beef were consumed, especially by members of the pastoralist Tutsi class, but this utilitarian function of cattle was overshadowed by a transformational function: to mark that social relations between people had changed from one state to another. A man became a husband by giving cattle to the bride's father. This exchange transformed not only the two members of the couple into husband and wife but also the relation between their respective families, making them long-term exchange partners. Cattle were essential in the forging of patron-client ties in the *ubuhake* relationship as well. One became a patron (*umushéebuja*) by the gift of usufruct rights in a cow to a client (*umugarágu*). The ultimate patron in this social system was the king (*umwaámi*), who was also the owner of all Rwanda's cattle and centrally important in ensuring their fertility. This idea is expressed in the following line from a famous dynastic poem, "En vue de multiplier les vaches, imaana a commencé par créer les rois" (Kagame 1951, 47).[4]

In the following myth reported by André Coupez and Thomas Kamanzi (1962, 79–83) and summarized by Luc de Heusch, the origin of cattle and the origin of hierarchy are depicted as intimately linked. The myth also characterizes the legendary Rwandan king, Gihanga—said to have been the Promethean inventor of fire crafts such as pottery making and ironworking—as the first king to have been favored by *Imáana* with the possession of cattle.

> L'épouse que Gihanga avait amenée du Burundi se trouva enceinte à son tour. Durant sa grossesse, une querelle s'éclata entre les femmes; elles se disputèrent la peau d'un animal tué par Gihanga. Nyirarucyaba, la fille ainée de celui-ci, blessa mortellement l'épouse rundi; atteinte au ventre d'un coup d'épieu, elle expira mais l'enfant, né prématurément, était sain et sauf. Gihanga l'appela Gafomo. Nyirarucyaba prit la fuite et se réfugia en forêt. Elle fut accueillie par un certain Kazigaba (éponyme du clan zigaba). Il l'épousa et ils eurent des enfants. Apprenant que son père était malade, Nyirarucyaba s'en affligea. Elle vit soudain des vaches sortir d'un lac. L'une des bêtes vint vêler devant sa porte et le veau fut pris dans les lianes de la forêt; la mère demeura auprès de son petit, tandis que les autres animaux se retiraient dans le lac. Nyirarucyaba pétrit des pots d'argile et s'en alla traire la vache. Constatant que le liquide aviat bon goût elle amena le veau près de l'entrée de la hutte et l'attacha. La vache suivit. Nyirarucyaba envoya le précieux breuvage qu'elle venait de découvrir à son père, par l'intermédiare de sa mère. Gihanga, agréablement surpris, fit venir sa fille, lui accordant son pardon. Nyirarucyaba apporta de nouvelles cruches. Le lait guérit Gihanga de son mal. Il exigea alors que son gendre lui envoie la vache. Celui-ci réfusa d'abord, mais Gihanga s'irrita. Nyirarucyaba finit par amener elle-même l'animal.
>
> Les vaches sauvages sortirent à nouveau du lac et Gihanga décida de s'en emparer. Mais Gafomo, effrayé par cet immense troupeau, poussa un cri d'alarme du haut de l'arbre où il s'était juché. Les vaches coururent se réfugier dans le lac qui se referma aussitôt. Et le narrateur conclut: "Il reste peu de vaches. Ce sont elles que les Rwanda ont élevées; si elles étaient venues nombreuses, aucun homme n'aurait été le suzerain d'un autre." (Cited by de Heusch 1982, 52)[5]

This myth is interesting for several reasons. First of all, as de Heusch points out, water is often depicted in Rwandan symbolism as a source of life and riches (1982, 107). In this instance, the lake is associated with bovine wealth. The story shows the aquatic origin of cattle (169), who are not simply metaphorically related to liquids, they are depicted as metonymically a part of a liquid, the terrestrial waters of a lake. This association is more complex, though, than the simple observation that cattle produce milk and thus have an obvious connection to liquids. In commodity economy language, the term *liquidity* refers to those assets that can be readily converted into other things; quite often, "liquidity" simply means cash. In a gift economy, there are also "assets" that can be converted into other things, although the process is usually slower. Here the transactions and the social meanings such assets participate in differ radically from those of a commodity economy, but the principle of convertibility is similar. In the Rwandan gift economy, the analogue of "liquidity" came to be embodied by cattle. Notice that in this myth, the first bridewealth exchange involving cattle takes place when Gihanga demands that his son-in-law send him a cow. There are, of course, certain natural properties of cattle that contribute to their value as an exchange medium: they can move easily from place to place, they produce useful products, and in the final instance, their flesh can be consumed.

These natural properties are not sufficient in themselves to make cattle coveted objects of possession and exchange, for other domesticated animals, such as sheep and goats, have them as well. Cattle also have the virtue of being the focus of cultural canons of value that make them desirable. Poems of praise are sung to them; beautiful young women are compared to them; young men freely risk death in battle to obtain cattle. In order to embrace such values, someone must convince someone else of their worthiness. Notice that in this myth Kazigaba is reluctant to send Gihanga a cow and finally, Nyirarucyaba must bring him the cow herself. Kazigaba is not just being stingy. Members of the Zigaba clan (*ubwóoko*) along with two other clans, the Singa and the Gesera, were termed *abasaangwabutaka* (literally, "those who were found upon the earth"). As autochthonous people whose occupancy of Rwanda predated the arrival of Gihanga and his predecessors—said to be of celestial origin—it was necessary for the latter to persuade the Zigaba that cattle should become the primary exchange medium in bridewealth and other socially significant transactions. This difference between autochthonous and celestial origin should also be interpreted as the difference between cultivating Hutu and cattle-herding Tutsi.[6] By accepting cattle as the foremost exchange medium, cultivators were placing themselves at a disadvantage, for eventually this acceptance would lead to their subjugation by Tutsi cattle owners, as the myth implies at the end. Perhaps Kazigaba foresees this, and thus has every reason to resist the blandishments of pastoralist values, in particular, the primacy of the cow. However, the state of scarcity described at the end has nothing to do with nature, but is the direct result of a human action, symbolized here by Gafomo's inopportune cry. Although the beneficence of *imáana* is potentially limitless, its descent to the earth and its materialization are inevitably impeded by human interference.

Finally, the legend evokes another recurrent theme in Rwandan mythical discourse, that of the *igishéegabo,* or virago (cf. Bigirumwami 1971, 348–49). Nyirarucyaba ignores the taboo that prevents men and women from employing objects belonging to the other sex. A man must never handle the large wooden spoon Rwandan women use to stir cooking food (and sometimes as a weapon) and a woman must never carry or use metal objects associated with hunting (P. Smith 1979a, 30). In Luba and other central African Bantu mythology, pointed, manufactured objects are frequently employed in opposition to natural openings (de Heusch 1972, 36). Although this symbolic value is operative here—spear vs. uterus (if we include its vaginal opening)—what is more important is that Nyirarucyaba transgresses the norms of her gender. De Heusch's interpretation in *Rois nés d'un coeur de vache* (1982) ignores this aspect of the legend and concentrates on Gihanga. The myth is important both for understanding Rwandan kingship and for gaining insight into Rwandan gender relations. Nyirarucyaba ignores a gender-demarcating prohibition by seizing a boar spear and then killing her stepmother (*mukase*) by slicing open her uterus. This action is the precipitant cause of the hapless Gafomo's birth.

In usurping a male prerogative, Nyirarucyaba is the immediate cause of a tragic being's birth and thus the ultimate cause of the impeded flow of milk upon the earth. Nyirarucyaba unwittingly deprives the world of a white fertility fluid (here milk is analogous to semen) by illegitimately assuming a male role. By "flowing" in the wrong direction, toward masculinity instead of femininity, Nyirarucyaba makes the cows flow the wrong way—back into instead of out of the lake. This observation is reinforced by Nyirarucyaba's role in bringing the cow that her father has demanded of her husband. Again Nyirarucyaba is assuming a male role: women do not act as their own agents nor as transactors in bridewealth exchange; they do not exchange themselves. The same idea is illustrated in a Rwandan prenuptial taboo analyzed by Pierre Smith (1979a: 28). This prohibition states that during the entire period that matrimonial negotiations are underway, the concerned girl must not take cattle paths when walking over the hillsides. As Smith points out, this is because the exchange destinies of women and cattle are opposed. Women flow in one direction, cattle flow in the opposite direction. Both are intended to be objects of exchange and never its agents.

THE KING AS A CONDUIT OF IMÁANA

The relation of kings, cattle, milk, men, and *imáana* is succinctly expressed in another dynastic poem cited by Alexis Kagame in *La philosophie bantu-rwandaise de l'être* (1956, 15):

> Le Roi n'est pas un homme,
> O hommes qu'il a enrichis de ses vaches . . .
> Il est homme avant sa désignation au trône . . .
> Eh oui! c'est certain:
> Celui-là cesse d'être un homme qui devient Roi!
> Le Roi, c'est lui Dieu
> Et il domine sur les humains . . .
> Je trouve qu'il est le Dieu accessible à nos supplications!
> L'autre Dieu, c'est lui qui le connaît,
> Nous ne voyons que ce Défenseur, quant à nous! . . .
> Le souverain que voiçi boit le lait trait par Dieu
> Et nous buvons celui qu'à son tour il trait pour nous![7]

In this poem, we see that the beneficence of *imáana* was once conceptualized as milk. As the earthly avatar of *Imáana*, the king received this bounty and channeled it downward to the rest of humanity. The Rwandan king, *umwaámi*, could be compared to a hollow conduit through which celestial beneficence passed, but the passage was never immediate nor direct. The king's body retarded the process of flow. The king's abdomen, for example, was sometimes referred to as an *igisaabo*, or butter churn (Jacob 1985, 6), which was a female implement. Pierre Smith refers to the butter churn as the "symbole par excellence de la féminité belle et féconde" (1975, 81).[8] The king catalyzed the descent of transformative power or *imáana*, but only by encompassing the powers of both genders. By temporarily blocking or arresting flow, he became like a butter churn or a uterus during pregnancy. (Rwandans compare the making of a child with the churning of butter; see the discussion of *gukúrakuza,* p. 68). He embodied the qualities of both conduit, through which things pass, and container, in which things are retained and transformed.

By retarding the descent of *imáana,* the king acted as a condensation of the flow/blockage process. Only by taking the risk of completely blocking the system, did the king's role in perpetuating flow became tangible and visible (M. Strathern, pers. comm.). In one legend that I heard in Rwanda in 1987, celestial beneficence passed through the king's alimentary canal according to this delayed rhythm; fertility was restored to the earth only after passing through the *umwaámi*'s digestive tract. The story concerns the semimythical Rwandan king, Ruganzu Ndori:

> Ruganzu Ndori was living in exile in the kingdom of Ndorwa, a neighboring kingdom to the north of Rwanda. There he had taken refuge with his FZ (*nyirasenge*) who was married to a man from the region. In the meantime, because the Rwandan throne was occupied by an illegitimate usurper, Rwanda was experiencing numerous calamities. The crops were dying, the cows were not giving milk, and the women were becoming sterile. Ruganzu's paternal aunt encouraged him to return to Rwanda to retake the throne and save his people from catastrophe. Ruganzu agreed. But before setting forth on his voyage to Rwanda, his FZ gave him the seeds (*imbúto*) of several cultivated plants (sorghum, gourds, and others) to restart Rwandan cultures. While en route to Rwanda, Ruganzu Ndori came under attack. Fearing that the *imbúto* would be captured, he swallowed the seeds with a long draught of milk. Once he regained the Rwandan throne, he defecated the milk and seed mixture upon the ground and the land became productive once again. Since that time all Rwandan kings are said to have been born clutching the seeds of the original *imbúto* in their hand.

Other inferences to be drawn from this legend concern the implicit and explicit associations linking the king to the productivity of the soil and to milk, prosperity, fertility, and continuity—associations that we have already seen in connection with the verbs *kwáama* and *gukáma.* The person of the *umwaámi* and his college of ritual specialists had to ensure that rain would fall in sufficient quantity, but without washing the kingdom away. Insufficient or excessive flow led to drought or inundation, with drought the more feared.

The cause of these calamities was always the same: ritual impurity (*ishyano*). The *umwaámi* was a defender of flow and an enemy of *ishyano.* This principle was imprinted upon his body. Ritualists saw to it that his physiological processes were kept in motion, for every morning the king imbibed a milky liquid called *isúbyo,* which was a powerful laxative (Bourgeois 1956, 173). The ostensible purpose of this daily practice was to purge the *umwaámi*'s body of any impurity he might have contacted, but the reasoning behind the custom goes deeper. The king's body was a metonym of the entire cosmological system. Since he was the conduit between sky and earth, his body had to be kept open.

The *umwaámi*'s enemies were the antithesis of "flowing beings"; they blocked production, exchange, and fertility. The Rwandan mythical archetype of the "blocked being" was a small old woman (*agakeecuru*), who harbored Death in her womb. *Imáana* and the king were associated with milk and fertility; Death was associated with blood and sterility, as depicted in the following legend, which recounts the origin of Death.

> In the beginning of time, there were four brothers: Lightning, the King, *Imáana,* and Death. One day the four were to receive their separate heritages. Lightning received his portion in the sky and in the forest. *Imáana* received his part upon the earth and in the sky. The King received his part on the earth, Rwanda. Death received blood. But Death was stymied in his attempts to enjoy his heritage, because each one of his brothers would protect those of his possessions which bled. In his attempts to obtain blood, Death even met with an accident and lost the sight of one eye. Dispirited and suffering from the lack of blood, Death returned to his father, the Creator,[9] to plead his case.
>
> The Creator (*Rurema*) tells Death that he shall possess whatever the others leave behind, neglect, or no longer want. Interpreting this very liberally, Death proceeds to ravage the possessions of his brothers. Finally, the three decide to join forces against Death and kill him. The King takes his bow and arrows, *Imáana* his heavy club, and Lightning himself. Cornering Death, the King shoots an arrow into his thigh, and when Death arights himself, Lightning slaps him. Nevertheless, Death manages to escape into a field where an *agakeécuru* (small old woman) is gathering gourds. Death pleads with her to hid him in the fold at the front of her dress and she complies. When Lightning and *Imáana* arrive to see what has happened, Lightning decides to kill the old woman and thus her charge as well, but *Imáana* prevents him, saying that his (*Imáana*'s) role is to oversee the multiplication of his creatures and not their demise. Besides, one day Death will have to leave his hiding place on his own and then he will be vulnerable. But Death decides that his new abode suits him well. He is protected from the rain, and he has all

the blood that he wants. Later the old woman transmits Death to all her progeny by eating with them; they in turn, take it to every corner of the earth. (In P. Smith 1975, 129–33)

In this tale we see the association between Death and beings who do not flow—old women, who do not menstruate. This association is not unique to Rwanda. Among other central African Bantu groups, such as the Yaka (cf. Devisch 1984) and the Komo (cf. de Mahieu 1985), symbolic connections link human fertility fluids to terrestrial waters. Here the connection is between menstrual blood and celestial water—rain. The old woman is an analogue of the dry season. Furthermore, her blood comes to nourish Death instead of life, for Death has sought refuge in the old woman's uterus. Like a witch, death parasitically sucks the blood of woman to sustain himself. Every woman following the original *agakeecuru* is born with Death already in her womb. Eventually Death destroys female fertility from within; he sucks away woman's blood and thus ultimately brings her capacity to produce new life to an end. Whereas male fertility can endure until a man's last breath, female fertility is limited.

We also learn from this tale that Death has an aversion to rain, which is part of the reason he remains sheltered within the old woman's body. Rain flows from heaven to earth and makes crops grow; this is counter to Death's activity, for Death dehydrates, it blocks the flow of substances that give rise to new life. The origin of Death is also the origin of witchcraft, for the old woman passes the contagion of Death on to others by eating with them.[10]

THE ROYAL RITUALS

Although most scholars who have studied Rwandan kingship agree upon the institution's central role in assuring fertility, the synchronic and diachronic implications of the kingship rituals remain a subject of controversy. Luc de Heusch's *Rois nés d'un coeur de vache* (1982) has been criticized by Jan Vansina (1983) for its tendency to decontextualize and to privilege structure over contingency and event. While many of Vansina's criticisms are justified, it would be wrong to discard the structural method as a possible tool in historical reconstruction. For example, many of the structures that de Heusch analyzes in *Le roi ivre* (1972) and

Rois nés and that he deduces from earlier ethnographic material (often minimally influenced by colonialism) have also been discovered among other present-day central African Bantu peoples (cf. Devisch 1984; de Mahieu 1985). De Heusch is justified in asserting that Bantu-speaking peoples share a common mythological base.

Nevertheless, Vansina is correct that structural analysis is most powerful where it is coupled with an analysis of actual social practices, and there is little of that in de Heusch's books. History is not the volitionless recapitulation in time of the same structures, but it is indeed influenced by the categories of mythical thought. To influence, however, does not mean to mold irrevocably. De Heusch's work does not satisfactorily address the question of the diachronic mutability of structures. In some cases (as subsequent chapters in this study will show), the reproduction of a structure may lead to its transformation (cf. Sahlins 1981). But transformation can only be discerned when some of the canons of structural analysis are transcended, when attention is focused upon the concrete manifestations of a particular structure at different moments in time. Such a structure also has to be sufficiently generalized in the culture so as to be present in a number of domains. Hence my focus upon liquids, for these mediate between physiological, sociological, and cosmological notions of causality.

In the seventeen royal rituals assembled in *La royauté sacrée de l'ancien Rwanda* (d'Hertefelt and Coupez 1964), the importance of liquid aliments is striking. There are dozens and dozens of references to milk (*amata*), mead (*ubúuki*), and honeyed sorghum beer (*inzogá y'inturire*), whereas there is only a single reference to beans, one of the peasantry's staple foods (17). An entire ritual is devoted to another staple crop, sorghum, but much of this grain was consumed in liquid form, either as beer (*ikigaáge*) or as a thick porridgy beverage (*igikóma*). The Rwandan king performed the royal rituals with the aid of his ritual specialists (*abíiru*), his wives (*abaámikazi*), and the occasional assistance of the queen mother (*umugabékazi*). These ceremonies continued to be enacted until the latter part of *umwaámi* Yuhi V Musinga's reign (he was deposed in 1931); some aspects of a few rituals survived under Yuhi's Christian successors.

All of the seventeen royal rituals directly or indirectly concerned fertility, and six of them dealt directly with things that flow. Two of the six, *Inzira ya Rukungugu* (the Path of Drought) and *Inzira ya Kivu* (the Path of Inundation) focused on rainfall extremes. *Inzira y'Inzuki* (the Path of the Bees) aimed at ensuring sufficient honey production, the necessary ingredient in Rwanda's most prized alcoholic beverages, honeyed sorghum beer and mead. *Inzira ya Muhekenyi* (the Path of Cattle Sickness) concerned the health of cattle and thus milk production. *Inzira y'Umuganura* (the Path of the First Fruits of Sorghum) celebrated the sorghum harvest. Probably the most important ritual, however, was *Inzira y'Ishoora* (the Path of the Watering). In this ceremony, performed at the beginning of each dynastic cycle of four kings by a "cowherd king," all the royal cattle herds were brought to the Nyabugogo River to be watered, an action that signified the ritual revivification of the entire magico-religious order of divine kingship.

Analysis of all the royal rituals would require too much space to be undertaken here, so I will use a few examples to elucidate Rwandan symbolic thought on the flow of bodily, celestial, and social media of exchange. All of these media interrelate in complex ways and with varying implications, but in most domains of Rwandan symbolism they reflect similar patterns. In the origin myth of Death, for example, we noted the relation posited between Death and postmenopausal women. A similar interplay of fertility and antifertility principles characterizes the royal rituals and practices related to the body. Although many of these practices have fallen or are falling into desuetude, their underlying logic forms the ideological substrate that continues to influence much of Rwandan behavior today.

In the Path of Inundation the problem of excessive celestial flow (rainfall) was ritually countered; once again, a woman figured prominently (d'Hertefelt and Coupez 1964, 27–31). In this instance, the king's ritualists were instructed to capture a Twa woman "without breasts or having passed childbearing age" from the forest just beyond the limits of the Rwandan kingdom (28). Later in the ritual her blood was shed along with other sacrificial victims: a black goat, a black bull, and a sterile cow. (Black in most contexts is associated with death, sterility, bad fortune, and nonproductivity. But it is also associated with the black clouds that announce rain.) Rwandan women without breasts (*impenébeere*) and girls who had reached childbearing age without ever having menstruated (*impa*) were considered sources of ritual impurity (*ishyano*) and thus infertility to all of Rwanda. One of the king's responsibilities was to ensure their elimination (286). Usually they were taken just beyond the limits of Rwanda and then killed; their blood as it flowed upon the earth was thought to vitiate the fertility of the foreign land, as well as bring it other forms of misfortune. Notice that in both instances these women were "blocked beings," that is, persons from whose bodies one of the two requisite fluids of female fertility, blood or maternal milk, did not flow. Because the productivity of their bodies was blocked, they were thought to threaten the productive integrity of the entire Rwandan polity. In the Path of Inundation, the Twa woman's body was perceived to be deficient in at least one of the fertility fluids. (The relation between menstrual blood and rain in *kumanikira amaráso* will be discussed in chapter 3.)

Members of the Twa ethnic group in Rwanda, less than 1 percent of the present population, have perennially been denigrated by the Tutsi and the Hutu. Part of the reason for this stemmed from their close association to the forest and to "wildness." The Twa were also despised for their alleged gluttony and lack of discrimination in eating. Twa, for example, ate mutton, a food spurned by both Tutsi and Hutu because they valued sheep for their pacific qualities. Sheep accompanied cattle herds and were thought to exert a calming influence upon them. (This practice persists today among many Rwandans.) Tutsi prided themselves on being able to consume a diet rich in liquids, especially milk and beer. Although they would occasionally eat beef and solid vegetable foods, their diet was more liquid than solid (d'Hertefelt and Coupez 1964, 17). Hutu consumed more grains and vegetable foodstuffs than Tutsi and more goat meat. Their diet was more solid than liquid, since they had less access to milk and the various alcoholic beverages available to the dominant Tutsi pastoralists. Twa reputedly ate just about everything, including foods gained through hunting and gathering, but they were least able to procure the esteemed aliments of milk and the various types of beer.

In terms of diet, then, as one descended the social hierarchy, solid foods became the norm. Furthermore, people on the lower rungs of the hierarchy had fewer possibilities to bestow things on others, having only their labor to give, whereas the dominant Tutsi could consider themselves as the ones who gave most to others—cattle, in particular—even though the gift of a cow usually implied the subordination of the receiver.

This hierarchy of consumption was also a hierarchy of production. Since the earth was associated with impurity, the most esteemed labor was that which involved the earth in the most mediated fashion, pastoral labor. The least respected labor was that which directly involved the earth, pottery making, the most common occupation of the Twa. The labor of the Hutu was midway between these extremes, for although they worked the land, they worked it with tools, rather than directly with their hands.

According to a Rwandan legend, this state of affairs was justified by the different behaviors of the three brothers Gatutsi, Gahutu, and Gatwa, sons of the mythical Rwandan king, Gihanga (P. Smith 1975, 39). Gihanga gave each of the brothers a pot of milk and told him to guard it during the night. But Gatwa became thirsty and drank his pot of milk. Gahutu became drowsy and in dozing off, spilled some of the contents of his pot. Only Gatutsi succeeded in keeping a full pot of milk until the next morning. For this reason, Gihanga decreed that Gatutsi should possess cattle and enjoy the right to rule. Gahutu would only be able to procure cattle by the work and services he performed for his brother Gatutsi. As for Gatwa, he would never possess cattle; alternate periods of gluttony and starvation were to be his lot. Presumably, it was only Tutsi who could be trusted to keep the milk pot, which was Rwanda, filled to its brim.

According to the logic of flow, therefore, a Twa woman without breasts or menopaused, who lived in the forest beyond the borders of the Rwandan kingdom, was a blocked being in both physical and social terms. She could not partake in the reproduction of human life, nor could she contribute to the productivity of Rwanda, because she lived beyond its political control and was a member of the ethnic group who, according to legend, had wasted milk by impetuous consumption. In a situation of disordered flow (e.g., excessive rainfall), such a woman, a symbol of counterproductivity, was appropriate as a sacrificial victim, because her body represented disordered flow, the absence of milk or blood or both. During times of general calamity, the king was concerned to exorcise the kingdom of impurity (*ishyano*). The Twa woman's blood must have been seen as particularly charged with impurity, for instead of being channeled toward the production of children, it was merely congealing its powers within a blocked body.

This power could be construed as Death. Since Twa are small in stature and the woman was probably old, the term *agakeécuru* (small old woman) could be applied to her. In comparison with the previously discussed myth concerning the origin of Death, this ritual recapitulates many of the same symbolic conditions encountered in the myth, with the exception that, in this instance, the blocked being harboring Death and representing misfortune was killed. I interpret this action to signify the king's counteracting of anomic celestial flow through his liberation of the blood of an extrasocial blocked being on earth.

THE PATH OF THE WATERING

The path of Inundation illustrates some of the possible symbolic interactions among the vehicles of fertility, notably blood, rain, milk, and women. The most important royal ritual, however, the Path of the Watering (*Inzira y'Ishoora*), encompasses a larger repertory of fluid imagery including that of the kingdom's two most symbolically significant rivers, the Nyabarongo and the Nyabugogo. The Path of the Watering was only accomplished by "cowherd kings," who inaugurated each dynastic cycle of four kings. Two "kings of the belt" (warrior kings) followed. The fourth king was said to be a "fire king," and it was his responsibility to renew the perpetually burning sacred fire at the end of the dynastic cycle, during the ritual called the Path of Fire. The following chart, representing two dynastic cycles, delineates this system of succession:

Name of king	Function	Ritual	Residence
1. Cyrima	peaceful (cowherd)	water	1st then 2d half (Nduga then Bwanacyambwe)
2. Kigeri	warrior (belt)	war	unconfined
3. Mibambwe	warrior (belt)	war	unconfined
4. Yuhi	peaceful	fire	1st half (Nduga)
5. Mutara	peaceful (cowherd)	water	1st then 2d half
6. Kigeri	warrior (belt)	war	unconfined
7. Mibambwe	warrior (belt)	war	unconfined
8. Yuhi	peaceful	fire	1st half

The Rwandan kingdom was divided into two sacred halves. The first consisted of the lands contained within the Nyabarongo River; the second comprised the lands immediately to the east (see map 1). Cowherd kings (Cyrima and Mutara) were obliged to remain within the confines of the first sacred half of the Rwandan kingdom until completing the Path of the Watering. They then crossed the Nyabarongo and took up residence in the second half. Kings of the belt (Kigeri and Mibambwe) had no restrictions placed on their movements and were expected to go beyond the borders of the kingdom to conquer new lands. The fire king (Yuhi) remained in the first sacred half of the kingdom for the entirety of his reign.

Every Rwandan king ruled in conjunction with the preceding deceased cowherd king, whose cadaver was mummified and kept in the half of the realm where the living king resided. The Path of the Watering marked the moment when the deceased cowherd king was transported to the second sacred half, to which the living cowherd king was moving. During the reign of a Mutara, for example, the preceding Cyrima's body was placed in a hut at Gaseke (first sacred half), where a group of ritualists watched over it. Cyrima was said to rule there as *imáana* for cattle and to ensure their multiplication. Mutara began his journey to the watering place from his capital, which was in the first half of the kingdom though not at Gaseke. When all the necessary preliminaries had been accomplished, Mutara dispatched the "ritual king" (one of the *abíiru* who was a member of the Tsoobe lineage) to Gaseke to "tell" Cyrima that he could now conduct the cattle in his care to their watering place. The symbiosis between living and dead kings was exemplified in the message from Mutara to Cyrima: "Water for him and he will water for you! Go, and conquer the epizootics of Rwanda" (d'Hertefelt and Coupez 1964, 131, ll. 740–41). Mutara was thought to water for Cyrima's benefit and vice versa. Both kings conducted their journey to their respective watering places in three stages and crossed the Nyabarongo at approximately the same time, though the living king traveled during the day and the deceased king traveled at night. Mutara then led his cattle to their watering place at Muhima, which is situated near Mount Kigali to one side of the Nyabugogo River. Cyrima's herd was conducted to its watering place at Gatsaata, on the other side of the Nyabugogo.

When Mutara died, he became the new *imáana* for cattle. Ritualists smoked the body at Museke (second half) and then transported it to Joma (second half), where his successor Kigeri was enthroned. At the end of the mourning period for Mutara, the preceding cowherd king, Cyrima, was definitively buried at Rutare (second half). During the

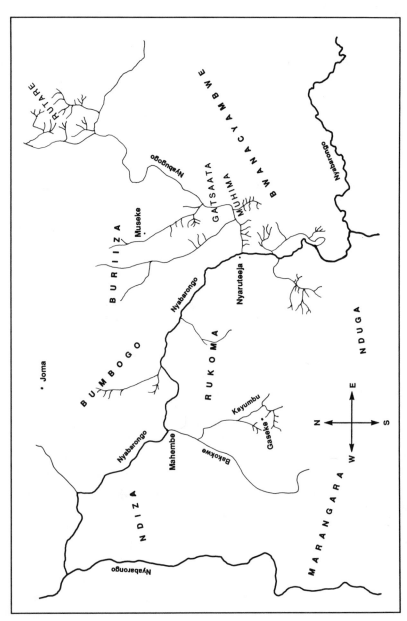

Map 1. *Central Rwanda. After a detail from M. Hertefelt and A. Coupez, La Royauté sacrée de l'ancien Rwanda (Tervuren: Musée Royal de l'Afrique Centrale, 1964).*

night of the day that Kigeri crossed the Nyabarongo to enter the first sacred half of the kingdom, ritualists took the mummified body of Mutara to Gaseke, where it remained as the *imáana* for cattle during the reigns of Kigeri, Mibambwe, and Yuhi. Upon Yuhi's demise, the dynastic cycle began again with a new Cyrima enthroned. After completing his watering ritual, the new cowherd king ordered that the deceased Mutara be transferred to the second sacred half to be buried at Rutare (d'Hertefelt and Coupez 1964, 52).

The mystical powers of Rwandan kingship were thus divided between a living and a dead ruler. The deceased cowherd king embodied active mystical force. Divination procedures often took place at his "throne" in order to consult with yet another avatar of *imáana*. This duality of mystical function within the kingship was paralleled by a duality of ritual function. Cowherd kings, the first in the dynastic cycle, had the responsibility of accomplishing a ritual that focused on water, the Path of the Watering. Fire kings, the last in the dynastic cycle, were entrusted with accomplishing the Path of Fire.[11] To some extent the duties of the peaceful kings—Cyrima, Mutara, and Yuhi—were redundant. For example, the Path of the Watering included a sequence intended to renew the sacred fire, though its emphasis was on watering the royal herds. This lesser fire ritual within a water ritual reflected the fact that cowherd kings, at least one of whom was always present (living or dead), encompassed all the other kings in the power of their *imáana,* just as water has the power to quench fire. Finally, the political functions of the Rwandan kings were also divided. Cowherd kings and fire kings were confined within the sacred portions of the realm. Kings of the belt, however, were not confined, but rather were encouraged to traverse the boundaries and conquer new territory. Thus two of the four rulers within each dynastic cycle had the responsibility of war and conquest, and the other two were charged with consolidation and renewal. The most sacred portion of the Rwandan polity, the first half, could be thought of as a container of kings, a vessel whose perimeter was defined by the Nyabarongo River. Like a gourd holding liquid, sometimes the gourd contained its kings, sometimes the gourd poured them out over new land.

Eight unmarried women figured prominently in the watering ritual as "promised wives" to deceased kings. Four of them belonged to the matridynastic clans from whom the queen mothers were selected. Called the *Ibibanda,* these clans were the Ega, the Kono, the Ha, and the Gesera. The other four were a representative of the Tsoobe clan (the group that held the ritual kingship), a woman from the Mugunga branch of the royal Nyiginya lineage (Sindi), one from the Munyiga branch, and one from the Cyambwe branch. All eight women were supposed to be "pure"—that is, untouched by death (with their parents still living)—and each was to be accompanied by a brother (d'Hertefelt and Coupez 1964, 105). Eight was thought to be an auspicious number, as were the even numbers two and four; all connoted perfection and happiness (282). Eight is also the number of reigns in a full cycle of kings (from one Cyirima to the next). In addition, an inheritance was called by the Kinyarwanda term for "eight," *umunaáni*. People explained to me that at one time, a father would leave groups of eight possessions to each of his children: eight cows, eight goats, and so on. Today though, Rwandans say that men are not sufficiently rich to leave groups of eight possessions to every child, but the term is still employed since it carries the connotation of plentitude.

The number nine was also thought to be powerful. Notice that in this ritual the eight "promised ones" and the king constituted a group of nine. In several instances during the watering ritual, a group of eight cows along with one bull, another set of nine, were presented to the king (142, 1.1030). This group was referred to as *isibo* ("a flow"), a term that derives from the verb *gusiba,* meaning "to obstruct."

One of the major events in the watering ritual occurred when the reigning cowherd king designated the son who would succeed him as Kigeri, as well as the future queen mother from the *Ibibanda* "promised" ones. Usually, though not always, the queen mother was also the genitrix of the future king. The queen mother of the present king was supposed to have died before her son accomplished the Watering ritual. If she were still alive and the king was growing old (an aging king meant that the kingdom was in danger of losing its vitality), and it was thus becoming urgent that he complete the ritual without delay, etiquette demanded that she commit suicide. This custom was an instance of the principle whereby members of the senior generation were supposed to relinquish gracefully their control over reproduction to members of the junior generation as the latter came of age.

One of the most revealing acts in the watering ritual occurred when the king poured milk into large gourds (*ibisaabo*) used as butter churns held by each one of the "promised ones," starting with the designated future queen mother. Then he began to churn the milk, agitating the gourd back and forth along with each woman and her brother in turn. The women then departed, handing the gourds to the king's ritualists, who would finish churning the milk into butter (d'Hertefelt and Coupez 1964, 139, 11.909–13). This portion of the ritual is important because it illustrates a simulacrum of the Rwandan theory of procreation. The king could here be thought of as a symbolic genitor. He began the procreation process by pouring milk, a white liquid, into a receptacle held by a ritual genitrix. The receptacle used was a butter churn, a gourd that symbolized the woman's uterus.

The king began the churning action alone and then was aided, first by the woman, and then by her brother. This symbolic coitus illustrates the Rwandan idea that conception occurs not merely from the father's "pouring" of semen into a container (the uterus of his wife), but from frequent intercourse during pregnancy. In effect, during pregnancy, the couple must conjoin their respective *intaanga* ("gifts of self") with more intensity than during ordinary conjugal life. They must cooperate in the sexual activity necessary to "churn" a child from the fusion of their bodily fluids (semen and blood). This idea is apparent in the verb used to describe the action of frequent intercourse during pregnancy, *gukúra-kuza*, which also means "to turn eggs in incubation" and "to put butter into lumps after churning."

The wife's brother was a participant in the ritual because sister's child and mother's brother had an important relationship: sister's child would belong to mother's brother were it not for the gift of cattle from husband to mother's brother's father (who is also, of course, wife's father). In this ritual the child was symbolized by the coagulating lump of butter, an association made clear when the king indicated the future queen mother by pouring milk into her churn first, meaning that the product of her "churn" (womb) had been his most important (pro)creation, the next king. The four principal ritual roles were the king as genitor and husband, each of the "promised ones" as symbolic wife and genitrix, each "wife's" brother, and finally, the king's son. The quadrad represented in this ritual was none other than the "atom of kinship" (see fig. 1) described by Claude Lévi-Strauss (1958, 37–62; 1976, 82–112). The watering ritual substantiates the assertion that the atom of kinship was an important concept in Rwandan thought as the society's most elementary unit of reproduction and not merely an artifact of analysis. After this coagulation of fertile fluids into new life, the guardians of Rwandan

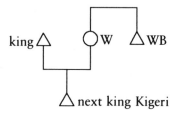

Fig. 1. Atom of kinship. Cf. Lévi-Strauss 1958, 37–62.

norms, beliefs, and values—the king's ritualists—entered the process in a second phase to continue the churning. This action symbolized the fashioning of the child into a socialized adult after his birth. The churning phase of the watering ritual thus appears to depict both the natural and the cultural components of the labor necessary to produce another human being: the sexual labor of procreation and the social labor of education.

The association among cattle, women, fertility, and the king as prime genitor for the entire Rwandan polity was reinforced when the enthroned king received a container with seeds (which would later be ritually sown), hoes, and the wooden receptacle belonging to the queen mother, into which were placed the eight lumps of butter churned by the "promised ones" (d'Hertefelt and Coupez 1964, 141–42, 11. 975–93). Next, cows belonging to the royal herd called the "Respectables" were brought forward and presented to the king. A ritualist began to milk them, and then the king would take the container and continue milking until it was full. Those present near the king would praise him, saying:

Ngo wuuzuz inka mu Rwanda
Wuuzuz amata mu Rwanda
Wuuzuz Urwanda rw'umwami.

(p. 140, 11. 984–96)

(May you fill Rwanda with cattle
May you fill Rwanda with milk
May you fill Rwanda with king.)

Rwanda was thus a container to be filled with the gifts of *imáana*—cattle, milk, and king—all of which were implicitly compared to fluids through the use of the verb *kuzuza* (to fill).

The king then entered his hut and drank some of the milk, perhaps in anticipation of the fluid he was about to spend. Next, he and one of his wives anointed each other with the eight lumps of butter from the future queen mother's receptacle, presented to him earlier, and they copulated. When he reemerged from the hut, he was acclaimed (*guhuunda*)[12] by a father's brother's daughter nursing a male child. In compensation for this service, she received a cow nursing a female calf.

Whereas up to this point in the ritual the milk that the king had poured into the churn held by the eight promised ones was treated as a symbolic equivalent with his semen, with the appearance of his FBD this symbolic identity becomes obscured. Milk and semen share the properties of fluidity and whiteness and can thus intersect in a metonymic relationship without contradiction (cf. Sapir 1977, 20). In this particular instance, however, intersection leads to differentiation. Fully conflating semen and milk would be tantamount to asserting that humanity is hermaphroditic, that it is possible for a single body to produce both substances, and furthermore, that it would be possible to reproduce human life without the sexual exchange of different fluids. Although this is of course impossible, the degree of closure in exogamous exchange (i.e., the degree of confluence of sexual fluids) was indeed a question that this ritual addressed.

When the watering ritual shifts emphasis from the qualities shared by milk and semen to their difference, it touches on the theme of incest and the confluence of milk, blood, and semen. The ritual probes the difference between women with whom the king may copulate—those to whom he may "give" his semen because he does not "share" their blood—and women with whom he may not copulate because of consanguinity.

The participation of a lactating FBD (patrilateral parallel cousin) is interesting because of her ambiguity. Does the milk that comes from her breasts represent an equivalent to the king's semen or does it represent a substance in opposition to his semen? Do the two fluids emanate from a single source? The ritual appears to be saying that the two substances are not equivalent, though they emanate from a single source—the king and his FBD share both FF and FM (see fig. 2). But a hint of the possibility of copulation between the king and his FBD persists. FBD (*mushiki*) is, in theory, off limits as a sexual or marital partner, but here she seems to be

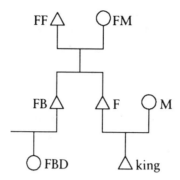

Fig. 2. Relationship of king and FBD in the Path of the Watering

vicariously participating in the king's ritual copulation with his wife by acclaiming him afterward. It is almost as if the ritual were experimenting with the possibility of the king's copulating with FBD in reality.

FBD is a classificatory sister, but she is not a real sister. In fact she is halfway between a prohibited kinswoman, a real sister (*mushiki*), and a sexually permitted one, a cross-cousin (*mubyara*, from *kubyara*, "to engender"; both FZD and MBD are called *mubyara*). Concerned with the themes of endogamy and exogamy, this ritual sequence is delineating the boundary between incestuous sex and nonincestuous sex by demonstrating that the king's semen and FBD's milk should follow separate paths and produce separate progeny. Hence the species and gender differences in the nature of their respective prestations: FBD brings a male child whom she is nursing, and she receives a cow nursing a female calf from the king in return.

Nevertheless, the possibility of incest with a classificatory sister was not unequivocally condemned in this ritual. Furthermore, Rwandan informants told me that, in the past, it was not uncommon for powerful Tutsi lords to marry FBDs (i.e., classificatory sisters [*mushiki, abashiki*]), though patrilateral parallel cousin (FBD) marriage did not occur among commoners. In the legends concerning the origin of divine kingship, marriages to real sisters appear. The first, mythical Rwandan king, Kigwa, married his sister, Nyampundu. Incestuous marriage leads to the confluence of milk and semen; it constitutes a form of "closed-circuit" exchange or partially blocked flow. In effect, the king's power in precolonial Rwanda arose from the capacity to control flow, to regulate the production and movement of substances along defined trajectories. But he could only control flow by blocking it, even though total blockage entailed drought, infertility, and death.

This imagery was not limited to the Rwandan king. In fact, it may have been common to Bantu symbolic thought in general. For example, among other central African Bantu peoples, the Luba carried closed-circuit exchange as a means of acquiring power to its farthest logical extreme.

> Le souverain luba s'affirme comme l'heritier ambigu de ce héros céleste aux moeurs raffinées et d'un ancien roi autochtone qui abusait de l'inceste comme du pouvoir. Il s'accouple en secret au moment de son avènement avec sa mère et ses soeurs dans une hutte sans porte ni fenê-tre, qualifiée de "maison de malheur." Cet édifice fermé sans ouverture sur le monde extérieur, est symboliquement coupé du circuit de l'échange exogamique. Il est par excellence le lieu de la transcendance maudite, le lieu où s'acquiert la sacralité du pouvoir comme élément étranger à la société. (De Heusch 1982, 27)[13]

De Heusch's interpretation of this custom underlines the extrasocial character of the Luba divine king. The king is a "deterritorialized be-ing," who acquires power over nature by violating ordinary social norms. Although I do not disagree with this interpretation, it is too gen-eral. I would add that we need to consider the specific symbolic images that are mobilized in order to evoke the king's acquisition of the condi-tion of extrasociality. These are images of closed-circuit flow or block-age: secrecy, M-S incest, B-Z incest, and a hut without windows or doors. The Luba king, like the Rwandan king, attained the power to con-trol flow by encompassing the quality of blockage.

Rwandan kings, living and dead, embodied *imáana*. As surrogates for the *umwaámi*, all sacrificial victims embodied it as well. *Imáana* as the principle of multiplication was the source of all beneficence to humanity. The king by virtue of his celestial origin but earthly enracination was the conduit through which material prosperity flowed. The king received the gift, then passed it downward. While he was the primary earthly receiver, he was also the ultimate debtor for humanity, the ultimate sacrificial victim, the ultimate blocked being in times of irreparable ca-lamity. Therefore his blood had to be shed at times to keep open the con-duit between sky and earth. Blocked beings, who impeded the flow of beneficence between divinity and mankind or who impeded it among men, were the *umwaámi*'s and *Imáana*'s enemy. Like the mythical *agakeecuru*, blocked beings harbored Death within them, and Death was the primordial nemesis of *Imáana*, the King, and Lightning. Blocked beings were also the "mothers" of witchcraft.

The flow of celestial beneficence had directionality; one had to move in consonance with its rhythms and peregrinations. Nyirarucyaba demonstrates the example of someone who moves contrary to it and thus indirectly brings scarcity, and ultimately hierarchy, to the earth. Diviners sought to discern the movement of *imáana* and to sensitize their supplicants to the paths and directions that their lives should take in order to move in harmony with the "diffuse, fecundating fluid." Inevitably though, Death would find ways to stymie the efforts of his brothers to ensure the unlimited reproduction of men and cattle, and so enjoy his inheritance.

The rituals of kingship underline the conjoined nature of flow/blockage symbolism. The king had to be able to stop the rain as well as to bring it. He had to impoverish certain people while enriching others. His body had to be both the image of an open conduit and that of a container capable of closure (a butter churn). Substances must circulate, but that circulation must be controlled. The body must be neither too closed nor too open. One can imagine social life without conflict or contradiction; one can imagine an environment that always provides for its inhabitants; one can imagine an immortal human body free from pathology; but one cannot live these states outside the imagination. The words *isibo* and *gusiba* reflect part of this recognition that one cannot have flow without blockage, just as one cannot milk (*gukáma*) without incurring the risk of depleting one's environment. Healers were Rwandan culture's tragicomic heroes, warriors in a battle whose outcome had already been written; they might postpone the inevitable, but they could never alter the fundamental nature of the creator Rurema's legacy to his sons.

CHAPTER 2

Religion and the Body Politic

In the previous chapter I sketched the outlines of pre-Christian and pre-colonial Rwandan symbolic thought. Before we can situate present-day Rwandan popular medicine and its symbolic concepts in historical time, we need to understand what became of Rwandan society between the late nineteenth century and the present. As elsewhere in Africa, this period was marked by colonialism and Christian evangelization. Catholic missionaries were probably the most influential agents of change in Rwanda. Their effect upon the society was political and economic, as well as religious.

Recent research on sub-Saharan Africa shows that Christian missionaries acted as the sometimes unwitting "culture brokers" (Geertz 1973) of European capitalist culture (Augé 1975; van Binsbergen 1979; Roberts 1984; Comaroff 1985). Rwanda, in its passage from a gift economy to a commodity economy, was no exception to this general pattern. Catholic missionaries offered Rwandans a first-hand model of commodity practices and concepts, such as wage labor, private property, contract, egalitarianism, and individualism. Most important on the question of misfortune, the missionary experience exposed Rwandans to the notion of essential human inadequacy: an image of the self divided between

51

a material, corruptible aspect—the body—and an immortal soul constantly in struggle with the body as the instigator of sins that accumulate and have to be confessed. Catholicism reinforced the individualistic tendencies of capitalism by insisting that the struggle with fleshly desire was a personal one; salvation was an individual achievement gained at the expense of life-long struggle with an egotistical, desiring body.

Nevertheless, changes in the politico-economic conditions of existence tended to outpace change in Rwandan symbolic thought. As case histories in subsequent chapters will show, in many contexts older explanatory models continue to be used to make sense of bodily experience. But with each passing day, Western cognitive categories and secular ideology are becoming more indelibly imprinted upon the Rwandan psyche. Notions of the person, the self, and the body are all in a state of flux. Not only is the soul being "re-cognized" in postcolonial Rwanda, so is the body.

The same can be said about the body politic, only more emphatically. Nothing remains of the Tutsi monarchy and the former condition of Tutsi dominance. Rwanda's Hutu majority managed to use the ties it developed with the Catholic Church to advance itself politically and economically. Today Rwanda's Hutu government remembers the debt it owes the Catholic Church, whose privileged status, temporal power, and success in discouraging heterodoxy seem likely to persist.

EARLY COLONIAL AND CHURCH HISTORY

The Church's beginnings in the early colonial days were more faltering than the present picture would suggest. Rwanda's entry into the "scramble for Africa" occurred relatively late in colonial history. In the negotiations among colonial powers in 1884–85 (the Berlin Conference), Ruanda-Urundi did not figure prominently. After Count von Götzen's discovery of Lake Kivu in 1894, the region became part of German East Africa (Louis 1963, 1–8).

In accordance with accepted colonial practice, the Germans set about to "effectively occupy" the land. In 1897 the king of Rwanda, *umwaámi* Yuhi V Musinga, who the previous year had usurped the throne from his half brother, Mibambwe Rutalindwa, accepted the offer of German protection (Linden 1977, 23). Within a few years he had been prevailed upon to accept the first missionaries, granting them permission in 1900 to establish a mission at Save, twenty kilometers away from the royal capital at Nyanza (Lugan 1978) (see map 2). Musinga's motivation in accepting missionaries stemmed from the fact that he was a usurper and felt the need for powerful outside supporters. He hoped to use the White Fathers to extend his influence into areas that were not fully under the Rwandan kingdom's control. Hence subsequent lands granted to them for missions tended to be in areas where the *umwaámi*'s influence was weak (Louis 1963, 122). He never realized that they would rapidly become the most numerous and widespread representatives of European culture.

With the influx of missionaries, Rwandan colonial politics became divided among three groups after 1905: Musinga and his court, the German Colonial Residency, and the Catholic missionaries. German aims were to reinforce the power of Musinga and his faction of the Rwandan ruling coterie and to rule indirectly through them. Musinga wanted German support in extending his control over the recalcitrant north. The missionaries were the "wild card." Although in theory they espoused the aim of evangelizing the Tutsi elite (Lugan 1978, 72) and thus appeared to be following a policy compatible with that of German colonialism, their aims were often at odds with those of the Rwandan court and those of the German Residency. Moreover, the official aims of the Church hierarchy did not always agree with the sentiments of rank-and-file missionaries, for often the latter sided with the dominated Hutu majority against the dominant Tutsi.

Tutsi cattle owners were Rwanda's most privileged indigenous inhabitants. Many of them were the patrons (*abashéebuja*) of agricultural Hutu clients (*abagarágu*) in the relationship known as *ubuhake*.[1] This clientship arrangement was not the only type extant in Rwanda, though it was quite common. Furthermore, it is probable that *ubuhake* merely reflected the inequality governing relations between Tutsi and Hutu and was not generative of this inequality (cf. Vidal 1969, 384–99). Outside of *ubuhake*, however, Hutu were more vulnerable to Tutsi exactions of corvée labor (*ubuléetwa*) than they were within *ubuhake*, for Hutu clients were protected by their patrons against the demands of other Tutsi. At the bottom of the social hierarchy in Rwanda were the least numerous group, the Twa. In northern Rwanda, where the stratified structure of central and southern Rwanda did not obtain, many Twa continued

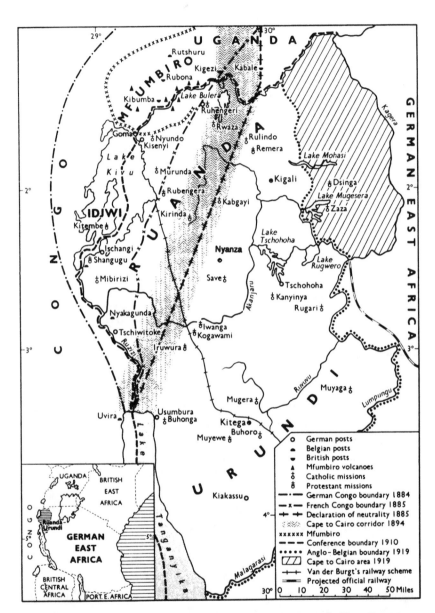

Map 2. *Ruanda-Urundi, 1884–1919. From R. Louis, Ruanda-Urundi, 1884–1919 (Oxford: Clarendon Press, 1963). Used by permission of Oxford University Press.*

to glean their living from the forest. In central and southern Rwanda, most of them were potters.

MUTUAL MISUNDERSTANDING

Missionary involvement in this complex social system was a source of moral conundrum to those priests whose sympathies resided with the Hutu masses. The Church directorate was committed to upholding the monarchy and Tutsi domination. The official policy of the Church favored the evangelization of the Tutsi elite, but *umwaámi* Yuhi Musinga discouraged this. Virtually no Tutsi nobles converted to Christianity until 1917 (Linden 1977, 131). Before then, new converts were overwhelming Hutu. The first ones tended to be the most impoverished among them, those without patrons and without protection. In fact, they often sought out missionaries as possible protectors.

Missionaries developed a "working misunderstanding" with their converts (Bohannan and Curtin 1964, 11), which was particularly evident in the realm of economic transactions. When priests acquired cattle, they often assigned them to the care of Hutu Christians, who sometimes understood the action to signify the cattle relationship, *ubuhake*. The priests' conceptions of these arrangements differed markedly: they saw their actions in terms of European commodity exchange.

Furthermore, although no one has noted how Rwandan converts first conceptualized money, it is known that missionaries began monetarily remunerating Hutu converts who worked for them at mission stations about 1912 (Linden 1977, 111). For many Rwandans this was their first exposure to the concept and practice of wage labor. Mission stations quickly became commercial centers, where the products of long-distance trade, cloth, and beads could be exchanged for local produce and livestock. Many Tutsi patrons in southern Rwanda complained bitterly that Hutu Christians were selling off cattle that should have remained within the *ubuhake* clientship arrangement.

To many Hutu, conversion to Christianity held out the possibility of a materially better life. At the very least, it offered an alternative to clientship under Tutsi patrons. Most significantly, white priests were weaning their Hutu converts away from Rwandan gift logic, a logic that implied Hutu subordination to Tutsi givers of cattle. A peasant church was developing in Rwanda, one whose success depended partly upon the fact that the actions of its agents offered loyal Hutu Christians the enhanced possibility of social advancement.

Yet there were many Rwandans who opposed the missionary presence. By 1904 mission stations had become small fiefdoms (Linden 1977, 52), each with a sizeable Hutu clientele, which were actively resented by *umwaámi* Musinga and his Tutsi chiefs. The Germans were also irritated with the White Fathers, both for their theocratic tendencies and because the majority were francophone and thus dubious agents of German imperialism. Some Hutu in southern Rwanda were disappointed with the priests for not going further to curb Tutsi excesses. In the north, leaders of the "traditional" religious cult known as Nyabingi (named after the goddess of fertility, health, and prosperity, whom they worshiped), firmly opposed missionization.

One of the more famous Nyabingi resistance leaders was the priestess Muhumusa, who also claimed to be one of the former wives of *umwaámi* Kigeri Rwabugiri, who died in 1895 (Chrétien 1972, 649). Rwabugiri had been Rwanda's most successful warrior king, and the king whom Musinga deposed in 1896, *umwaámi* Mibambwe Rutalindwa, had been Rwabugiri's designated successor. Muhumusa had followers in the north and even in central Rwanda, for she challenged Musinga's legitimacy on the basis that Mibambwe Rutalindwa had been Rwabugiri's rightful heir. Many Rwandans recognized the validity of Muhumusa's claim and referred to her respectfully as the "queen of Ndorwa," since she had taken refuge in the north after Rutalindwa's deposition.[2] Because the German Residency was committed to imposing central Rwandan authority upon the north, the German military had begun conducting punitive raids in the area. In May 1909, Muhumusa was captured and brought to Kigali (Linden 1977, 85).

Although Musinga might be expected to have been pleased with the capture of Muhumusa, by bringing her to Kigali the Germans had unwittingly reinforced the woman's claim to legitimacy. Kigali is situated within the sacred half of the Rwandan kingdom called Bwanacyambwe (see map 1). By keeping Muhumusa in sacred Rwandan territory rather than in a peripheral region, the Germans had enhanced the credibility of her claim to the spiritual powers of kingship. Two competitive sources of kingly *imáana* could not invest sacred Rwandan territory at the same time. Musinga thus interpreted the German action as an attempted coup d'état against him, but he turned his wrath against the missionaries instead, by unleashing rampaging Tutsi youths on their recently established administrative school at Nyanza. Realizing the gravity of their error, the Germans quickly transferred Muhumusa away from central Rwanda and teaching resumed at the Nyanza school (Chrétien 1972, 647). Nevertheless, the incident underscored Musinga's vulnerability. He had not dared to attack the Germans directly, for his armies were no match for them. The missionaries were apparently a less formidable adversary, but they could not be easily dislodged from their settlements either. They tended to be well armed and well protected by their Hutu followers. Musinga had betrayed his inability to defend the inviolability of Rwanda's sacred halves (see pp. 40–43).

Following the defeat of Muhumusa and later of her son Ndungutse in 1912, Tutsi loyal to Musinga entered the north in vengeance, pillaging the regions of Bumbogo, Kibali, and Buhoma (Linden 1977, 109), areas where Nyabingi-inspired resistance had been most active. Many Tutsi stayed behind in the northern areas to consolidate their gains and to develop *ubuhake* ties with the Hutu population. With the aid of German military might and the tacit support of Catholic missionaries, central Rwandan Tutsi accomplished in a few years what it had taken them several centuries to achieve in southern and central Rwanda, but they would live to regret it.

During the subjugation of northern Rwanda, the Germans, the missionaries, and the Rwandan monarchy had forged a tenuous political alliance. Economically, however, the three groups' interests diverged. After 1912 conflict of an economic nature became more apparent.

The Rwandan economy was becoming monetized, and the German Colonial Residency encouraged this tendency by levying a head tax in 1914 (Louis 1963, 160). Musinga opposed the tax as an attempt to diminish his influence, for the Tutsi patron caste extracted its share of the products of Hutu labor in kind, rather than through the abstract medium of money. Many Hutu, however, welcomed the new tax, realizing that it would partially release them from indenturedness to Tutsi patrons. In opposition to the Tutsi version of gift logic imposed upon them by their patrons, Hutu cultivators were embracing commodity logic as a means of circumventing Tutsi domination. Furthermore, by introducing an alternative "tribute" system, the German Residency had to erect a bureaucratic structure to administer it. Eventually this structure began to conflict with Musinga's administration, and a split soon developed between the "modernist" opposition and "traditionalist" supporters. Economic changes accompanied bureaucratic ones. Trade in cattle products, ivory, and animal skins between Rwanda and the outside world was increasing. It was also about this time that the German Resident, Dr. Richard Kandt, began advocating the growing of coffee as a cash crop in Ruanda-Urundi (175). The idea of turning Ruanda-Urundi into coffee lands, though, would have to await the outcome of World War I.

Concerning the war, little need be said except that it came to a quick end in this area when Belgian troops from the Congo easily overcame small German garrisons stationed in Ruanda-Urundi. At war's end, Belgium was awarded a League of Nations mandate over the region.

CATHOLIC HEGEMONY

The immediate postwar years were a period of confusion. The new Belgian colonist class sought a coherent policy, one committed either to reform or return to the status quo ante. Overtures were made in both directions. Some Belgians took the statements of pro-Hutu White Fathers seriously and toyed briefly with the idea of reforming the Rwandan system in favor of the Hutu peasantry, hoping thereby to increase agricultural production through monetary incentives (Louis 1963, 129). By the end of 1917, however, many Belgians and the upper echelons of the Church hierarchy had gravitated back to the German strategy of indirect rule (which favored the Tutsi elite). The tripartite political arrangement (the *umwaámi*, the Colonial Residency, and the Church) that had prevailed before the war reemerged, but with the important difference that the *umwaámi* was much weaker than before.

As Musinga's influence waned, some Tutsi began to go their own way in religious matters. The first nobles were baptized in 1917; other Tutsi started to frequent mission schools. At about this time, several Catholic missionaries—Fathers Arnoux, Hurel, Pagès, and Schumacher—began the first serious studies of Rwandan society (Louis 1963, 137). The intention of these studies (with the notable exception of that of Pagès) was to investigate how the Rwandan social system might be reformed and made more equitable to the Hutu. Thoughts of reform were dashed in 1919, however, with the arrival of the new Belgian Colonial Resident, who was firmly committed to the policy of indirect rule maintaining Tutsi privilege. A deaf ear was turned toward the reform-minded priests.

From 1922 to 1930, Tutsi converted to Catholicism in large numbers as a pro-Tutsi "tilt" of the Church was felt in education. The first class of students (all Tutsi) graduated from the administrative school at

Nyanza in 1923. With Tutsi beginning to enter the Church, Rwandan Tutsi as a whole became divided along pro- and anti-Church factions. The former were "modernists" who sought education and the new bureaucratic, cash economy route to power and patronage; the latter were "traditionalists" like Musinga. The *umwaámi* sensed the erosion of his influence with members of his own ethnic group and made some conciliatory gestures toward the Church, but by 1924 the Church and the Belgian administration had grown bold enough to talk of a "bourgeois revolution" (Louis 1963, 154–55), which meant the replacement of traditionalists with an educated elite made up of both Tutsi and Hutu.

Ritual erosion of the Rwandan system accompanied the political and economic change. The years 1924–25 witnessed the demise of several royal rituals, as Musinga, concerned with appearing "pagan," neglected to perform them. Despite his efforts, by 1927 the Belgians considered deposing him and replacing him with a mission-educated *umwaámi*.

The Church exerted pervasive influence over Rwandan society through education, by which it was becoming the guarantor of the Tutsi-Hutu division. As more Tutsi received mission school educations, the number of Hutu occupying lower- and middle-level colonial administrative positions declined. Those Hutu who did manage to live under the tutelage of a mission settlement were considerably more fortunate than other Hutu. Many had begun to grow cash crops, such as coffee and tobacco, on land sheltered from Tutsi exactions (Louis 1963, 169). By embracing the cash economy as well as Catholicism, these Hutu achieved a degree of autonomy from the Tutsi-dominated system. Furthermore, many pro-Hutu priests approved the privatization of land, seeing it as a way their Hutu followers could permanently evade subjugation to the Tutsi.

In 1931 the sword of Damocles that had been hovering over *umwaámi* Yuhi V Musinga's head ever since the first White Father set foot on Rwandan soil finally fell. The traditionalist king was deposed and replaced by his son, who was proclaimed *umwaámi* Mutara IV Rudahigwa. Both the governor-general of the Belgian Congo and the elitist head of the Rwandan Catholic Church, Monsignor Classe, participated in naming Rudahigwa king. All brakes on Tutsi conversion were now removed; the pro-Tutsi faction among Catholic missionaries had prevailed over the pro-Hutu faction, and once again Tutsi had outflanked Hutu.

Following the deposition of Musinga, what remained of the tripartite feudal hierarchy, which had afforded leeway to many Hutu in allowing them to use the patronage of one chief to counter the exactions of another, was now scrapped as inefficient. In its place a system was installed wherein a single chain of command descended from the colonial governor-general to the *umwaámi* and then through Tutsi administrative chiefs down to the lowliest Hutu and Twa.[3] In the north, where Tutsi dominance had only recently been established, these changes were bitterly resented by the Hutu majority.

Furthermore, many Hutu in central Rwanda began to grow disillusioned with the Catholic Church. Hundreds converted to Protestantism, particularly Seventh-day Adventism. In parts of northern Rwanda, the Balokole movement, a syncretistic spin-off from the Church Missionary Society (Episcopalian) in Uganda, began to attract followers. This movement remained confined to Uganda and a few areas in northern Rwanda.

During the 1950s a new crop of missionaries entered Rwanda. These priests reinforced the populist wing of the Rwandan Catholic Church, for they were concerned with the issue of social justice in Rwanda and embarrassed by the Church's inconsistent position on it. Many felt that *ubuhake* had to be eliminated. In 1954, *umwaámi* Rudahigwa agreed and *ubuhake* was indeed abolished. This change, although cosmetically important, did not significantly alter the unequal relation between Tutsi and Hutu, because Tutsi administrators continued to dominate the indirect-rule state apparatus and to control the land. The abolition of *ubuhake* was clearly not enough to satisfy Hutu bent upon fundamental change.

In 1957 several mission-educated Hutu, including Gregoire Kayibanda, published the "Bahutu Manifesto," which called for basic reforms in Rwandan society but remained supportive of the Catholic Church (Louis 1963, 250). This document signified unity between the educated Hutu elite and the Hutu masses. But *umwaámi* Mutara Rudahigwa paid it no attention, and when a Hutu delegation visited him in April 1958, he insulted them by calling them *inyanga rwanda* ("haters of Rwanda"). This act disabused many Hutu of the widely held belief that the *umwaámi* was the protector of all.

After ethnic violence broke out in 1959, a UN trusteeship authority entered Rwanda in March 1960 to oversee elections. In July 1960 these resulted in an overwhelming victory for the Hutu parties. The Tutsi monarchy was abolished and Kayibanda was named the first prime minister. Official independence from Belgium came in July 1962. Some Tutsi exiles continued to organize sporadic raids into Rwanda from camps in Burundi and Zaire, but these raids only provoked reprisals against noncombatant Tutsi still living on Rwandan soil. Tens of thousands of Rwandan Tutsi were killed, and many more fled as refugees and remain today in Burundi, Zaire, Uganda, Tanzania, Europe, and elsewhere.

Tension between Tutsi and Hutu continued into the early 1970s. In schools students would have their fingers measured for length and their noses measured for width. Those found to be Tutsi—identified by their longer, thinner fingers, longer heads, and narrower noses—would be beaten (Linden 1977, 284). When the democratic government proved unable to control these incidents, the military took over in 1973 to restore order. The new military government, composed of several army officers from the north (Gisenyi and Ruhengeri prefectures), opposed the overrepresentation in parliament by members from the south and center of Rwanda, but supported the privileged position of the Catholic Church. It also discouraged further acts of persecution against Rwandan Tutsi. Since that time, the condition of Rwandan Tutsi has improved. In effect, the events of 1973 signified that the predominantly Hutu regions of northern Rwanda, through the army and with the tacit support of the Catholic Church, had done what Muhumusa, Ndungutse, and their Nyabingi followers had been unable to do. They had crossed the Nyabarongo River and taken control of the entirety of Rwanda.

RECENT HISTORY

The Church was spared throughout the upheaval, having changed its position at a critical moment in the 1950s from preserver of the status quo to defender of social justice. Today that image lingers. President Juvénal Habyarimana, leader of the 1973 military coup, and the present government uphold the privileged position of the Catholic Church, and there is no evidence indicating that its status will decline in the near future. The Church-sponsored newspaper, *Kinyamateka* (in Kinyarwanda), once an organ of the Hutu revolution, continues to be widely read.

In Burundi, by contrast, the Catholic Church is viewed with suspicion. Tutsi government leaders there clearly perceived that the Rwandan Catholic Church eventually supported Hutu emancipation, and they do not want the same thing to happen in Burundi. In the 1960s and 1970s the hint of developing class consciousness among Hutu in Burundi was brutally repressed. As many as two hundred thousand Hutu were killed. Hutu intellectuals were particularly singled out for persecution and the definition of Hutu intellectual was quite wide: anyone with a smattering of education qualified. Many Hutu refugees fled to Rwanda and elsewhere. Although the Burundi government has not made Catholicism illegal, it was clear in 1983, when I lived in neighboring Rwanda, that they did not want any more Catholic missionaries who might have pro-Hutu sympathies. Those already present were encouraged to leave; their visas were not extended after they came due.

Education remains largely in the hands of Catholic Church officials in Rwanda, especially at the primary and secondary school level. Today there is evidence of the Church's presence in most areas of Rwanda, including the rural regions. It operates urban and rural health dispensaries and nutritional centers staffed by both European and Rwandan health technicians. These centers act as focal points for the dissemination of Western biomedical concepts concerning illness and the body.

Furthermore, because of its influence and temporal power, the Church has stifled the development of syncretic religious sects in Rwanda, though it has had to tolerate Protestant evangelism. Catholic leaders in Rwanda saw the example of Kimbanguism in the Congo and they learned from it. The Balokole movement apparently continues to function in the Kigezi District of southwestern Uganda, but I neither encountered it in northern Rwanda nor heard it spoken of in other parts of Rwanda. Protestant missions do exist in many parts of Rwanda, particularly in the south and center, and include Seventh-day Adventist, Pentecostalist, Methodist, and Baptist denominations. Protestantism and Islam, however, are not as widely followed as Catholicism. Instead of "new religions," Rwandans follow either a mission religion or a "traditional religion (Nyabingi in the north, Ryangombe in the south and center) or both.

Northern Rwanda and central-southern Rwanda have continued to play antagonistic roles. Rwanda's brief parliamentary democracy was dominated by central Rwandan personalities; today's military government is dominated by northerners. The south and center were being incorporated into the central Rwandan Tutsi kingdom since at least the sixteenth century A.D.; in the north, the last Hutu polity remained independent until 1928. There were fewer Tutsi in the north, and those who were present were seldom able to dominate the Hutu agriculturalist population for long (Ndorwa was briefly controlled by the pastoralist Abashambo [cf. Freedman 1984]). People in the north never became as accustomed to the Tutsi regime as the people in the south and center.

When this regime was imposed upon them in the twentieth century, they were the ones who reacted most bitterly. The first major violent incidents against Tutsi took place in the north during the events of 1959–61. Today the split between northern and southern Rwanda is perhaps as important as the split between Tutsi, Hutu, and Twa.

It is not useful to consider religious change apart from economic and political change. In Rwanda evidence shows that the Catholic Church influenced the capitalization of the Rwandan body politic. This development, whereby commodity logic came to predominate over gift logic, has succeeded because for the Hutu majority gift logic entailed subjugation to Tutsi patrons, whereas commodity logic held out the prospect of liberation from them.

NEW RELIGIONS

The pace of political and economic change has been swift in Rwanda. The process has led to numerous conflicts, both social and individual. Elsewhere in Africa, dealing with these difficulties has become an important function of popular religious and therapeutic movements. "New religions," or syncretic religious movements, have arisen in response to the exigencies and contradictions of the colonial and postcolonial world (Jules-Rosette 1979). In most cases these innovative religions have attempted to bridge the gap between the old and the new, the accepted and the foreign. In some instances these movements have resisted the changes brought with colonialism (cf. van Binsbergen 1979; Comaroff 1985).

One prime area of focus in popular therapy and innovative religion concerns the explanation of misfortune. For example, many new religions exhibit a marked tendency to replace explanatory models of misfortune that concentrate on causes external to the sufferer with ones that emphasize internal causes. Similarly, these movements also tend to replace healing techniques that involve accusation with those that call for confession. The Ivory Coast religion known as Harrism manifests these tendencies in a particularly dramatic way (Augé 1975; Zempleni 1975; Walker 1979). One suffers because of one's own witchcraft desires rather than because one is the victim of witchcraft. Instead of using such healing procedures as ordeals and divination that aim at discovering the identity of the witch in one's social nexus, Harrism has its adherents confess to their own witchcraft. Although Harrism seems to depart radically from precolonial models of misfortune explanation that emphasize external causes, it really forms a bridge between the old and the new. Although the person becomes self-afflicting in Harrism, the cult uses the precolonial notion of witchcraft to explain the novel in terms of the old.

Other African new religions such as the Zambian "Masowe Vapostori" (Kileff and Kileff 1979), merely add the notion of internal causation to the notion of external causation. Witches and spirits (external causes) may afflict people with misfortune, but devotion to Christ leaves one less vulnerable to their attack. Misfortune can also be visited upon a sufferer as punishment for sin (an internal cause), prodding him or her to repent.

Another new religion, called Jamaa in Katanga (cf. Fabian 1971), confronts the problem of separation and alienation in the copper-producing regions of Zaire. While Jamaa acknowledges the problematic nature of separation, it provides a framework for conceptualizing this phenomenon through the use of Bantu categories. Jamaa appears to say that individuals have become isolated in the postcolonial world, not so much because of the new social and economic conditions as from their failure to uphold precolonial values. Jamaa provides a way of accommodating the new by obfuscating the differences between the old and the new.

As we shall see, the themes that have emerged in the context of new African religions are also major issues in Rwandan popular therapy. One issue concerns how Rwandans define themselves in relation to their own society and to the outside world. Another concerns the determination of causality in misfortune.

CHAPTER 3

Accusatory Therapy in Northern Rwanda

~~~~~~

Flow/blockage imagery has been relatively well preserved in northern Rwandan therapies of accusation that focus upon the causal notion of poisoning. Images of "blocked flow" and "hemorrhagic flow" permeate the illness episodes of Rwandans afflicted by poisoning (*uburozi*).[1] Poisoning is related to the ideology of the gift, for witches or poisoners (*abarozi*) are those who do not abide by reciprocity. They are those who take, but do not give. Breaching the morality of gift logic compromises social relations and can lead to illness.

When illness or misfortune occurs, the healer or diviner first establishes whether it is ordinary or extraordinary. If the illness is extraordinary, he attempts to determine if it is of spiritual or human origin. These categories are not mutually exclusive, for humans can enlist the aid of various spirits to afflict others. If the sickness has been sent by another person, the healer attempts to discover who that person is, and how the charms or poisons used can best be neutralized. This type of therapy relies on a "persecutorial" view of misfortune (cf. Zempleni 1975); that is, it orients the sufferer's suspicions toward those with whom he or she has difficult social relations.

Fluids are central to Rwandan concepts of physiology and the body's insertion into social life. Employed symbolically, they are interconnected with notions of production and exchange. The body itself is partially constituted by fluids that are consumed and exchanged by people in circumstances ranging from the quotidian to the ceremonial.

In this chapter, I discuss fluids and their relation to the body, conflictual social relationships in Rwanda, the cultural particularity of northern Rwanda, the theories and remedies used by Butaro healers in treating illness attributed to *uburozi* (poisoning), and case histories in Butaro illustrating the interdependence between the healing theories and local notions of sociality.

FLUIDS IN HEALTH, LOVE, ILLNESS, AND DEATH

The first humor that one observes playing an important role in Rwandan popular medicine is saliva (*amacáandwé*). Since it is thought to embody the person's nature or essence (*kamere muntu*), saliva is used in divination. In most divinatory practices today the client spits upon some object used in the procedure before the procedure begins. When Rwanda was ruled by the *umwaámi*, court ritualists employed the king's saliva in divination (de Heusch 1982, 118). Royal sputum was introduced into the mouths of sacrificial bulls. After a bull's death, ritualists opened its abdomen and "read" its entrails. One ritualist had the responsibility of obtaining the king's saliva and keeping it in a special container. *Imáana*'s saliva was also imbued with extraordinary properties; *Imáana* was said to have given life to the first man by using his spittle to fashion a clay simulacrum of man from the earth. Healers sometimes use their saliva in therapeutic practices, especially when the disease they are treating is a skin disease. It is not unusual to see them expectorate directly on the skin lesion. Some healers say that saliva is a by-product of the brain resulting from its normal action. People that are mad, for example, are said to have mouths that are dry. In other words, they are lacking in a necessary bodily humor: the one that is thought to contain the "nature" of the person, his *kamere muntu*.

Probably the most important humor in cases of poisoning, however, is blood (*amaráso*). Poisons attack the blood first. In many instances poisons interrupt the flow of blood between the heart (*umutíma*) and the brain (*ubwonko*) (cf. Habimana 1988), which are believed to work together in producing and maintaining consciousness. When Rwandans speak of "losing heart," they usually mean loss of consciousness or fainting. The heart is the seat of reason, volition, and desire; the brain aids the heart in these functions. Blood is thought to be involved in tactile sensibility. Blood coursing through the veins allows the heart and the brain to sense whether something that one touches is hot or cold, soft or hard.

Healers state that *amarozi* (poisons) diminish the total volume of blood in the body; they dehydrate the body, or cause blood to exit abnormally from a bodily orifice. A poisoning can decrease the volume of blood in the body by as much as one half without yet killing the victim. When someone dies from an *uburozi* (poisoning), it is because he or she has lost all blood.

Male semen (*amasohoro*) is also thought to be blood, but in a purified form. Some healers state that semen production begins within the brain and then passes through the spinal cord into the scrotum. Others say that semen production occurs within the scrotum alone. A healthy diet that includes such beverages as *igikóma* (a thick beverage made from sorghum), *ikigaáge* (sorghum beer), and *amata* (milk) helps produce strong semen in good quantity. Beverages that are stronger in alcoholic content than *ikigaáge*, such as *urwáagwá* (banana beer), Primus (a brand of Rwandan bottled beer), and whiskey, are detrimental to the production of semen when drunk to excess. Overindulgence in such beverages dehydrates the body and delays ejaculation. *Urwáagwá*, however, is thought to be more masculine than any beverage made with sorghum. Women tend to do most of the work associated with sorghum cultivation and the brewing of *ikigaáge*, whereas men tend to do most of the work associated with bananas and *urwáagwá* brewing.

Contained within semen is its active principle, *intaanga* ("gift of self," from the verb *gutáanga*, "to possess, to give"), which gives semen its power to impregnate. Unhealthy semen embodies "bad" *intaanga* and lacks the power to fertilize; other kinds are like gasoline and can either burn the woman's uterus or dehydrate the child in her womb if she is already pregnant.

Women also possess *intaanga*, which is in their blood, but is not considered to be as strong as that of the male. Because of this, some healers say that the sentient and moral qualities of the person—situated primarily within the heart (*umutíma*), though also in the brain (*ubwonko*)—are inherited from the father. Others, more often female than male, state that the contributions of mother and father to the child's makeup are equal. Healers say that male *intaanga* and female *intaanga* join together most effectively after both the man and the woman have had orgasm during coitus. A favorable time for conception to occur is within the first week after the woman has had her period. Rwandans conceive of sexual intercourse not only as an activity to procure pleasure but also as a productive act, one in which the partners' *intaanga,* their two "gifts of self," fuse together to create a child. Many healers add that a couple must have frequent intercourse during pregnancy to permit the two types of *intaanga* to continue to fuse. This practice is especially important during the later stages of pregnancy. Rwandans call it *gukúrakuza,* which in other instances means "to slowly agitate milk during churning so as to separate out the butter" (Jacob 1987, 304). This concept demonstrates that Rwandans metaphorically link sexual reproduction to productive activity involving milk.

Other healers, more influenced by Western biomedical ideas of health and hygiene, dispute the idea that semen has any long-term constitutive effect on the fetus. Instead they say that semen fortifies the woman by "adding" to her blood. According to them and many Westernized Rwandans, women who have had frequent intercourse with their husbands during pregnancy are less likely to miscarry or suffer problems during childbirth, for they have blood in sufficient quantity. Moreover, after childbirth the husband's semen is said to aid in healing any lesions the woman may have sustained during parturition. Both "traditional" and many Westernized Rwandans agree, therefore, that sustained sexual activity during pregnancy is desirable. Semen is a productive fluid, which either directly contributes to the fetus's growth within the womb (the older idea) or contributes to the woman's health before and after giving birth (the more recent idea).

Before today's widespread practice of giving birth in a hospital or a rural dispensary, the position during parturition consisted of the woman kneeling on all fours. Someone behind the woman attempted to grasp the baby as it began to emerge. If the baby showed difficulty in exiting the birth canal, healers told me that they sometimes covered the woman's mouth and nose. In effect, her body is analogous to an open-ended conduit, movement of substances within it can proceed in either of two directions, toward the upper orifices or toward the lower ones. By blocking the upper orifices during parturition, the fetus is prevented from moving upward and remaining within the abdomen; instead it is forced downward and out. By blocking the top, flow to the bottom is encouraged.

Once the woman gives birth, she is secluded for a four- or eight-day period called *ikilili*. Thereafter the couple should resume intercourse, though not with the same frequency as before parturition. Some healers say that the vaginal intake of semen directly aids the rise of maternal milk (*amashéreka*) in the breasts. But this may be an idiosyncratic idea. Others claim that the action of intercourse indirectly aids lactation, rather than any direct effect of semen. A woman's breasts consist of fat that, according to these healers, must melt in order for *amashéreka* (maternal milk) to be produced. Intercourse with her husband develops a feeling of congeniality, of human warmth (*ubushyuúhe*) on the part of the woman. It is this warmth that helps the fat in the breasts to melt and turn into milk.

The new mother's lactation is a social as well as a private concern of the family. After *ikilili*, people come to see the mother and bring her gifts, a custom called *guhéemba* (to recompense). Representatives from both the husband's and wife's families make speeches. The wife's parents perform a special kind of *guhéemba*. They bring the couple a goat, cow's milk, beer, and especially, a quantity of sorghum porridge (*igikóma*). The idea behind this custom is that if the woman drinks *igikóma* in sufficient quantity, she will have abundant maternal milk (*amashéreka*), because sorghum porridge is thought to stimulate the production of milk. The wife's parents, therefore, will have indirectly participated in the production of their daughter's child's body through their gift. Both this custom and the sorghum beverage brought as a gift have the name *igikóma cy'umubyéeyi* (the *igikóma* of the relative). *Guhéemba* manifests the cooperation that should obtain between agnatic and uterine kin in assuring the baby's development.

When the mother's seclusion ends, the newborn child is brought out and shown to the other members of the family and immediate community (*gusohora umwáana*). But this rite of passage can only be performed after the child's body has been examined and found to be free of anal malformations. People present at this occasion receive a meal, especially the children who are given favorite foods. The meal given to the children is termed *kurya ubunnyano*, meaning "to eat the baby's excrement," for it is sometimes said that a small quantity of the baby's fecal matter is mixed with the food. This appellation may seem ironic, but in reality it celebrates the fact that the baby's body, in similar fashion to the body of the king in former days, has been found to be an open conduit, an adequate vessel for perpetuating the process of flow. If the baby's body were closed at the anal end, it would be able to receive but not pass on that which it had received. In a sense, the baby's feces are its first gift and the members of his age class are its first recipients. The children incorporate the child into their social group by symbolically ingesting one of his bodily products. These children in turn bestow a nickname on the newborn. Several months later, the parents will give the child another name (*kwiita izína*), but the children will continue to call the infant by their name. Their act of naming manifests their acceptance and reciprocity of the infant's "gift."

Mother's milk is the principal sustenance of Rwandan infants, and children may continue to nurse until they are three or four, though most babies are weaned earlier, between the ages of one and a half and two and a half. Obtaining maternal milk (*amashéreka*) in sufficient quantity is often a matter of life and death for Rwandan children; the protein deficiency disorder known as Kwashiorkor is most frequently observed among those who are no longer being breast-fed. A woman who lacks *amashéreka* is called *igihama,* a term that also applies to women who lack vaginal secretions (*amanyáaré*) during intercourse. The noun *igihama* comes from the verb *guhaama,* "to cultivate a field hardened by the sun; to have sexual relations with a woman who lacks vaginal secretions" (Jacob 1984, 437).[2] Although someone outside the context of Rwandan culture might not see any connection between a woman who lacks maternal milk after childbirth and one who lacks vaginal secretions during intercourse, Rwandans explicitly equate the two in *igihama.* Both women lack an important bodily fluid, in one case the fluid that passes from a woman to her child, and in the other case that which passes between a woman and her husband. In both instances the deficiency compromises the woman's and the household's fertility.

A woman can become *igihama* in several ways. According to some healers, the condition can be congenital. In other instances, menopause, parasites, or the Rwandan disease called *ifuumbi* can cause it. In yet other cases, *uburozi* (poisoning) may be the basis. Poisoning is thought to be common among women who share the same husband. If one wife succeeds in stealing her rival's urine (*inkáli*) or some of the fluid (*amanyáaré*) that she produces during intercourse, she may poison it in order to make her rival become *igihama*. She might also use her victim's menstrual blood. One possible treatment for a woman who has become *igihama* involves ingesting the plants *umunkamba* (*Clematis* var. sp.); *umukuzanyana* (*Clerodendrum rotundifolium*), a plant that is frequently given to calves because its name derives from the words *gukúza* (to make something grow) and *inyana* (calf); *umusange* (*Entada abyssinica*); and *igihungeri* (*Philippia benguellensis*). These medicines act by restoring "heat" (*ubushyuúhe*) to the woman's blood. With sufficient "heat" the woman will be able to melt the fat in her body, either to lactate or to produce vaginal secretions in sufficient quantity.

Vaginal secretion is extremely important, because the Rwandan fashion of making love, called *kunyáaza*, requires that the woman produce copious secretions (*inyáaré*, *amanyáaré*) during intercourse. *Kunyáaza* comes from the verb *kunyáara* (to urinate) and means "to make urinate"; that is, the man is supposed to make the woman "urinate," cause her orgasm and profuse secretion.[3] In former times, a woman was not supposed to eat anything solid after midday; she could only drink, in order that she be as "wet" as possible at night during intercourse. Elongated labia (*imishino*) were also thought by some to aid secretion (pubescent Rwandan girls practice the manipulation of their labia in order to make them longer—*gukuna imishino*). Intercourse is considered most fruitful when both partners produce a fluid contribution, for conception is thought to be most probable after both partners have had orgasm.

Ifuumbi, which is probably the most common ordinary malady of women treated by Rwandan popular healers, can cause a woman to become *igihama*. It can provoke miscarriage as well. *Ifuumbi* is not caused by poisoning, nor is it propagated by everyday contact among people. Some healers say that *ifuumbi* is caused by the eggs of parasitic worms such as *Tenia*. Others are extremely vague about the disorder's causes. The illness attacks the lower part of the abdomen first, causing pain especially during pregnancy or preceding menstruation. It can cause a woman to bleed from the vagina during pregnancy or at moments when she should not be menstruating.

Though more common in women, it can also afflict men. Nosebleeds are a frequent symptom among men who have *ifuumbi*. Furthermore, when a man contracts *ifuumbi*, he may have difficulty urinating, his testicles may swell, and he will often lose the power to ejaculate, though not necessarily the capacity to have an erection. Without treatment, such a man can become permanently impotent, for *ifuumbi* is said to be able to "buckle" its victims. In men and women, *ifuumbi* can cause vomiting, constipation, bladder problems, and sterility. The symptoms of both sexes are thus characterized by a similar disruption in bodily flow—excessive flow or blockage.

After attacking the lower abdomen, *ifuumbi* enters the blood and begins to damage it. The sufferer experiences feelings of generalized pain, weakness, or dizziness. Though the sickness can become localized in the lower abdomen or in the legs and cause swelling, *ifuumbi* may move upward in the body, passing through the spinal column into the mouth and head. The teeth can also be attacked; their color can change, or they can rot away completely if the disease is not checked. Once *ifuumbi* has moved to the head area via the spinal column, it can propagate along tendons, veins, and nerves, causing dizziness, diminished eyesight, and even mental debility. Though some of these symptoms may resemble syphillis, healers are quick to point out that *ifuumbi* and syphillis differ. The latter is accompanied by sores; the former is not.

The medicinal plants already mentioned as being used to treat women who have become *igihama* can also be employed to treat *ifuumbi*. Such medicines follow the course of the disease in the body. They begin their action in the lower abdomen and then move along the spinal column, nerves, tendons, and so on. Another Rwandan medicine that is often used to prevent and to cure *ifuumbi* in girls and women consists of a somewhat complex mixture of several plants and clay. This medicine is called *inkuri* and it is frequently administered to pregnant women as a prophylactic measure against *ifuumbi* and other sicknesses.

One of the recipes for *inkuri* includes the following plants: *igihoondohoondo, umusene, inyabarasanya, nkurimwonga, igicuncu, umushishiro, umuravumba, umunkamba, kazigashya, akanyamapfundo, umuzigangole, umushaariita, igifûmbafûmba,* and *umwanzuranya. Igihoondohoondo (Dracaena steudneri)* is a tree that has yellow wood and white flowers; the word for yellow, *umuhoondo,* resembles this tree's name and also designates the first milk a cow gives after calving. *Umusene (Ficus asperifolia)* is a plant that has yellow fruit. *Inyabarasanya (Bidens pilosa)* is a plant which has white and yellow flowers. *Nkurimwonga (Thunbergia alata)* has whitish-yellow flowers, as does *umushishiro (Zehnaria scabre). Umuravumba (Tetradenia riparia), umunkamba (Clematis hirsuta), akanyamapfundo (Leucas martinicensis), umuzigangole (Pauridiantha paucinervis),* and *umwanzuranya (Di-*

coma anomala) all have white flowers. *Kazigashya* (*Ranunculus multifidus*) has yellow flowers. *Igifûmbafûmba* (*Rumex abyssinicus*) is a plant with flowers of green, yellow, and white, and it is used in preparing a yellow dye.

Notice that most of the above plants are associated with the colors white or yellow. Yellow, one of the colors of the present-day Rwandan flag, is often used to symbolize peace. White is the color of milk and semen. It is used to symbolize purity, fertility, and the termination of mourning (*kwéera*, "to whiten"). It is not fortuitous to find these plants, whose flowers evoke two important fertility fluids, used against a sickness whose symptoms involve a generalized, perturbed flow of bodily humors.

The clay used to prepare *inkuri* reinforces the symbolic efficacity associated with the colors white and yellow. It is found in areas where cattle drink and urinate, activity that is an image of flow, for the waters the cattle drink enter, then exit, then reenter their bodies. According to some legends, cattle originated from the terrestrial waters of a lake (see pp. 29–32). When cattle go to drink at a lake, they are returning to their place of origin. Such places can be thought to be particularly auspicious repositories of *imáana*. Furthermore, when cattle ingest these waters, excrete, then reingest them, *imáana* becomes concentrated. Drying out the mud and adding herbs to it potentiates this concentration. *Ifuumbi* is thus treated by medicines that evoke associations with the flow media of water, milk, semen, and cattle.

Cattle are always positively valued in Rwandan culture, as is anything associated with them. Cow's urine, for example, is often used directly as a remedy or mixed with other substances in popular medicine. Cattle were celestial *Imáana*'s gift to terrestrial humanity. They unite the elements of sky, water, and earth. The gift of cattle originated in the sky, for at one time only *imáana* possessed them. This gift then passed from the sky through the waters of a lake onto the land. Cattle mediate between sky and earth, just as rain passes from sky to earth. As with rain, the circulation of cattle has to be socially ordered.

Bovine blood is another valued cattle product and is sometimes drunk by woman who has just given birth. A cow is bled and then the blood is added to the juice of cooked meat. The woman drinks this mixture with the intention of restoring the blood that she lost during parturition. This blood is also believed to help provoke the new mother's lactation (*guhéembera*).

When a man wishes to marry, cattle are required as bridewealth. One cow (sometimes two, if the woman has received higher education) is given to the bride's father as a brideprice (*inkwáano*). Later when the bridewealth cow calves, one female calf will be returned to the husband's father for each cow that he gave as *inkwáano*. This return gift of a cow from the bride's father to the husband's father is called *indoongoranyo*. Today the custom of offering this return gift is falling into desuetude, an indication that the system of prestations and counterprestations that once characterized relations between the families of the husband and the wife is also disappearing (see appendix A).

Another marital custom that has disappeared was called *kwaambika umwishywa*. Until the 1940s or 1950s, the groom adorned the bride with *umwishywa* (*Momoridica foetida*), a plant also used in the royal rituals. *Umwishywa* was clearly associated with fertility fluids, for its flowers are white and its small gourdlike fruit, at maturity, are red. In the marriage ceremony, the husband placed a garland of *umwishywa* around the bride's head. Then he expectorated a mixture of milk and herbs either in her face or between her breasts, an act called *gucíira imbazi* (Ndekezi n.d., 62–63). This action of adorning the bride, then spitting milk upon her, evoked the fertility powers associated with milk and *umwishywa* as two powerful images of surrogate semen—one bovine, the other botanical. The garland symbolized the bride's containment within a ring of "semen," that is, within her husband's patrilineal group, the group to whom her reproductive potential was transferred. The expectorated milk represented the seed that the bride would eventually contain in order to produce new life. As a wife, a woman was both contained and container. Her body should swell like the gourdlike fruit of *umwishywa* and became as flowing as that of a lactating cow, once it received the husband's semen.

Today instead of *kwaambika umwishywa* and *gucíira imbazi,* the husband and wife sit on opposite sides of a calabash of sorghum beer and drink from it at the same time. Then all the other participants at the wedding ceremony come forward and drink from the calabash in turn.

Drinking and the values that surround it lie at the core of Rwandan notions of sociability (see appendix B). These notions continue to be important in present-day rural Rwandan society. Drinking of *urwáagwá* (banana beer), *ikigaáge* (sorghum beer), or bottled pilsner beer remains the foremost social activity in Rwanda. It is also the context where one clearly witnesses the division between Tutsi and Hutu, on one hand, and

Twa, on the other. Although Tutsi and Hutu will drink together and openly share the same container (*igicumá*) or drinking straw (*umuhehá*), neither ethnic group will do so with Twa who happen to be present. Twa may drink and receive beverage in the company of Hutu or Tutsi, but the containers and straws that they use must be separate. Once this was pointed out to me, with some embarrassed tittering, as I proceeded to pass on a calabash of *ikigaáge* to a Twa who was sitting beside me. "No," a friend of mine said, "he receives his portion separately." Then someone handed him a cup of *ikigaáge*, which he kept to himself. Not to have given him anything to drink at all would have been a serious breach of etiquette.

Fluid exchange is important even in the most ordinary context of social interaction. When someone comes to visit, the host will usually offer the visitor beer to drink. If the host possesses beer, but refuses to offer some to a guest (*kwíima inzoga*), though others are present drinking, it is considered a very serious affront, tantamount to saying that good social relations no longer exist with that person.

Even at the end of life the values associated with fluid gifts emerge. In the past cow's milk was sometimes given to dying people in order to put an end to their suffering. The family took milk and poured it down the dying person's throat until he choked. The most compassionate manner of dying in Rwandan culture was thus being drowned in its most cherished liquid aliment.

PROBLEMATIC SOCIAL RELATIONSHIPS IN RWANDA

The previous discussion delineated Rwandan popular thought about fluids and their relation to the body. It should be emphasized, though, that conflictual social life perennially disrupts orderly fluid movement. We thus need to address the question of who is responsible for interrupting flow: Who is poisoning whom? In many accusatory therapies, determining the identity of one's persecutor (witch or *umurozi*) is the therapy's first aim. This is true not only of *kuraguza amaheémbe* in Butaro (northern Rwanda), where it is particularly manifest, but also of accusatory therapies practiced in southern Rwanda.

It is thus of interest to consider the specific social relationships most frequently implicated in poisoning cases in Rwanda as a whole. Some minor differences between the two regions exist with regard to problematic social relationships, but here I only wish to underline certain general tendencies that do not fundamentally differ between the north and the south.

All told, I was able to elicit information on forty-one cases of poisoning in Rwanda. Although this number of cases may not constitute a sufficiently large sample for statistical purposes, one can discern trends, even within this small corpus (see table 1). The majority of informants were Hutu, some were Tutsi, and one or two were Twa. Tutsi infor-

TABLE I
Relation of Poisoner to Victim

Relationship	Number of cases	Percentage of total
Collaterals		
FZ (*nyirasenge*)	1	2.4
FB (*data wacu*)	4	9.8
B or B/2 (*mukuru, muramuna*)	9	22.0
FW (*mukase*)	5	12.2
FZS (*mubyara*)	1	2.4
Inzu member (exact relation unknown)	1	2.4
Total collaterals	21	51.2
Other relationships		
Neighbors	5	12.2
Occupational or professional associates or rivals	4	9.8
Husband's family against wife[a]	3	7.3
Co-spouses against each other	2	4.9
Wife against husband	2	4.9
MBW against her husband's ZS	2	4.9
Wife against husband's father	1	2.4
Matrimonial rivals[b]	1	2.4

[a] Includes one case of a husband's mother against the wife.
[b] In this instance, a woman against another woman.

mants, whether as patients or healers, showed no difference from Hutu in the type of healing practice that they followed. Whether the Twa differ appreciably in their healing theories and techniques, I do not know. To-day many Tutsi and Hutu prefer to deemphasize the differences that dis-tinguished them in the past. Rarely does one find Tutsi, for example, who practice cattle husbandry to the exclusion of cultivation. Some Tutsi, however, especially among those who are older, continue to insist that they drink more than they eat.

Following Max Marwick's hypothesis (1965) that high frequencies of witchcraft tend to correlate with areas of social tension, it would appear that relations between collaterals are the most conflictual in rural Rwanda. Next most troublesome are relations with neighbors, and then those with occupational rivals or associates. Of the four cases involving occupational rivals or associates, three occurred in the south and one in the north.

The above figures also confirm Claudine Vidal's observation that re-lationships among collaterals in Rwanda are the most problematic (1978, 117). The reason for this is that collaterals often find themselves at odds over land. This is not surprising given that Rwanda's population, which is 95 percent agricultural, presently occupies the entirety of the country's arable land (66 percent of the total surface). Rwanda's popu-lation density of $715/mi^2$, which continues to grow at an annual rate of 3–3.5 percent, is one of the highest on the African continent (*World Al-manac 1991, 746*). Land is frequently the source of friction between neighbors as well, especially where the boundaries of fields are con-cerned. Sometimes, though, conflict may focus upon some other produc-tive asset (e.g., banana plants, coffee plants, cattle, or other livestock) in-herited from a predecessor.

Other motives in poisoning cases are also encountered. Someone may be jealous of a neighbor because the latter has children, whereas the former does not. As for occupational associates, the source of conflict usually concerns wealth or success, including ability in brewing and sell-ing beer, knowledge and patronage as a popular healer, having a salaried job or not. Unpaid or unreciprocated debts are also a cause of social ten-sion. Conflicts develop in political affairs too. Sometimes politicians sus-pect their rivals of having used poisoning to corrupt ballot box supervi-sors and vote counters.[4] Finally, conflict arising from sexual jealousy and marital infidelity is also an important factor; seven of the above cases showed this. Some cases combined a sexual and an economic motive, including one case involving a MBW.

Notice that the largest subgroup among collaterals is the brother–half brother category. This is not surprising since brothers, half brothers, and male parallel cousins (also classified as "brothers") tend to be pushed into competition over land and other resources belonging to a single *inzu* or *umuryaango* (see pp. 16–17). Furthermore, within a household, it is generally impossible for a father to pay the educational costs beyond primary school for all his children. More specialized schooling beyond that level is even less of a possibility. Usually, a rural Rwandan father cannot be completely democratic in rationing family resources, and privileges bestowed on other sons and daughters are never forgotten by those to whom they were denied. Moreover, wives in a polygynous household favor the interests of their own children over the children of cospouses. This fact accounts for the high number of FWs or stepmothers (*mukase*) implicated in poisoning cases.

BUTARO, ITS HEALERS, AND *KURAGUZA AMAHEÉMBE*

The healers who most exemplify the accusatory mode in popular Rwandan therapy are those who employ a technique of divination and healing called *kuraguza amaheémbe* (to divine by horns). I was able to spend about nine months working with several of these healers in the commune of Butaro (Ruhengeri Prefecture) in northern Rwanda, where this technique is widely practiced.

Butaro is considered unprogressive by many central Rwandans and "backward" by others. In 1984 an article appeared in the Rwandan daily newspaper, *Kinyamateka*, describing the region as an enclave, possessing cultural particularities not found in the rest of the country, such as the cult of Nyabingi. Butaro is indeed linguistically and historically unique. Linguistically the area is characterized by a large number of Rukiga speakers, though Kinyarwanda is still more prevalent, and the inhabitants of this region are usually referred to as Bakiga by Rwandans to the south. Many people are bilingual and have relatives who live north of the border in Uganda where Rukiga is more frequently employed than Kinyarwanda. Historically, the area was once a part of the interlacustrine kingdom called Ndorwa. This name is often used by inhabitants of Butaro to designate the larger area of which they once were a part. By the same token, they frequently refer to central Rwanda by the pre-colonial name Nduga.

Ndorwa was once ruled by the pastoralist Abashambo, but their dominance and influence waned toward the end of the eighteenth century in favor of the Hutu cultivating population (Freedman 1984). These Hutu do not appear to have been interested in establishing a strong state; instead their political efforts were oriented more toward preserving their autonomy in the face of strong neighboring kingdoms, such as Bunyoro and Rwanda. Their efforts were relatively successful. During the latter half of the nineteenth century, however, the Rwandan king Kigeri Rwabugiri succeeded in subduing large portions of the north including parts of Ndorwa. After his death in 1895, these areas once again began to drift away from Rwandan control. The end of Rwabugiri's reign witnessed the arrival of German colonialists, and the new king, Yuhi V Musinga, thought he could use the Germans to help consolidate the territories that had been won during Rwabugiri's tenure (Linden 1977, 22–24).

Before the arrival of the Germans, Tutsi penetration into the area had proceeded slowly and tenuously. The process accelerated during the early twentieth century as Tutsi ethnic hegemony spread over the agricultural Hutu into areas where it had not existed before. This policy was bitterly resented by Hutu and so it is not surprising that the first widespread violence that took place during the Rwandan Revolution (1959–61) occurred in the northern prefectures of Ruhengeri and Gisenyi (Atterbury 1970). As a result, most of the Tutsi population fled the region. Butaro thus differs from central Rwanda in that few Tutsi reside there. Today perhaps only a handful of Tutsi families live in the entire commune.

Even before the revolution, however, Hutu in the northern regions resisted the incorporation process emanating from the south. Instrumental in leading this resistance against the encroaching kingdom of Rwanda, and later against European colonialism, were Nyabingi *abagirwá* (priests), who today remain active in northern Rwanda and particularly in Butaro. The cult of Nyabingi in some respects resembles the indigenous religion practiced in southern and central Rwanda known as Ryangombe, or *kubaandwa*.[5] Both cults address themselves to problems of health, fertility, and prosperity. The term *Nyabingi* comes from Rukiga and means "she who possesses very much"; the goddess is sometimes referred to by her Kinyarwanda name of *Nyabyinshi,* which means the same thing. Female fertility is an important concern in both Nyabingi and Ryangombe.

Kubaandwa, however, has a more esoteric cast to it than the cult of Nyabingi. Whereas *abagirwá* openly practice their vocation and Nyabingi temples (*ingoro*) dot the hillsides, nothing of this nature occurs in regions where the cult of Ryangombe is practiced. People have to undergo initiation into the cult of Ryangombe; ceremonies occur at night and are often held outdoors beneath an *umukó* tree (*Erythrina abyssinica*). Access to Ryangombe practices as an outsider is difficult, but one can usually find Nyabingi *abagirwá* who will discuss their practices and beliefs. No formal initiation procedure is required to become associated with a particular Nyabingi priest.

Nyabingi priests do not usually play a direct role in healing although occasionally one may find *abagirwá* who, by coincidence, are also healers. Instead most *abagirwá* tend to envision their role in misfortune as secondary and supportive. One consults a Nyabingi priest and gives an offering to Nyabingi to solicit the goddess's benevolence and to reinforce one's mystical strength and resistance, but the participation of the *umugirwá* in this procedure is as an intermediary between the goddess and the supplicant. Quite often diviners refer their clients to specific Nyabingi priests, for the diviner (*umupfumu*) is usually the first person consulted in misfortune. He determines whether a particular misfortune is the result of an angered ancestor (*umuzímu*), poisoning (*uburozi*), or Nyabingi's wrath. In the last instance, which is exceptional, the Nyabingi priest's role as a therapist becomes important. He will recommend that the sufferer make a sacrifice to Nyabingi (a sheep or a cow) or that the person "give" a daughter to the Nyabingi priest. In cases where the sufferer is a young girl, her illness is often taken as a sign that Nyabingi has chosen her to become a medium and that she should leave her parents and take up residence with a Nyabingi priest.

Girls who become members of an *umugirwá*'s household in these two manners are later given as wives to followers of the *umugirwá* who cannot afford the high bridewealth payments that predominate in northern Rwanda. Whereas one might pay the equivalent of 100,000 to 200,000 Rwandan francs (US$1,000 to $2,000) for a wife in northern Rwanda, someone who receives a wife from a Nyabingi *umugirwá* pays considerably less and sometimes nothing at all. Despite the obvious advantage in obtaining a wife from a Nyabingi priest, most marriages in the north are not transacted through them. Nyabingi priests control a very small proportion of marriageable women. In southern Rwanda, bridewealth payments are much lower, anywhere from 30,000 to 100,000 Rwandan francs ($300 to $1,000). The reason for this difference is that in the south bridewealth is slowly losing its significance, becoming a final payment for a wife, rather than a single exchange within a relatively long cycle of reciprocal exchanges between the two families (see appendix A).

Courtship practices also differ in the two regions. In the north a young man does not directly court a woman; instead he manifests his desire to wed a certain girl to his father, who then approaches the girl's family to begin matrimonial negotiations. In the south a man may often begin to court a girl before negotiations with her family get underway. Couples often form out of mutual preference in the south. The north is more conservative in its mores than the south. Bridewealth payments are higher in the north, and reciprocal exchange obligations between the two families are usually observed more carefully.

POPULAR HEALING SPECIALISTS

The first popular specialist consulted in misfortune in both the north and the south is the *umupfumu* (diviner), who provides the initial orientation to the sufferer's quest for therapy. Frequently in Butaro, diviners recommend that their clients visit a particular Nyabingi priest and bring him a gift. A diviner may also tell his client to visit a specific healer. Nyabingi priests in Butaro sometimes recommend specific diviners or healers to their followers. A degree of cooperation thus obtains between Nyabingi priests on the one hand and healers and diviners on the other. People say that a remedy (*umuti*) obtained from a healer may be very good, but without the favorable disposition of Nyabingi, it could be useless. The role of *umugirwa* is more clearly delineated than those of healer and diviner, though all three enter into contact with the spiritual world. Nyabingi priests are morally the least ambiguous of these three personages. Their role is to uphold local morality. *Abagirwá* are respected by most members of the community, even by Christians; some *abagirwá* are spoken of in glowing terms as people who help those in need.[6]

The social role of healers and diviners of Butaro is more liminal. Many people respect them, but many suspect them of witchcraft as well. They encounter the more unseemly side of people's personalities—jealousy, hate, avarice, and the desire for power—as well as the brighter side—the desire to find a husband or wife, to bring children into the world and to care for them properly, and to maintain peaceful relations with one's family and neighbors. Although most healers and diviners claim that they never send poisons against others, people tend not to believe them. Most Rwandans say that sending poisons requires the expertise of specialists in the domain of the supernatural in order to be effective. Thus healers are frequently suspected of complicity in poisoning.

In many instances, the role of healer and diviner is also not clearly distinct. This is especially true of those who perform *kuraguza amaheémbe* (to divine by horns), for this practice is divinatory as well as therapeutic. The use of *amaheémbe* (horns) is doubly ambiguous, because the horns can be used to cure a sufferer's affliction or to send an affliction against someone else (*kwohereza amaheémbe*, "to send horns"). *Kuraguza amaheémbe* is quite widely practiced in Butaro and in other parts of northern Rwanda and southern Uganda. It may be the origin of central Rwandan beliefs about the malevolent *amaheémbe* spell (see pp. 147–148). Just as beliefs in *nyabingi* spirit possession in southern and central Rwanda are based on the Nyabingi cult in the north, central and southern Rwandans have probably focused more on the antisocial rather than the curative use of *amaheémbe*.

The procedure for employing the *amaheémbe* in curing varies somewhat from healer to healer, but tends to follow a general pattern. First the healer determines whether his patient's problem is the result of an *uburozi*. If the patient has already consulted another diviner and poisoning has been confirmed, the healer proceeds directly to *kuraguza amaheémbe*. If poisoning has not yet been determined, the healer may employ a separate divinatory procedure to establish the nature of his patient's disorder. One healer employs a weight wrapped in a piece of cloth, an apparatus that he called *ihiriza*. He asks a "yes"-or-"no" question, then shakes the *ihiriza* inside an animal skin pouch and throws it on a circular basket-woven utensil that is ordinarily used to toss grain into the air to separate it from the chaff. If the *ihiriza* comes to rest in an erect position, the answer is "yes," if it comes to rest in a reclining position, the answer is "no." Sometimes a healer will also administer an emetic as both a divinatory and a healing procedure. If the patient vomits within a few minutes after ingesting the medicine, he is considered to have been the victim of poisoning. If the patient does not vomit, that means the medicine has not "found" any poison in his body. The following is an example of a

The hut that Baudouin uses to perform kuragura amahéembe.

healer's (named Albert) use of the *ihiriza* in the case of a man who came to consult him for impotence:

> Q: Do you have impotence?
> Albert shakes the *ihiriza* and then throws it. It rolls, bobbles about, and then comes to rest standing up—an affirmative reply.
> Q: Do you have a wife?
> Affirmative reply from the *ihiriza*.
> Q: You sold a field recently, you received almost 100,000 Rwandan francs?
> Once again affirmative.
> Q: Your wife, before leaving you, attacked and injured you with a knife; two of her brothers helped her?
> Affirmative.
> Q: You had refused to give her money?
> Affirmative.
> Q: Your wife took your underpants to do something to them to make you impotent?
> The *ihiriza* says yes. This is the only bit of information that the patient had not already revealed to Albert in talking with him. The man seemed surprised by the *ihiriza*'s precise determination of the method used to make him impotent.

Kuraguza ihiriza is but one method of preliminary divination; others may also be used before resorting to the *amaheémbe*. After preliminary divination, the patient may decide that he or she has been the victim of poisoning and choose to have divination (*gushikisha*) performed by the "talking horns" (*amaheémbe*). (The healer is said to perform *gushika*,[7] i.e., to divine with the *amaheémbe*; the patient is said to do *gushikisha*.) The object of sending the *amaheémbe* is to capture the voice of one's persecutor (or the object of one's desire or curiosity), while that person sleeps at night, and to bring the voice back so that the healer and his patient can interrogate it. The aural aspect of the method has earned it the jocular title by which healers sometimes refer to it, *telefoni y'ikinyarwanda* (Rwandan telephone). To perform *gushika*, the healer invokes the *amaheémbe* spirits and instructs them to seek out the enemy of his client.[8] Usually there is a pause at this point, for the horns must be allowed time to find the enemy. Since the poisoner may reside far from the healer's residence—in another Rwandan prefecture, for example, or in Uganda, Burundi, Tanzania, or Zaire—this pause may last over an hour.

Often the healer occupies himself with other matters during this time, though frequently he waits with his clients, talking, joking, and drinking with them. A healer in Butaro named Samuel sometimes uses a talisman (*impigi*) if the *amaheémbe* delay in returning. He puts the *impigi*, a piece of horn that comes from an animal called *indibatizi*, under the patient's foot.

The *iheémbe* itself consists of a horn taken from an *inzobe* (*Limnotragus spekii*), an antelope that lives in swampy areas, or from an *impoongo* (*Tragelaphus scriptus*) (cf. P. Smith 1975, 186), an antelope that is also found in low-lying areas, is frequently seen walking in water, and is said to drink water through its legs. It may be that these animals are used because of their association with water, the most flowing element. If witches are blocking beings, it is logical to use things associated with fluidity to counteract them. This may also be the reason why certain healers prefer to use the *impoongo*, for water supposedly permeates this antelope's legs so that it does not even need to lower its head to drink. The *impoongo* has only to enter the water and it becomes, in a sense, continuous with the water. Its association with fluidity thus goes beyond the qualities of its habitat and extends to a property of its body. Another type of horn, less frequently employed, is that of a blind cow that has given birth to both a male and a female calf.

Possessing one of these horns is not, in itself, sufficient to exercise the power to perform *gushika*. This power must be acquired from someone else who possesses it. The healer must purchase not only the power but also the necessary medicines to make the *iheémbe* work. The healer must also make frequent sacrifices to his ancestors so that they continue to protect and aid him in his endeavors. A healer named Albert explained to me that his *iheémbe* had not been functioning well. He attributed this to an adulterous wife in his household, who had inspired the enmity of Nyabingi and Albert's ancestors. This episode in Albert's life disturbed his relation to the spiritual world and diminished the effectiveness of his *iheémbe*. Now he was temporarily abstaining from performing *gushika* and was waiting until he had sufficient money to purchase a goat as a sacrifice for his ancestors and a bull for Nyabingi. This action, he claimed, would restore his powers with the *amaheémbe*.

Another healer in Butaro, named Baudouin, explained to me that one also requires the aid of spirits (*imaándwa*) besides one's ancestors to perform *gushika*.[9] One such spirit is Nzamuzinda, who speaks at night and especially about problems concerning *abazímu* (ancestors) or Nyabingi.

Baudouin explained to me that, because this spirit cannot speak in the presence of fire, he could not employ him as his personal *iheémbe* spirit, for Baudouin always has a fire burning in the hut where his patients consult him and where he performs *gushika*. Instead Baudouin uses a spirit called Munihuzi to aid him in doing *kuragura amaheémbe*. Baudouin purchased the power to communicate with and employ Munihuzi from another healer in the Gisaka region (southeastern Rwanda). Without Munihuzi's cooperation, Baudouin would be unable to perform *gushika*.

Kuraguza amaheémbe is supposed to be performed at night, or in darkness behind closed windows and doors. Often, healers in both northern and southern Rwanda who do not require darkness disparage those who perform *kuragura amaheémbe* and other nonempirical procedures, referring to them by the French word, "féticheurs." Such healers, who only work during the day or in well-lit places, eschew magic and claim to rely only on medicinal plants (see chapter 4).

Kuraguza amaheémbe begins when the client spits on the *iheémbe* and then hands it back to the healer. The client's spittle is referred to here, and in most divinatory circumstances, as *imbúto*, a word that in other contexts means "seed," "child" (in reference to his parents), or "sperm" (Jacob 1985, 147).[10] The healer takes the *iheémbe* and places it in a small sack made from the pelt of an animal called *intutuzi*. The sack is attached at midpoint on a spear that is inserted into the ground blade upward. The healer asks his client to state his or her name, the nature of the problem, and what he or she desires to learn from the *iheémbe*. If someone has sent an *uburozi* (poison, spell) against the client, the *iheémbe* will be asked to seek out the poisoner. When the *iheémbe* returns with the voice of the *umurozi* (poisoner), the healer and his client will ask what poisons were used, what the motivation behind the malevolent act was, how the poison(s) can be neutralized, and what other members or property of the client's household, wife, children, livestock, or fields, have been touched by the *uburozi*. In some instances the *iheémbe* retrieves the *uburozi* itself. In these cases, the poison is later found somewhere within the healer's *urugó* (living compound, enclosure).

When the *iheémbe* returns, either with the enemy's voice or the poison (*uburozi*), many healers claim to see a streak of light that comes and places itself in the *intutuzi* pelt. Another way of discerning its return is the sound of an approaching motorbike that cannot be seen. Sometimes the participants are alerted to the *iheémbe*'s return by a squeaking sound, which is said to be the voice of one's enemy captured in the horn. The patient and the healer interrogate the voice, which never poses questions of its interrogators, and together they interpret its squeaky replies. A session may last up to two hours. The price of this treatment varies, but it can cost as much as 2,000 Rw.Frs. (about US$20), with an average fee of about 500 Rw.Frs. If the healer's ministrations resolve the patient's problem, the client is expected to pay another visit to the healer and reward him more generously. Patients tend to respect this stipulation: I often encountered people whose problems had ameliorated and who were merely visiting the healer a second time to bring him a gift of felicitation.

Here is the incantation that Baudouin uses in *kuragura amaheémbe* (an explanation of proper nouns follows). When reciting it, he shakes a gourd rattle and speaks toward the spear that holds the *iheémbe*.

> 1. Ngwino Bambuka, ngwino Sigigi, ngwino Sigiti,
>   (come Bambuka, come Sigigi, come Sigiti,)
>   ngwino Igewuza-Banguza, ngwino Mbanirubusa,
>   (come . . . , come . . . ,)
>   ngwino Bacucubikana-Balibucube,
>   (come . . . ,)
>   ngwino Musibyarugendo wa Nyenkangwa,
>   (come . . . ,)
>   iyo umugabo azindutse, undi arasibiraga.
>   (when one man sets forth [on a journey], another man adjourns his.)

> 2. Simpamagaye umuzímu, simpamagaye Nyabingi,
>   (I'm not calling an ancestor spirit, I'm not calling Nyabingi,)
>   mpamagaye umuntu wanga ——— ,
>   (I'm calling the person who hates [client's name],)
>   akamwanga ku manywa na nijoro,
>   (he [the poisoner] hates him in full daylight and at night,)
>   agatekereza ko azamuroga cyangwa akazamutwikira mu nzu.
>   (he [the client] thinks that [the poisoner] will poison him or
>   set fire to his house.)
>   Ndamuhamagaye ngo atebuke vuba vuba,
>   (I call him so that he come back quickly,)
>   aze ambwire amagambo ye na ——— .
>   (so that he come tell me his words with [client's name].)
>   Namara kubimbwira ndamurekura,
>   (when he has finished telling me, I will let him go,)

agende nta kindi cyo nshaka,
(he will go without my wanting anything else from him,)
ndashaka amagambo ye na —————— .
(I want his words with [client's name].)

3. Watindaganya, nakuhurabuliza,
(If you delay coming, I'll mistreat you,)
nakuburanganya nyiza kulyama,
(I'll prevent you from resting well,)
guhinduka no guhindukuliza,
([you will be] turning and turning [in bed],)
Umwahuro nakwahura igihugu naguteranya,
(the "brew" [poison] that I deliver to you, will make the country
turn against you,)
n'abagore naguteranya, n'abagabo,
(women will be turned against you, and men,)
naguterereza ibisazi, ukaziruka,
(I will throw madness at you, you will wander aimlessly)
naguterereza umwitwaro, ukazagwa kure.
(I'll throw banishment at you, you will die far away.)

4. Ngwino mitima nyangwe, nyangaragura,
(come hearts that hate, that mistreat [others])
umubambure ku nsengo z'imitima,
(so that you lift the siege against the hearts [of my client],)
ndamurekura agende nta kindi cyo nshaka,
(I'll let him [the enemy] go, without asking anything else,)
ndashaka amagambo ye na —————— .
(I want his words with [client's name].)

Then after the interrogation has been completed, the "poisoner" is instructed to touch his head so that he will forget the interaction.

5. Ubyibagirwe, wishime mu mutwe,
(Now forget it, scratch your head,)
ntugire uwo ubwira, urabeho, ntugaruke,
(have no other thing to say, good-bye, don't come back,)
haguruke undi uramukiwe.
(so that another may come whose turn it is).

An explanation of the proper nouns in the first stanza is critical for our
understanding of its meaning and tone.

LINE 1: *Bambuka*—"the one ready to get up, the one ready to go." From *kubambuka*—"to get up, to take off, to come unglued" (Jacob 1984, 72). *Sigigi*—"the one who is not coiled up or compressed." From *kugiga*—"to compress, to squeeze, to push into a small space" (Jacob 1984, 362). *Sigiti*—"the one who is not a tree." From the noun *igiti*—"plant, tree."

The idea in this verse seems to be, to arouse the attention of someone who is resting or sleeping, to coax him or her to action.

LINE 2: *Igewuza-Banguza*—"the one who causes understandings or agreements to come undone, but who borrows from me"; i.e., he does not honor his debts, he does not abide by reciprocity. *Igewuza* comes from *kugewuka*—"to fail to respect an understanding or agreement made with someone, to refuse or hate something or someone that previously had been accepted or loved" (Jacob 1984, 360). (When the *-za* suffix is put at the end of a verb, it makes it causative.) *Banguza*—"the one who borrows from me." From *kuguza*—"to ask for a loan, or a credit" (Jacob 1984, 414). *Mbanirubusa*—"I am with those who do not matter."

The cajolery of the first verse gives way to the first hint of a threat, the tone that characterizes the remaining part of the invocation. Here the healer's incantation begins to enumerate the moral flaws of his patient's persecutor: someone who abrogates understandings or agreements, who injects hate where once there was love, who does not honor his debts, and who thinks nothing of the people around him or her.

LINE 3: *Bacucubikana-Balibucube*—"the one who is sweating profusely, but who then is calmed, neutralized." *Bacucubikana* comes from *gucucubikana*—"to be sweating profusely, to be involved in work that requires a great deal of effort" (Jacob 1984, 196). *Balibucube* comes from *gucuba*—"to become quiescent after being very angry (person); to become placid after boiling (liquid)" (Jacob 1984, 194).

Notice here the use of a liquid metaphor that draws an analogy to the affective state of the *umurozi*, who is sweating profusely and is "boiling" in envy or anger while he performs his work, but who will eventually be calmed or neutralized. The healer is again threatening the *umurozi*. He is saying, in effect, "You spend your efforts uselessly in trying to poison my client, for you will only be neutralized in the end."

LINE 4: *Musibyarugendo wa Nyenkangwa*—"the one who interrupts the journey of someone who is afraid." *Musibyarugendo* comes from *gusibya*—"to impede, or to adjourn" (Jacob 1985, 170)—and *urugendo*—"journey, voyage." *Nyenkangwa* comes from *gukanga*, "to cause fear." The -*wa* suffix makes it passive. Here the full meaning of *Nyenkangwa* would be the "son of someone who has been made afraid," i.e., the "son of fear itself."

The imagery of impeding someone's journey, recalls the idea of blocking someone's path. Here the victim, "the one who is afraid," has had his way blocked by the "one who interrupts a journey," i.e., the *umurozi*. This is not far from the idea of *gusiba inzira* (literally, "to block the path"), which means to lose one's daughter through death, that is, to lose the possibility of entering into a matrimonial alliance with another family through the gift of one's daughter as a wife to another man (see the discussion of *isibo* on pp. 10–12).

LINE 5: The first stanza ends *iyo umugabo azindutse, undi arasibiraga*. This proverbial expression means that two people cannot take the same path at the same time, that is, rivals avoid each other, and what one gains another loses.

In summary, the invocation expresses several important ideas. First, the offending party, the poisoner, is compared to someone who does not abide by the moral notions of gift logic. He does not honor agreements. He takes, he borrows, but does not reciprocate. He changes love into hate. The people with whom he lives, his neighbors and his family, mean nothing to him. Consumed with hate and jealousy, he is not a flowing being but a boiling one, who expends his efforts and his fluids (perspiration) in the pursuit of evil against others. Furthermore, he interrupts the journeys of others and instills fear in them. He is thus a blocking being, who arrests movement along the path of life and fertility.

The following conversation is an excerpt from an interview with a poisoner solicited through the *iheémbe* of Baudouin. The conversation took place between the poisoner and his victim. I was unable to collect many interactions of this sort because most patients would not allow me to tape record the conversations that they had with their persecutors through *gushika*. Often though, they would relate the essential points of the conversation afterward. Here the questioning is done either by the healer or his patient, the answers were in the form of squeaks emanating from the *iheémbe*.

> Q: Where do you live?
> A: Not far from you.
> Q: What is your name?
> A: Ndekezi Salatien.

Q: Are you a Christian?

A: Yes.

Q: What have you come here to do?

A: I have come to tell you that I poisoned your wife.

Q: How did you poison her?

A: I used a cat and a pile of ants.

Q: Did you make her swallow it?

A: No, she only had to walk over the spot where I buried it.

Q: Is there any way of curing her?

A: No, unless you find an expert healer. The poison that I sent against her will kill her by eating away at her stomach.

Q: Do you dance at night?[11]

A: Even last night I came and danced at your house. During the dance I took earth from a grave and threw it on your house.

Q: Is this earth dangerous?

A: Yes, because it enters the flesh of my victim. It will cause her to urinate blood and then die.

COMMENT: The poisoning in this case is of the type healers call *umutáambikiro*. The *umurozi* digs a hole in the ground and then buries medicines in it. When the intended victim walks over the spot, he or she will contract an illness. Only the intended victim can contract this illness; an uninvolved party cannot get it. In this instance, the poisoner has accentuated his efforts by coming to the victim's house and performing *gucyúuragura* ("dancing at night") nearby.

The specific identification of the poisoner is also worthy of comment. The squeaking sounds are liberally interpreted by both the healer and the patient. In fact, the latter often offers his or her interpretation as to what the *iheémbe* has just said before the healer does, and in so doing, frequently reveals what and who it is that is feared.

The third point to be noted in this conversation is the action of the poison. It supposedly acts by causing the victim to lose her most vital fluid, blood, through urination.

Kuruguza amaheémbe is employed for a number of disorders. With all of these illnesses, though, it must first be established that a human agent has been responsible. No healer that I met in Butaro performed *kuruguza amaheémbe* in instances other than those involving human intervention, which in most cases meant *uburozi* (poisoning). Baudouin indicated to me that with the *imaándwa* spirit Nzamuzinda it is possible to diagnose and treat problems involving *abazímu* and the goddess

Nyabingi by *gushika,* but he did not possess Nzamuzinda. Munihuzi was the spirit at his disposal, and so his therapeutic action through *gushika* was restricted to afflictions of human origin.

POISONINGS EMPLOYED IN BUTARO

Kuzinga Abakoobwa

This poisoning prevents a girl from finding a husband. Most often, it is women and girls that afflict their rivals with this disorder. To send the spell, one takes a piece of the girl's undergarment, or some of her hair that has been caught in a comb, and burns it. One takes the ashes, adds medicines, and then wraps the mixture in a piece of rubber and conceals the packet beneath a rock where rainwater cannot touch it.

All the healers in Butaro who do *gushika* commonly encounter this poisoning. Samuel says that most of the poisoning victims who consult him are girls afflicted with this spell. He sends his *iheémbe* to find the person who attacked his patient so that he or she will have a conversation with the patient similar to that indicated above. Sometimes he also sends the *iheémbe* to find the malevolent charm and bring it back, so that his patient can see it. He charges 6,000 Rw. Frs. (about $60) for lifting this spell, a sum of about 1,000 Frs. in advance, and the rest when the patient has recovered.

COMMENT: This spell employs metonymic representations of the girl's sexuality, a piece of her underclothing or some of her hair. The hair from her comb is related metonymically, because it is a part of the body used to represent the sexual persona of the whole. A girl's hair and its grooming is one of the attributes she uses to announce her marital status.[12]

The logic of burning either the piece of garment or her hair is to induce the forced dessication of her body, the drying up of her sexual fluids. This idea is reinforced by the act of sealing the ashes along with medicines in something waterproof, and then secreting this packet in a location where rainfall will be unable to touch it. Not only will the girl's fertility substances be dried up through fire, they will be contained (in the rubber packet), and then removed from the circuit of fertility flow from sky to earth, since rain will be unable to touch them.

TREATMENT: Remedies vary from healer to healer, and even from patient to patient among those treated by a single healer. One way Baudouin treats this disorder is by taking an aquatic plant that grows at the fringes of lakes called *amarebé*, a queen bee, a plant called *umusinga*, and beans that sometimes grow spontaneously on the thatched roofs of traditional Rwandan houses. These ingredients are made into a concoction that is drunk by the afflicted woman.

COMMENT: *Amarebé* (sing. *irebé*) is used because of its homonymy with the word for the entry to a traditional Rwandan hut, *irebé*. *Mu irebé* means "to be at the entry of the hut." The image evoked here is that, after the cure, the girl should find herself at the doorway to a house (*inzu*), that is, ready to enter it with her newly found husband. Since the term *inzu* is also used to signify the minor lineage segment of three-generations depth, the girl's fertility or ability to produce new *inzu* members is implied as well.

Baudouin also gave the girl a queen bee, so that, as he put it, the girl would be admired by many men. This use may also stem from the fact that bees produce honey, a liquid whose production is closely associated with general ideas concerning fertility (see chapter 1). Honey is used in the manufacture of the alcoholic beverages that are important gifts in matrimonial transactions. Furthermore, since Rwandans have always been avid practitioners of apiculture, bees live and produce their fluids in "houses" partly of their own and partly of human manufacture.

The imagery of the house, and of founding a new household, is apparent in the third element Baudouin used: *umusinga*, a plant that grows on rocks. In precolonial Rwanda, when a person erected a house, he solicited the assistance of someone who belonged to the *abasaangwabutaka* ("those who were found upon the earth," i.e., the autochthonous clans), someone from the *Abasinga, Abazigaaba,* or *Abagesera.* Since members of these clans were thought to be the first to occupy the land, subsequent settlement by members of other clans had to be ritually approved and consecrated by them (d'Hertefelt 1971, 4–5). For example, when one built a house, the first stakes put into the earth had to be placed there by an *umusinga*, an *umuzigaba*, or an *umugesera*, since the earth was theirs.

The final component of Baudouin's treatment, the beans, reinforces this imagery of a new and fertile household. Here the logic has to do with the gender coding of the house. Projecting from the roof of a traditional house is a spire made of wood, called *agasoongero*. This spire suggests masculinity, for when the head of the household dies, the spire is taken down and discarded. Beneath the spire and surrounding it, one finds the thatching that drapes over the edges of the circular wall. This

thatched part of the roof is a female encompassing element—a matrix—
from which the phallic *agasoongero* projects. Beans that take root and
then begin to grow in this thatching, where they have not been intention-
ally sown, express gratuitous, exuberant fertility. How can the woman of
the household fail to be fertile and productive, when beans grow even
from the roof of her hut?

Kumanikira Amaráso

This poisoning, whose name literally means "to suspend blood," impedes a woman from delivering her baby. Sometimes it prevents her from
conceiving. Samuel explained that among pregnant women, the poisoning causes the baby to rise toward the heart instead of descending toward
the birth canal. Another healer, a woman named Antoinette, told me
that many pregnant women are victims of this spell, which causes the
baby to become turned transversally in the womb.

One method of poisoning a woman in this way is to obtain some of
the blood and other fluid that exuded from her womb during a previous childbirth. The fluid, called *igisaanza,* is then placed in a packet
along with other medicines and then suspended from the rafters of a
house. This form of the spell prevents the woman from being able to deliver again.

Another version of this poisoning, involves obtaining the woman's
menstrual blood (*iruungu*), vaginal secretions (*amanyáaré*), urine
(*inkáli*), or, if none of these bodily fluids is available, a piece of her clothing. This is put in a packet with medicines and then placed in a cave or
suspended from the rafters of a house or inserted among rocks on the
summit of a high hill, where rain cannot touch it. As a result, the victim's
menstrual flow is stopped and she becomes sterile. An interesting variant
of this poisoning entails putting the blood, along with medicines, into a
stream of fast-moving water. The woman's menstrual flow then becomes
hemorrhagic, which causes sterility and can be life-threatening. Some
healers refer to this last variant as *umuvu;* others consider it a form of
kumanikira.

COMMENT: The symbolic nature of this poisoning should be clear. In
effect, by suspending a woman's blood or other fluids involved in sexuality or reproduction, the woman's reproductive functions are also "suspended." Either she becomes unable to deliver the baby already in her
womb or menstruation stops and she becomes sterile. By suspending the

woman's bodily fluids in a position between sky and earth, or in a place where rain cannot touch them, the woman's body becomes blocked. When her fluids are put into a body of fast-moving water, her menses become dangerously abundant, an example of hemorrhagic flow.

TREATMENT: Healers vary in their treatment of this poisoning, but these variations possess features in common. One healer has the woman lie on her back while naked. He takes medicines and sprinkles them in a line from the woman's forehead, over the middle of her face, over her chest and abdomen, down to her genitals. The logic behind this treatment appears to be that movement must be encouraged from the top of the body to the bottom.

Antoinette uses another method. Although she does not employ *amaheémbe* in therapy, her treatment of *kumanikira* follows a similar line of symbolic reasoning to the previous treatment, but it engages more elements from the macrocosmic sphere in which the female body, as microcosm, is embedded: house, earth, sky, and rain.

Antoinette has the woman remove her clothes and then lie in a supine position inside her own house. Someone climbs upon the roof of the house, parts the thatch, and then pours an aqueous mixture of medicines through the opening in the roof onto the woman's abdomen. Another person inside the house then rubs the woman's stomach with the medicinal mixture.

COMMENT: In this treatment the blockage within the woman's body is treated as if it were an obstacle between sky and earth, for it is countered by someone's actually moving to the sky position, opening the female part of the roof, and then pouring fluids earthward. This time, however, the downward movement of fluids includes the woman's body in the circuit of flow from sky to earth, for the fluids contact the woman's abdomen before draining to the earthen floor. The cure is virtually a one-to-one homeopathic reversal of the symbolic operations accomplished in the poisoning, which removed the woman's body from the circuit of moving fluids by suspending her blood. In this cure, an analogic relation is established between the female body, its social locus—inside a house— and the elemental forces of nature. Then the woman's body is reinserted into the normal cycle of social and cosmic flow.

ANOTHER TREATMENT: Baudouin's treatment of *kumanikira* follows his diagnosis of the poisoning through the method of *gushika*. In one case he gave the afflicted woman, who was unable to deliver despite being pregnant, water with a piece of hippopotamus (*imvubu*) skin in it. In addition, he gave the woman a remedy concocted from the *umuhaanga* plant (*Kotschya aeschynomenoides; Kotschya strigosa* var. *grandiflora; Maesa lanceolata*) (Jacob 1984, 449). The name of this plant comes from the verb *guhaanga*, which means "to create, to restore, to invent; to occupy a place first; to germinate, to blossom; to have one's first menstrual period." He also gave her a plant called *umumanurankubá*, a name that comes from the words *kumanura*, "to make something descend, or to depend on," and *inkubá*, "thunder." The full meaning of the name of this plant would be "to make thunder descend, to depend on thunder." That is, to make rain fall.

COMMENT: Once again this is an image of restoring the sky to earth movement of rainfall, and by analogy, restoring normal fluid movement to the woman's body. In restoring this movement, the healer renders the woman capable of (pro)creating, capable of blossoming. The use of the hippopotamus seems to derive from its aquatic nature and its bellowing, which resembles thunder.

Urukarango (or Umukobwa Utajya Mu Mihango)

Afflicting a girl who cannot menstruate, or whose menstruation has been stopped, this spell is similar to the *kumanikira amaráso*, and some healers consider it to be a variant. According to Baudouin, though, the procedure used to cast the spell is different. Baudouin said that a poisoner can inflict *urukarango* by taking some of the girl's urine, or her menstrual blood, adding medicines to it, and then cooking the mixture on a piece of broken pottery from a vessel that has never been used (*urujo*). The mixture is cooked until the liquid evaporates. As a result, the girl stops menstruating and becomes sterile.

COMMENT: The girl's fluids are forcibly dessicated by fire. The *urujo* is a shard from a cooking vessel whose productive life has been prematurely ended by the act of breakage. It has never fulfilled its functions of containing and pouring out liquids involved in cooking.

TREATMENT: Baudouin usually treats this spell with the powder of a dried insect called *impanguzi*, which lives among plants called *imvúra idahita*. This is added to other plants, including *umurasanka* and *amarebe*.

COMMENT: As in the treatment of *kuzinga abakoobwa*, *amarebe* (sing. *irebe*) is used because of its homonymy with *irebe*, which means "entry of a Rwandan house." Why *umurasanka* is used is not clear. The healer's use of the *impanguzi* is due to the fact that its name is derived from the verb *guhaanguura,* one of whose meanings is "to impregnate a woman previously thought sterile" (Jacob 1984, 456). Furthermore, this insect's habitat is *imvúra idahita,* which means "rain that does not cease falling." In this instance, the symbolic reasoning is that, after treatment, the girl's menstruation should never fail again. In summary, a girl treated for *umukoobwa utajya mu mihango* should recover her capacity to menstruate and consequently her fertility, and then she will find herself at the doorway to a hut, that is, married and producing children.

Ubureémba

Women, especially wives belonging to a polygynous household, are wont to poison their husbands in this way, although sometimes a woman may afflict her lover when she suspects him of infidelity. The man's semen (*amasohoro*) or urine (*inkáli*) is taken and put into a small container. This vessel is placed beneath a larger one containing water. This does not prevent the man from being potent with the woman who poisons him in this way; it only keeps him from being potent with other women.

Antoinette says that one type of impotence, *ubureémba* proper, is congenital and cannot be cured. Another type, *akareémba* ("small impotence"), is more common and is caused by poisoning. In *akareémba,* the woman takes a piece of the mat that her husband and a co-wife sleep on and puts it into a jug of cold water. As long as the piece of mat remains in the jug of cold water, the man will be impotent with that wife.

COMMENT: The object of this poisoning is to contain the man's sexual fluids and then to immobilize them beneath a larger container of fluid. The larger container represents the woman doing the poisoning. By placing the man's semen or urine in a small vessel, his sexual capacity is contained. By placing this vessel beneath a larger one, a static body of water, the man's sexual capacity is "pinned" beneath, or subordinated to that of the woman.

In the second variant described by Antoinette, the object of the spell is both to contain and to "cool" the husband's (or lover's) sexual capacity.

TREATMENT: Antoinette says that she administers medicines that "reheat" the man slowly. If possible, the poison should be discovered and the water from the larger container poured out. In difficult cases, where the man does not respond to medicinal reheating and the poison cannot be found, she sends the man to Baudouin who will do *gushika* to ferret out and retrieve the poison.

Albert administers an emetic called *umwiha* and then gives medicines dissolved in lamb's urine in order to reheat the body. Sometimes he also gives *imumba,* a mixture of several plants. Lamb's urine is used because Rwandan women carry their babies strapped to their backs in sheepskins called *ingobyi* (placenta). A gift from the husband to the wife, the *ingobyi* is also an acknowledgment on the husband's part that the baby born by the woman is his legitimate offspring. Drinking lamb's urine, therefore, would reinforce the man's ability to give a lamb's skin, that is, his ability to be potent and produce legitimate offspring.

Umugabo Udashyúukwa

This is another poisoning intended to cause impotence (*umugabo* means "man," *gushyúukwa* means "to have an erection," and adding the negative infix -*da*- yields "a man who cannot have an erection"). Women who are not married to men with whom they have sex and from whom they receive gifts afflict those who either stop coming to see them or stop giving them gifts. A woman does this by luring the man to her another time, having sex with him, then taking his sperm and putting it on a cloth. Later she obtains the man's urine and puts drops of it on the cloth as well. She then takes the cloth and puts it into cold water obtained the day before (the water cannot be freshly obtained). This part of the poisoning is intended to make the man cold like the water (and perhaps stale as well).

After this mixture of sperm, urine, and cold water has been prepared, the woman pours it onto a piece of pottery (*urujo*) that has broken off an unused vessel. She takes this piece of pottery and puts it over a fire until the liquid has been completely boiled away. Finally the potsherd is placed in a bottle, wrapped in a piece of rubber to make it waterproof, and then buried. As soon as this packet is buried, the man becomes impotent.

COMMENT: The man's sexual fluids are captured and then cooled. In this respect the spell resembles the previous one. Here, however, another operation involving pottery and fire is employed to accentuate the spell's force. The *urujo* is used in conjunction with fire to dessicate the man's sexual fluids. When the shard is sealed within a bottle and then wrapped within a piece of rubber, the intention is to render it impervious to rain. This vestige of the man's sexual fluids must be kept away from any natural flow process, for contact with the rain would reinsert the man's sexual fluids into the macrocosmic cycle of flow and consequently nullify the spell. Finally, the male victim's sexual capacity is treated as if it were dead; it is buried.

TREATMENT: Samuel says that he treats seven to ten men per year who have been afflicted with this poisoning. He charges 10,000 Rw. Frs. (about $100) once the patient has been cured. First Samuel sends the *iheémbe* (i.e., performs *gushika*) to seek out the poisoner and determine where the poison (*uburozi*) has been buried. When this has been determined, the *iheémbe* finds the *uburozi* itself and brings it to Samuel's living enclosure (*urugó*). This can take minutes, hours, days, or even a week. The client must wait at Samuel's home while this takes place.

After the poison has been found, Samuel administers medicines to the patient. He uses material from a tree called *umuboró,* which he pulverizes and adds to fresh (i.e., obtained the same day) water. He pours the resultant mixture into a drinking cup and places this in front of the doorjamb (*umuryáango*) of his house. The patient goes to the opposite end of the courtyard facing the door. Then without looking behind him, the patient runs up to the cup and drinks the mixture all at once.

COMMENT: The name of the plant remedy used in this instance, *umuboró,* resembles the word for penis, which is *imboró.* By running up to the mixture of *umuboró* and fresh water, and not looking behind him, the man turns his back on his impotent past. The man then reinserts himself into the macrocosmic cycle of flow, for he revivifies his own fluids by drinking fresh water. In drinking a medicine prepared from the *umuboró* tree, he drinks back the capacity to have his penis stand up again, like the tree. That this healing ritual takes place before the doorway to a house is also significant. The word for doorjamb, *umuryáango,* closely resembles the word for the patrilineal segment of about six generations in depth, *umuryaango.* An impotent man cannot add descendants to his *umuryaango.* A potent man can cross the threshold of the doorjamb, for he can add descendants. He can even be the apical ancestor of his own *umuryaango.*

The association between the home and the capacity for socially approved sexuality is quite common in Rwandan culture. It is not unusual for Rwandan men who are brothers, very close friends, or "blood brothers" to agree to sleep with each other's wives. This practice is called *guhana ingó,* which literally means "to reciprocally give one another one's home" (P. Smith 1975, 384).

Kurotsa Igisaanza

The name of this poisoning means "to put the liquid that exudes from the birth canal after parturition into someone's drink or food." A poisoner can use the fluid from a human female, a dog, or any other non-comestible animal. The victim develops symptoms including stomach pains, odorous breath, coughing, and reddishness of skin.

TREATMENT: An emetic is given to make the victim regurgitate the poison. Or a laxative is given to make the victim defecate the poison. The healer examines the egested material to see if it has the color of a placenta or if there is blood in it. If either condition is confirmed, then the healer administers concoctions prepared from the roots of a tree called *umusorooza*. He shaves off bits of the root, extracts the liquid, and uses it. He also obtains a liquid from a plant called *karungu* (which resembles leeks). These two liquids are then added to *umuhoko* (*Phytolacca dodecandra; Strychnos usambarensis*), a plant that is otherwise used as an abortive and against venereal diseases (Jacob 1984, 538).

COMMENT: Once again this spell demonstrates the power associated with reproductive fluids. Ingesting *igisaanza* is sufficient to cause the victim to manifest symptoms that resemble the fluid itself: redness and odorousness.

The logic of treatment follows the idea that the poison must first be evacuated. Thereafter, if it is determined that the body is flowing abnormally—that is, if blood is present in either the feces or in the vomit—then a procedure must be followed to reinstate normal flow. This underlies the reasoning behind the use of *umusorooza*, whose name is related to the verb *gusorooza*, meaning "to collect offerings for the rainmaker" (Jacob 1985, 207). When one prepares to give a gift to the rainmaker, one anticipates that a period of abnormal celestial flow—drought or inundation—will come to an end. By analogy, one anticipates that abnormal bodily flow will terminate when one ingests a remedy whose name evokes the custom of giving gifts to one of the most important ritual regulators of flow in traditional Rwanda.[13]

POISONINGS TREATED BY BUTARO HEALERS

A patient named Marcel who came to see Albert in Butaro, was recently poisoned by his FZS (*mubyara wanjye*). He is also hated by his father's brothers (*data wacu*) and was once physically assaulted by an FBS (*mwene data wacu*). This affair began in August 1984 when one FB "poisoned" him. Later all his FBs and his FBSs colluded to pay someone to attack Marcel while walking on a pathway. He escaped with minor injuries when people unrelated to him came to his assistance.

Marcel is involved in litigation with his FBs over possession of the land and banana plants that belonged to his father. Since Marcel's father died while Marcel was quite young, his mother decided to return to her own *inzu* ("house") and bring her son with her. When Marcel became old enough, he decided to return to his father's land and claim his inheritance.

Several years had elapsed since Marcel's departure, and in the meantime, his FBs were using their deceased brother's land. Marcel's FZS had also taken a portion of the land to use as his own. Normally, the FZS would inherit land from his own father (FZH in relation to ego) and not from his mother (FZ to ego), but inheriting land from one's mother's side of the family may occur when one is unable to inherit land from one's father and one's mother's family possesses sufficient land. All these men—FBs, FBSs, and FZS—hoped to retain the land and deprive Marcel of his rightful inheritance. There is little chance that their claim would ever be supported by an official Rwandan court or by the more traditional, though less formal, familial adjudicatory body (*gacaáca*).

COMMENT: This case illustrates one of the most common forms of social conflict in rural Rwandan society, rivalry among collaterals over land. There is an added complexity here in the participation of a FZS. He appears to be centrally involved, for he is the one actually accused of having committed the poisoning. Since FZS's claim to the land passes through a matrilateral link, his hold over land that he now wrongfully occupies at the expense of Marcel is tenuous. No paternal link binds him to the land. His interest in eliminating Marcel is thus quite comprehensible.

Besides collaterals, a commonly accused kinsperson in cases of poisoning is a father's wife who is not one's own mother, *mukase* (stepmother). Rwandans themselves explain this as a natural corollary to polygyny. Mothers tend to favor the interests of their own children over those of their co-wives, and they usually resent any material advantage that a husband may bestow on the children of another wife. Rwandan folklore richly develops the theme of the jealous stepmother (see chapter 4). This antagonism is often perpetuated among the children. Thus half siblings, especially half brothers, tend to find themselves having to compete over a limited patrimony.

When a stepmother strikes against a female child of a co-wife, she often attacks the girl's fertility. One adolescent girl came to Baudouin in order to seek treatment for arrested menstruation, a spell known as *urukarango*. Through *kuragura amaheémbe* Baudouin determined that a FW of the girl had been responsible. The FW inflicted her stepdaughter with this spell by roasting her urine or menstrual blood on an *urujo*. Ingredients used in curing the girl included *impanguzi*, an insect found among plants called *imvúra idahita*, and plants called *umurasanka* and *amarebe*.

A man from Nyakinama, which is in the prefecture of Ruhengeri, but is rather far from Butaro, came to see Albert for the problem of impotence (*ubureémba*). The man was married in 1982; his impotence started in February 1984. It has persisted since then, though the problem has ameliorated somewhat after consulting Albert. From divination, it was determined that the man's MBW was responsible. She took her victim's urine and placed it beneath a jug of cold water. She did this in order to alienate the man's wife from him, so that she (MBW) would be able to take her rival's place. She wants this man, because he is richer than her present husband (the victim's maternal uncle). The man is richer than his MB (*marume*), because he brews *urwáagwa* (banana beer) and sells it in a cabaret. The victim complains that his business has suffered since all this began. He has been forced to spend time and money on treatment that he would otherwise spend on his business.

The man's MB has never had bad relations with the victim, nor has he ever been jealous of his ZS (*umwishywa wanjye*). His MBW, however, invited the victim to her house on several occasions when her husband was away and gave him something to drink. When she did not succeed in seducing him, she decided to take some of his urine and poison him. The victim's wife and his MBW have never gotten along. But the latter's actions to undermine the marriage have come close to succeeding, for the man's wife thought he was refusing her voluntarily. She has threatened to leave him because of it. Since consulting Albert and periodically obtaining medicines from him, the man's condition has improved and his wife has shown understanding. MB is unaware of both his wife's actions and Albert's treatment of his ZS.

COMMENT: If one considers the movement of cattle exchanged in the bridewealth transactions involving the two men's families, one gains a clearer picture of the gift logic relation binding the two men and the potential rivalry between their wives.

The fact that the relation between the victim's wife and his MBW might be singled out as problematic by the technique of *kuraguza amaheémbe* is not difficult to understand when we consider that, in this region of Rwanda, MB and ZS have a special relationship. The cow that ego's father paid to obtain his wife (ego's mother), went to MBF, who then probably gave it to one of his sons (i.e., an MB to ego) to obtain a bride in turn. In other words, ego's MB has a wife, because ego's father indirectly paid for her. Thus she is also, in a sense, ego's wife (see fig. 3). This is consistent with the logic of gifts, for debts in a gift economy often persist and do not revert to zero.

Stated briefly, MB owes his ZS, his wife. Thus the ZS could conceivably demand wifely services from his MBW, sexual and culinary. (It is said that MBW is supposed to cook for ego when he visits.) MB has to be somewhat wary of a ZS when the latter visits; a ZS who sits on his MB's chair is said to usurp the latter's position as head of the household. ZS is not supposed to look into the grain silo (*ikigega*) of his MB, nor to tend his cattle, for fear ZS would make these possessions diminish.

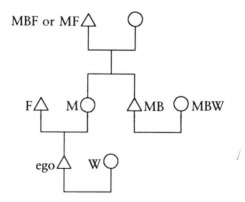

Fig. 3. *The movement of cattle in a bridewealth transaction. 1. A cow went from F to MBF to pay for FW (here labeled "M"). 2. A cow went from MBF to MB to pay for MBW. 3. F also gave a cow to ego, so that he could obtain a wife (W). 4. therefore W = MBW.*

Whether temporary sexual encounters often occur between MBW and ZS is a moot point. Although this is sometimes hinted at, and may have been accepted in the past, it is not consistent with today's Christian-influenced morality. Hence there is ample cause for jealousy between ego's wife and his MBW, for in some ways they are symbolically equivalent. The hint of an unpaid debt will always remain between their husbands and this debt is in the favor of the ZS.

In a similar case, a pregnant woman named Mercianne visited Baudouin with symptoms of vaginal bleeding. Earlier, in June 1982, she had gone to the hospital in Ruhengeri where they had to remove a deceased fetus from her womb by surgery. Later, a diviner established that the cause had been poisoning. Because of this precedent the woman and her husband, despite their being devout Christians and their skepticism concerning sorcery, immediately suspected poisoning at the first symptoms in this recent episode. Baudouin confirmed this, determining through use of the *iheémbe,* that the woman's HMBW was responsible.

From the *iheémbe* it was learned that the poisoner took some of Mercianne's urine, part of the stone called *inkurungu,* a plant named *ikigorogoro,* and a fetus taken from a pregnant sheep slaughtered before giving birth (*igitorogano cy'intama*). The poisoner buried these objects under her victim's bed. The poisoner also stated through the *iheémbe* that the reason she had poisoned Mercianne was because she coveted the victim's husband, Charles. Mercianne says that she and her husband live near his MB and his wife, but that she never suspected her HMBW. Although the woman frequently attends the catechism classes that Charles teaches at the nearby Catholic church, she never found this unusual.

COMMENT: The comments on the possible symbolic equivalence between a man's wife and his MBW made in the previous case apply here as well. The reason for using the stone called *inkurungu* stems from the fact that stones are frequently used in poisonings to symbolize "obstacles" (Bourgeois 1956, 190), that is, the idea of blockage. Added to this notion is the suggestion of pollution through uncleanliness, for the verb related to *inkurungu* is *gukurungu,* which means "to become dirty." The use of *ikigorogoro* is due to its also being the name of an object that is long and twisted. The noun is related to the verb *kugorama,* which means "to be twisted." Any fetus in the woman's womb will become twisted in its own umbilical cord.

The use of the fetus of an unborn sheep recalls the idea that a sheep-skin, *ingobyi*, is used by Rwandan women to carry babies on their backs. The word *ingobyi* is also sometimes used to mean "placenta." In other words, the sack that carries the baby on the outside of the woman's body is, in some contexts, equivalent to the one that carries the baby inside the woman's body before birth.

The conjunction of these elements in this poisoning is intended to symbolize obstacles in the placenta and the twisting of the fetus's umbilical cord. This has already caused her the loss of one child and now abnormal flow, vaginal bleeding. As a result, the woman's fetus, like that of the sheep, should never see the light of day; it will be dead before it is born.

CONCLUSION

Rwandans construct social relationships through the fluids they exchange in celebration, hospitality, and ordinary social interaction. Men and women produce new life from the conjoining of sexual fluids. The sky fertilizes the earth with its rain. Maintaining the continuity of this flow is necessary to biological and social reproduction. Bodily fluids (blood, semen, maternal milk), "social" fluids (cow's milk, sorghum porridge, beer), and rainfall are analogues of one another. The individual is metaphorically and metonymically implicated within three homologous matrices of flow: his or her own body, that of society, and that of the cosmos.

Fluids mediate productive and reproductive transformations by passing through socially ordered phases of containment and decontainment. The person's implication in social life is not bounded by the limits of his body, because his "nature" suffuses the liquid substances his body exudes. Fluids establish social and ontological connectedness by bridging the boundaries between self and other, microcosm and macrocosm. According to gift logic, bodily fluids are dangerous when they become separated or alienated from the body. When this occurs, fluids can be contained or decontained according to malevolent intention rather than socially ordered process. Poisoners accomplish their deeds through these acts of separation. Just as the *umwaámi*'s power derived from his capacity to open or close the conduits of flow, so the witch's power derives from his ability to interdict the movement of fluids among human beings and between man and the spirits. Butaro healers, their patients, and their therapy manifest these principles in a more exemplary fashion than any other healers with whom I worked in Rwanda.

CHAPTER 4

The Case of Maria and Beatrice

~~~~~~

*One day the discovery was made that the symptoms
of disease in certain nervous patients have meaning.*

SIGMUND FREUD

In the previous chapter I emphasized that in culturally conservative parts
of northern Rwanda flow/blockage imagery permeates Rwandan representations of the body, of the body's insertion into social life, of pathology, and of cure. I will now follow a specific case history from central
Rwanda, an area that was touched earlier and more profoundly by missionization and colonialism. Despite this, a specifically Rwandan way of
interpreting illness has survived into the present. Many of the mythic
themes analyzed in chapter 1 continue to pervade the explanatory models used by sufferers and the healers who try to cure them.

This case of spirit possession centers on two female sufferers, one married and one unmarried. The therapeutic procedures employed by the
healers are of interest, for in contrast to those of the Butaro healers, they
are not solely accusatorial. They combine the techniques of accusation

and confession. This case demonstrates some of the complex ways in which the cognitive constructs of earlier Rwandan culture interact with those of today.

THE CENTER FOR TRADITIONAL MEDICINE AT BARE

Two young women, Maria and Beatrice, were treated by healers affiliated with the Center for Traditional Medicine at Bare (near Kibungu in southeastern Rwanda). A Catholic priest named Telesphore Kayinamura founded this dispensary, *Ivuliro Lya Kinyarwanda,* in the early 1980s. Here Rwandan popular healers of various specialties consult patients three days per week. Their dispensary is quite impressive—a solid brick building with cement floors and dormitory rooms for patients who need to stay overnight. Patients meet with their respective healers, who all wear blue lab coats, in separate chambers in the new building. Nearby, medicinal plants grow in a well-tended garden surrounded by a locked chain-link fence. People from all areas of Rwanda frequent the Bare dispensary, for it has gained a certain reknown. Indeed, the president of the Rwandan Republic himself, General Juvénal Habyarimana, came to inaugurate it in July 1984. This action was significant. It illustrates the policy of revalorizing "traditional medicine" in Rwanda (as does the existence of the Curphametra research group).[1] Funds come from the Rwandan government and external sources. Fees at the dispensary are reasonable and are closely regulated by the center's director, Father Kayinamura.[2] Patients are interviewed and then directed to any one of about a dozen healers, according to their sickness.

Father Kayinamura's original intention in founding the center was to restrict practice to healers who rely solely on medicinal plants and who do not resort to magical procedures. He once explained to me that he had wanted to exclude healers "qui emploient des rites ou la magie, ou bien qui travaillent la nuit. S'ils sont de vrais guérisseurs, pourquoi ils peuvent pas faire cela en plein jour. . . . pourtant j'avoue que quelques-uns sont efficaces dans certains cas."[3] His remarks reflect a distinction, which I often heard in Rwanda, between healers of the day and healers of the night. According to daytime healers, healers of the night employ illusionist techniques of a theatrical nature. Healers who work at night, however, justify this practice on the basis that bad spirits are most active after dark: they "dance at night" (*gucyúuragura*). Thus to effectively combat them, they claim, one must work at night.

One such healer of the night was a thirty-seven-year-old man named Frederick, who was somewhat defensive about his marginal status among the coterie of healers that gravitated around Kayinamura at Bare. He never practiced, for example, within any of the rooms at the center, nor were any of his patients entitled to lodging in the center's six-room dormitory. Sometimes Frederick was openly mocked by a daytime healer named Mutabazi (who officially practiced at the Bare center), but occasionally the two worked effectively together. At these times, Mutabazi might play a light role, a cajoling, nonthreatening healer who could defeat the spirits through his refusal to take them seriously. Frederick, on the other hand, who often mentioned to me, "I taught Mutabazi everything he knows," took spirit possession quite seriously. It was grave business to him, involving threat not only to the patient's life but to the healer's as well. Frederick explained that he always carried an *impigi* (protective talisman) when he worked. A healer could be killed if a patient's possessing spirit decided to attack the healer immediately after exorcism. With recalcitrant cases, this was an ever-present possibility. Refractory cases, moreover, seemed to be Frederick's lot; Kayinamura solicited his help only on such occasions. The easier ones could be treated directly at the center by daytime healers.

When Frederick and Mutabazi worked together, they combined the opposed viewpoints of belief and doubt concerning the spirits. In some respects, this dialectical tension between them may have been a more-or-less empirically derived, pragmatic, therapeutic technique intended to mirror the internal schismatic state experienced by the sufferers themselves. Whereas Mutabazi might occasionally display irony toward illnesses of spiritual origin, Frederick treated possession cases with singular fervor. Sometimes he might appear on the verge of violence when a spirit would persist in concealing its identity or its origin. Mutabazi might occasionally explode into unabashed mocking laughter, but he was never openly threatening. Frederick, on the other hand, yelled menacingly at patients, stating that he would kill the spirit if it did not quit the victim's body immediately. Frederick justified his technique by explaining that it was really the spirit that suffered and not the patient.

Frederick's marginal status at the dispensary was not merely a question of bedside manner; it was also a problem of whether to attribute credence to a spiritual discourse that was in conflict with many aspects of Western Christian discourse. Father Kayinamura's attitude was ambivalent. As a Catholic priest he represented an acculturative force that as an institution claimed to embody the principles of modern Western rationalism, but that as a belief system and a social practice admitted the validity of phenomena transcending the canons of ordinary rationality: apparitions, miracles, resurrection. Kayinamura's dilemma resembled that of the Kwakiutl shaman, Quesalid, discussed by Lévi-Strauss (1958, 192–203): whether to purge "traditional medicine" of its irrationalist burden or to accept without question the healer's morally and rationally ambiguous position as actor in the liminal regions between darkness and light, sickness and health. Although he had serious reservations about Frederick's techniques, Kayinamura once mentioned to me that he might integrate him into the team at Bare anyway, because of his effectiveness as a healer and because they already worked with him on some occasions.

Kayinamura's dilemma reflected in some ways that of the Catholic Church. While the Church has built itself upon the ideas of thinkers as meticulously rational as Pascal, it might never have gained a following in the West without the popular appeal of the miraculous, nor the credence it attributed to witchcraft in the fifteenth to eighteenth centuries. Rwanda's experience with Catholicism is less than one hundred years old, and it is interesting to note that Rwanda is one of the few places in the world today where there are periodic apparitions of the Virgin and even of Christ (cf. Maindron 1984). These occurrences are announced on the radio and fervently attended by thousands of Rwandans. Kayinamura knew that there was no systematic way to resolve the dilemma of belief and doubt in reference to the nature of the unseen and the nonempirical. He also knew that sometimes magic could be put to good use. A therapeutic policy systematically abolishing it might have as much chance to succeed as a priest abolishing ritual and prayer in his ministrations to the faithful.

The affliction of the two young women in the following case history could also be characterized as a dilemma, one that in many ways encompasses that of Kayinamura and Quesalid.

THE CASE OF MARIA AND BEATRICE: DESCRIPTION

I saw Maria for the first time, in February 1984 at the Center for Traditional Medicine at Bare, where she was treated by Mutabazi. Maria had been brought to the center by her maternal uncle, Zacharie, who also employed Maria's husband, Elihu, at a small, wholesale used clothing business in Butare. Elihu rented a tiny flat directly across from the room that served as the business's storage and sales area. One weekend per month Elihu visited his wife at their small farm in Remera. Maria had been brought to the center with the following symptoms: often she was extremely agitated and could not be restrained from running about aimlessly on the hillsides near her home, and she had nightmares and occasional headaches. Maria's sister-in-law, Beatrice, was treated at Bare at the same time for similar symptoms: she had nightmares from which she would wake up screaming and then attempt to go outside to run.

Through the use of burning powder, Mutabazi determined that the disorders of Maria and Beatrice were due to a spirit called *nyabingi*. (Weeks later, spirits termed *imaándwa y'isunzu* were determined to have been the culprits.) Mutabazi's diagnosis had been formulated by using a powder made of pangolin scales added to a combination of herbal substances.[4] The mixture would be burned close to the patient, who would cover her head with a cloth to better capture the smoke from the smoldering mixture. Fumes from the burning powder had the property of being able to induce possessing spirits to speak. As the victim inhaled the fumes, the healer interrogated the spirit(s). According to Mutabazi, spirits could not resist the power of the smoke; they would identify themselves and state how they had come to afflict their victim. They would also state their demands. If they resisted speaking, they would die.

Mutabazi used this powder as a truth serum to treat Maria and Beatrice. Under the influence of the powder's smoke, both victims accused an older woman named Hester of being their poisoner. Hester was Beatrice's stepmother (FW, *mukase*) and Maria's mother-in-law (HM, *maabukwé*). Hester lived near Maria with her husband Simon, who was at least ninety-one. Hester, about sixty, was Simon's twelfth wife; all the others had either died or been separated from Simon. He was the father, by different wives, of several principal actors in this case: Elihu, Beatrice, Edouard, and Habimana (see fig. 4). After treating Maria and Beatrice at Bare, Mutabazi said that he needed to go with Frederick to treat Hester at her home. He needed to neutralize the spirits at their source in order to prevent their return, an action called *gutsírika*. To undertake this treatment, Mutabazi asked Father Kayinamura's permission and the latter accorded it.

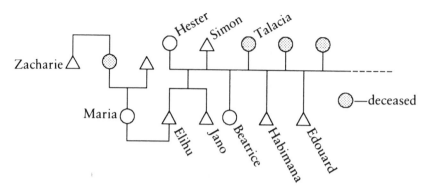

Fig. 4. Relationships in the case of Maria and Beatrice.

THE EXORCISM OF HESTER

The healing ritual took place in February 1984 near Remera. I arrived first at Zacharie's, Maria's maternal uncle (*marume*) and the employer of her husband. Zacharie had a relatively large house for this peasant area. The walls were painted, and there were cement floors and a roof of corrugated iron sheets. Zacharie also had a late-model car in good condition. Obviously, he was the most prosperous member of the family. His wife Helena lived permanently at this house, occupying herself with the crops and the livestock (a few head of cattle and several goats). Zacharie returned home almost every weekend to visit his wife, delegating the supervision of his business to Elihu. The journey by car took about an hour and a half; by bush taxi, it could take anywhere from two to five hours. The long voyage, the necessity of guarding the business, and financial exigencies kept Elihu at Butare for most weekends.

At Zacharie's house I was received by him, his wife Helena, and another son of Simon's, Edouard, a Protestant preacher in the town of Kibuye, a little over a half hour's drive to the north of Remera. Maria's maternal grandfather (MF, *sogo-kuru*) also came to welcome us. He was about seventy years old, and he had raised Maria from infancy to adulthood after her mother died in 1960. Although Maria's father was still alive, he rarely showed up in the area. Because he was a Tutsi and had been a patron (*umushéebuja*) of several Hutu clients (*abagarágu*), he had been compelled to flee Rwanda in 1960 during the revolution that saw the overthrow of Tutsi domination. In 1976 he returned to Rwanda, but not to live in the same area. Because Maria's mother was Hutu, he had never recognized her as an official wife. Maria was thus an illegitimate, quasi-orphan child.

After Maria's marriage to Elihu, Maria's father showed up to claim the bridewealth cow (*inkwáano*) that had been given to the grandfather. According to Maria, if the father had appealed to the informal familial court (*gacaáca*), instead of to an administrative one, there never would have been any question of his taking the cow. But because he had bribed the magistrates, he succeeded. The grandfather maintained that sooner or later he would win the cow back by appeal to another court. Maria also stated that the return gift of a cow (*indoongoranyo*) had not yet been given to Simon, Elihu's father, because Maria's older sister, who had been married before her, had not yet had an *indoongoranyo* given to her husband's father.[5]

The fact that Maria was an illegitimate daughter—the result of a Tutsi-Hutu union in which the Tutsi partner had dramatically lost his former social status and where the Hutu partner was now dead—made her less attractive as a potential daughter-in-law. Simon and Hester would not be able to count on Maria's relatives to offer the gifts that pass between the two sets of affines after a marriage (see appendix A). Although Hester used this argument to oppose Maria, ultimately it was overridden by other members of the family. But Hester was determined. She also pointed out that Maria was premaritally pregnant. Moreover, she suspected that someone other than her son had been responsible for Maria's pregnancy. Premarital pregnancy was once severely punished in Rwanda. In some instances unwed mothers were killed. Although this is no longer the case, unwed mothers continue to be stigmatized.

Beatrice had also had disputes with Hester. It was thus not surprising that during the smoke inhalation treatment at Bare, she also accused Hester of having sent spirits against her. Beatrice's symptoms consisted of frequent nightmares in which she saw a girl named Giteega, who sucked blood from inanimate objects.[6] Blood exuded from everything Giteega pressed her lips against. When Giteega approached Beatrice, she would feel trapped and awaken screaming. Sometimes upon awakening, she ran outside the house.

Beatrice lived with her half brother Edouard and his wife and children. She was twenty-five, somewhat old for an unmarried rural Rwandan

girl. This unfortunate status she also blamed on Hester, who, she maintained, had sent a spell against her to prevent her from finding a husband
(*kuzinga abakoobwa*). She had had three prospective fiancés, but each
one reneged long before serious marriage negotiations began. Beatrice
had also lived with several other members of the family before moving in
with Edouard. Often she would go from one to another, leaving the preceding guardian after misunderstandings. According to Maria, she had a
lamentable tendency to recount to her new hosts all the faults, quarrels,
and indiscreet remarks of the previous ones. This trait seemed only to
accentuate the instability of her living situation.

Once Zacharie, Helena, and Edouard had welcomed me, I left for Simon and Hester's. I found them there along with the two victims, Maria
and Beatrice; Maria's husband, Elihu; and the two healers, Mutabazi
and Frederick. Hester was vehemently protesting her innocence and refusing to submit to treatment; it looked as if we might have come for
naught. This seemed strange, however, as Hester had already given her
consent that the healers from Bare come to treat her. Several people began to argue; at one point Elihu raised his hand as if he were prepared to
slap Hester, his own mother, if necessary to make her submit to the treatment. (This gesture seems all the more significant because, after getting
to know Elihu better, I realized that he was not at all someone easily
aroused to such heights of passion.) As for Simon, he steadfastly supported the innocence of his wife. Seeing that his words had no effect, he
returned inside the house.

Mutabazi yelled at Hester. Later, I found out something he had said in
my absence, "I've brought this *umuzúungu*[7] here by order of the president of Rwanda. If you don't submit to treatment, he'll take you to
Europe and kill you!" Finally, Mutabazi and Frederick took Hester by
the arm after she gave no further signs of protest. They stripped off the
cloth garment covering her torso and proceeded to place one cupping
glass against her lower back and another against her cheek. Cupping
(*kurúmika*) is a procedure that is often employed in popular Rwandan
medicine. A bit of kerosene is poured into an ordinary drinking glass—a
hollow animal horn or small gourd (*inguunga*) used to be employed—
and a bit of lit paper is then inserted to start the kerosene burning.
While the glass continues to flame, it is applied directly to the skin.
Suction develops as the flame is extinguished and this causes the glass
to adhere to the skin. According to Mutabazi, one places cupping glasses
on various parts of the body, but especially on the back, in order to

immobilize and capture the bad spirits afflicting a sufferer. The glass applied to Hester's back served that purpose. The one clinging to her cheek was used as a means of persuasion. When Frederick or Mutabazi asked Hester questions to which she did not respond quickly enough, Frederick grabbed the glass and pulled on it, an action that Hester obviously found painful.

Frederick and Mutabazi had a curious way of working together. Mutabazi asked numerous questions, but never menaced Hester. Often, though, the woman's responses provoked his mocking laughter. Mutabazi acted as if the spirits were there only to be ridiculed and that his therapy consisted of destroying their credibility. Once, he challenged Hester saying, "If you really are capable of summoning spirits to harm others, make this child sick right now!" as he pointed to a young boy in the arms of his mother seated nearby. But just as he said this, Maria's grandfather arose and, propping himself against his walking stick, said in a dignified but adamant way, "No, leave that child alone! We've had enough of all these *amashitáani*.[8] We want this to end, right now and forever!" After the old man's interjection, Mutabazi desisted. This seemed to reinforce, at least for the moment, the onlookers' conviction that Hester indeed possessed the ability to harness and to use the power of the spirits. Mutabazi's strategy in this instance had not worked.

Whereas Mutabazi's technique sometimes aimed at destroying the spirits' credibility among those who appeared to believe in them, Frederick followed an entirely different strategy. He never mocked the belief, nor the believer. Instead Frederick insisted on showing that his own power was superior to that of the spirits and could therefore defeat them. He was more direct, more tenacious, more vehement in confronting the spirit world and those who were either under its influence or possessed its powers. He was the more menacing toward Hester. It was he who would most often berate her and then tug spitefully at the cupping glass clinging to her cheek.

Sometimes during the ritual, one of the members of the family tried to chase away the numerous onlookers gathered around the perimeter of the *urugó* (enclosure) to peer through the fencelike surrounding vegetation. Soon this attempt was abandoned, for it required too much effort and there were more important things going on. Soon people began filtering into the *urugó* itself, forming a kind of Greek chorus that eventually participated by offering its opinions on the proceedings. During this whole time, Hester, half-naked and with cupping glasses hanging from her back and the right side of her face, answered questions put to her by the healers:

"What are these spirits called?"

"*Imaándwa y'isunzu*," replied Hester. These spirits are similar to those worshiped in the *kubaandwa* cult—dedicated to the adoration of Ryangombe and the Bacwezi—but they are specifically those persons among one's lineal ancestors (of either side) who formerly were Ryangombe cult adepts. In further questioning, Hester specified that the spirits came to possess her through her paternal grandmother (*nyogo-kuru*). She showed objects that she used in her ministrations to these spirits: pieces of broken pottery, two horns made from stone or pottery, a small bell usually hung around a dog's neck. All were objects that had at one time belonged to the *imaándwa y'isunzu*. Then the healers made her demonstrate to everyone how she made offerings to the spirits. She showed how she would sing a short refrain and then ring the small bell. She would give the spirits morsels of goat or beef and drops of *urwáagwá* (banana wine). Just at this moment one of the spectators in the crowd of fifty to one hundred persons arose and stated that if anyone else employed spirits in a manner similar to Hester, they should declare themselves now and be treated while the healers were present. No one volunteered.

At another point during the proceedings, question arose concerning a small cooking vessel called *urweeso*. Ordinarily, this small pot is used to stopper the larger vessel or *inkóno*, which is placed on the fire. According to Maria's words at Bare, while under the influence of Mutabazi's smoke, Hester retained the spirit *nyabingi* in just such a vessel. Maria had specifically referred to it as *urweeso rwa nyabingi* (the small pot of *nyabingi*). Hester denied its existence, but Frederick was insistent. Taking a bunch of dried grass, Frederick sprinkled it with an herbal medication intended to aid in finding the *urweeso*. Agitating the bundle of grass in his two hands, he spoke almost violently as he hurried from place to place searching within the *urugó*, within the house, and even in the immediate vicinity outside the *urugó* (enclosure). But Frederick managed to turn up nothing, nor was Hester intimidated into yielding another object.

Finally, all the objects that Hester used in her devotions to her familial spirits were gathered together in front of her. With hands raised above her head and naked torso, she was forced to declare that never again would she make offerings to these spirits or contact them. After this avowal the cupping glasses were removed, first the one on her back, then the one on her right cheek. Mutabazi later explained that without Hester's confession and promise to desist from spirit worship, the ritual would have served no purpose. There would have been no way to liberate Hester from the hold that the spirits had over her. When the glass on her cheek was removed, a blistered and swollen surface was revealed. Frederick and Mutabazi applied herbal medication to the burned area (healers at Bare usually do not reveal the constituents of their remedies). Then Hester was instructed to pour kerosene on the spirit objects and to set them on fire. When the fire was out, she was told to throw them into the latrine.

Once the objects were discarded, Mutabazi and Frederick proceeded to scatter herbs over their right shoulders and in front of themselves. This was intended to protect them against the vanquished spirits who might be hungry for revenge. Then they took dried grass, placed it in a wooden trough, and set it on fire. They sprinkled herbs over the fire and brought it into the house. Spirits might still be in the house and the medicated fire would chase them away. They passed into every corner of the house dropping medicines as they went. Next they treated Beatrice and Maria by cutting incisions (*indasaago*) on their feet, their hands, upon their foreheads, on the upper part of Maria's breasts and on her back. Into these incisions the healers rubbed a medicine called *urugombora*, consisting of the ashes of herbs and pangolin scale, the same medicine they had used on Hester's cheek. Beatrice, still unmarried, was not treated on the breasts and back. These parts of the body, one to nourish, the other to carry a baby, were not yet in need of protection.

With all the ritual procedures completed, we headed back to Zacharie's house. A few neighbors stopped us and asked the healers to come and examine their houses, fearing that Hester might have sent spirits against them as well. Mutabazi declined, explaining that no other treatments were necessary. The spirits had been neutralized once and for all. Hadn't Hester given her word that she would never contact them again? Didn't they see her throw all the objects into the latrine? It was time to leave this woman alone; she was finished with this business. He seemed to be implying that people should not suspect Hester every time some new misfortune occurred. During the ritual, a few people had been eager to attribute other adversities to her influence. Now the healers seemed concerned that people leave Hester in peace and take no further action against her.

Walking back on the path to Zacharie's, I asked Edouard if he thought the ritual would be effective. Earlier he had expressed skepticism about belief in non-Christian spirits and any action based on that belief. The only spirit that existed was God. Now his objection was quite different. He felt that the ritual would prove useless because the healers had not found the container, *urweeso rwa nyabingi*. This meant that Hester could still summon the spirits at will. He seemed unaware that this statement contradicted his earlier attitude denying the efficacy of all non-Christian ritual. Now he doubted the ritual's effects because of an error in its execution. According to him, both Beatrice and Maria were still vulnerable to spirit attack emanating from Hester.

RECONSTRUCTING THE ANTECEDENT CONDITIONS

Although I had been allowed to attend Hester's exorcism, I had only a dim understanding of the events and conditions leading up to it. To gain a clearer idea of what was going on, I decided to interview the principal participants one by one. Since their homes were widely separated, these interviews required considerable time and travel. For example, Elihu and Zacharie spent most of their time in Butare, Maria lived near Remera, and Beatrice lived with Edouard near Kibuye. Moreover, facts and opinions tended to change over time. In some instances this reflected a desire to furnish new details, ones that an informant might have been unwilling to reveal before arriving at a certain level of confidence with the ethnographer; in other instances it betrayed a desire to dissimulate the participant's role in the events.

I began with Edouard and Beatrice, who lived near the small Protestant church where Edouard was preacher. I visited them in March, about two weeks after the healing ritual in Remera. Edouard brought me up to date on the background of the family and the two young women's troubles. Simon was his father by a wife now deceased. Hester was Simon's most recent wife. Before her, Beatrice's mother, Talacia, had lived with Simon.

From the moment Hester entered the household, problems had arisen. Finally Talacia left and returned to her natal family bringing her baby daughter, Beatrice, with her. When Beatrice was about four or five, Simon came to reclaim her and bring her back to his home (in the case of divorce, children belong to the father). Occasionally, Talacia came to visit Beatrice, but she died before her daughter turned eighteen. According to Beatrice, her mother died shortly after a visit to Simon's household. Beatrice maintained that Hester had poisoned Talacia. Soon thereafter Beatrice manifested symptoms (e.g., nightmares).

Edouard agreed with Beatrice's accusation of Hester concerning Talacia's death. He also felt that Hester was jealous of him, because her own sons, Jano and Elihu, had been unable to pursue higher studies and he had. Every mother in a polygynous household tends to favor the interests of her own children, explained Edouard: she resents the privileges and favors accorded to children of co-spouses.

Although Beatrice's symptoms became more severe shortly after her mother's death, her problems had begun earlier, at the age of fifteen, two years before the death of her mother in 1977. She had occasional nightmares; frequently she was silent and uncommunicative. After Talacia's death, Beatrice's condition took a more dramatic turn. Her nightmares became more frequent; she often quarreled bitterly with Hester. Finally she left her father's home to live with Habimana, a married son of Simon's who resided near his father. In 1980, after Edouard's marriage, she moved in with him and his wife in Kibuye. These moves did not assuage her problems.

As for Maria, her symptoms began much later than those of Beatrice. After the birth of her first child, she experienced problems of lactation, *igihama*. At this time she and Beatrice decided to consult a diviner. He told them that their illnesses originated from a relative who had sent spirits against them. Realizing that both Beatrice and Maria suspected her, Hester hired a diviner to diagnose Maria. He concocted the dubious proposition that Maria's father had sent *abazímu* (ancestor spirits) against her. This explanation satisfied only Hester; no one could accept the idea that a father would bewitch his own daughter, even an irresponsible father like that of Maria. He had been guilty of negligence toward her, that was certain, but not outright malevolence.

In January 1984, the two young women were brought to Bare for the first time, and Mutabazi treated them. Both seemed much better the next day and were brought home—Maria to Remera, Beatrice to Kibuye. Later that day, however, Maria saw Hester and had a crisis that night. Two weeks later Beatrice came to visit Maria in Remera and became afflicted again. On February 11, Maria's uncle Zacharie came to Edouard's house in Kibuye with the news that Maria had again taken ill.

That night, Beatrice had a nightmare and ran out of the house screaming. Edouard had to pursue her to bring her home.

The next day, Zacharie brought both women to Bare again. Mutabazi employed the smoke treatment and learned from the spirits afflicting Beatrice that they had come from Hester. Ultimately they intended to kill Beatrice and it was also because of them that she would never find a husband. During Maria's treatment, the cooking vessel in which the spirits were kept was mentioned for the first time. After a few days, Beatrice and Maria, much improved, left Bare to return to their homes. As a result of this second treatment session, the healers decided that the spirits had to be stopped at their source—Hester would have to be treated.

AFTER HESTER'S TREATMENT AT REMERA

Edouard continued to maintain that the healer's exorcism of Hester had been ineffective. First of all, the container had never been found. Second, Edouard heard that after the ritual certain people had congratulated Hester for having succeeded in concealing her secret. Most important, Beatrice's symptoms continued to persist. These included nightmares in which she saw people dressed in white carrying flowers, who would attract her and then try to strangle her when she approached, and visions of water in which she wanted to drown herself. In other dreams she reviewed the bloodsucking Giteega.

Hester and her spirits still had the upper hand. Simon was under their influence too, explained Edouard, for she had given him an *uruzaratsi* (pl. *inzaratsi*), a love charm, which had rendered him blind to her nefarious activities. Allegedly, she had taken a sweet potato (*ikijumba*) and inserted it into her vagina before cooking it. Ingesting Hester's vaginal fluids while eating the potato, Simon had become her slave. This explained why he preferred his wife to his children.

Moreover, the spirits that Hester admitted worshiping during the healing ritual, *imaándwa y'isunzu*, were not at all the ones from whom Hester derived her powers. According to Edouard, Hester worshiped the goddess Nyabingi,[9] who is venerated by northern Rwandans. Friends of Hester's also allegedly worshiped Nyabingi and assisted Hester in casting bad spells. It was from Nyabingi that Hester had acquired the power to befuddle Simon, kill Talacia, keep Beatrice husbandless, stop Maria's lactation, and kill one of Maria's children.

After seeing Edouard and Beatrice, I visited Simon and Hester several days later. Their opinion as to the disagreement in the family was very different. According to Simon, the family's problem had been instigated by one of his sons, Habimana, a married man about fifty years old and father of six children. Habimana had been the author of the accusations against Hester. When Maria's second child died, it was Habimana who circulated rumors stating that Hester had been responsible. He impugned his father's wife, because he was jealous of her and her children, thinking that they enjoyed exaggerated favor with Simon.

Supposedly, Habimana had also influenced his half brothers. Once, during Edouard's Protestant seminary training in another African country, Habimana wrote him a letter stating that Hester was a witch (*umurozi*). Edouard responded by saying that he would heed this warning, but did not feel menaced at the present time. Someone else in the family intercepted the return letter from Edouard and brought it to Simon's attention. Simon presented this matter to the informal adjudicatory body, *gacaáca*. No action was taken, however, because proof of Habimana's action was lacking. Habimana had not only sown disagreement among Simon's children, he had purportedly also succeeded in alienating Simon's brothers from him. They no longer came to visit him. Simon blamed Habimana for having subverted his authority with his and Hester's youngest son, Jano, age twenty, who did not work hard enough for his aged parents.

Simon's opinion about Maria's sickness was that it was a sickness of the head, a sickness like any other and thus curable through proper treatment. If the healers were successful, it was because their medications were effective, not because their explanation of the illness was correct. Simon did not believe that ancestor spirits (*abazímu*) could cause illness or misfortune. One healer in the area had diagnosed Maria's problem as *ibisazi* (psychosis); at Bare they had diagnosed her as having *nyabingi* possession. Before that, yet another healer had said that she suffered from *abazímu* affliction. How could you believe one healer rather than another? To Simon healing was simply a matter of effective or ineffective medication, and that's all. The spirits did not exist. Habimana had simply used the episode of Maria's and Beatrice's illnesses to antagonize his stepmother again. Since Beatrice's animosity toward Hester was of long standing, it was easy for him to manipulate the situation to Hester's detriment. As for the healers, they had only been the foils of this manipulation.

Hester defended herself by stating that the practices to which she had confessed were really quite commonplace for many Rwandans. Every Rwandan household is protected by ancestral spirits called *abakúraambere* (the ones that came first). They are paternal ancestors whose ascendance may go back several generations. The rite of *gutérekeera* is performed for them, and occasionally even by Christian Rwandans. Objects that belonged to the ancestors are often passed down through the family and may be used in *gutérekeera*. These were the objects that Hester surrendered during the healing ritual. Included among one's ancestors are initiates in the *kubaandwa* cult (the cult of Ryangombe), who are particularly important in *gutérekeera* and may be referred to as *imaándwa y'isunzu*.

Nevertheless, the practice of *gutérekeera* and the objects used in it are not of danger to anyone. She confessed to these practices merely to terminate the healers' ritual, which had been humiliating and physically painful. The only reason that she had submitted to the ritual was that she wanted life to return to normal. Hester's opinion concerning the possible effectiveness of the ritual mirrored her husband's; if the two women improved, it had to be due to the medicines that were administered and nothing else.

A few days later I visited Habimana, who asserted that there never was any letter accusing Hester of being a witch or poisoner. There had indeed been three family "trials" (*gacaáca*) where the question of Habimana's slandering of Hester had been brought up, but each time Habimana had been judged innocent for lack of proof. He has been involved in many conflicts in his father's household, both with Hester and before that with another of his father's wives. For that reason he had left the household in 1952 to work in East Africa (Tanganyika). He returned in 1963, got married that same year, and started a family.

As for the *gacaáca* trials, the first one occurred in 1978. Habimana explained that this trial came as a complete surprise to him, since he had never done anything against Hester. Moreover, one of his children had lived with Hester and Simon. (Often a young child will live with his grandparents and help with small tasks, such as fetching water.) Maria presently had a child living with Hester and Simon, just as Habimana had had before her. Would he have allowed his own child to live with Hester if he had thought she was a witch? Like his father, he believed that Maria's sickness was an ordinary illness and that there was no spiritual basis to it. As for Beatrice's illness, it started after she left Simon and Hester, so there was little possibility of her having been afflicted by Hester. Ironically, despite Habimana's poor relationship with his father, both claimed to be skeptical about stories of mystic involvement.

The next family member I visited was Maria. She informed me that now it was Hester who was ill. She would hear voices at night. When these voices spoke, they would ask her to open the door, but when she went to the door, nobody would be there. But Maria, like Edouard, believed that Hester was still dangerous. She had never given up the *ur-weeso*. Some of Maria's symptoms were persistent; she continued to have headaches and a feeling of malaise when she was in the company of other people. She was not satisfied with the action of the healers. Sometimes her daughter, her husband, and even a goat suffered from illnesses that she believed were caused by spirits. Her husband had bad dreams where he would see a half-human–half-animal who would try to suffocate him. Her daughter would leave the bed at night and try to go outside, or she would sleep in an inverted position in her bed. Maria continued to spend a lot of time at Hester and Simon's according to the custom whereby a daughter-in-law renders services for her parents-in-law. But Hester was never happy with Maria. She resented her bringing healers who had only humiliated her.

Maria traced the origin of her troubles back to the time of her marriage. Hester had opposed Maria's marriage to her son Elihu, for instead of allowing the parents to take a major role in the selection, Maria and Elihu had chosen each other by sentiment. Furthermore, Maria was visibly pregnant and Hester suspected that someone other than her son was responsible. Finally, Hester's opposition was overridden. After the marriage Maria gave birth to a daughter, but experienced problems of lactation. Despite this, the child survived. At the moment of this investigation the girl was about four. Twenty-one months after the birth of the first child a second child was born, a boy, but he died not long after his birth. Eighteen months after the death of this boy, she gave birth to fraternal twins, a boy and a girl. (They were about twenty-two months old when I met them in 1984.) Once again she experienced problems of lactation. Moreover, the female twin had frequent health problems. Maria attributed all this to Hester's poisoning of her.

Most important of all during this enumeration of her problems, Maria revealed that she had had an adulterous liaison with her husband's half brother, Edouard, the Protestant preacher. He was the father of the twins. During her illness she confessed this infidelity to her husband while she was semidelirious. She also mentioned that while under the influence of the smoke at Bare, she had revealed this information. At Bare, however, the confession had taken the form of an accusation against Hester, for she held Hester responsible for having sent Edouard to seduce her in a time of vulnerability, to destroy a marriage that she had always opposed.

It was true that Maria's twins closely resembled their father, Edouard, and did not look at all like Elihu. This fact had undoubtedly been perceived by others. One of the favorite subjects for gossip after a birth on a Rwandan hillside is guessing which man the child looks like, and the resemblance between the male twin and Edouard was remarkable. When Elihu learned of his wife's adultery, he confronted Edouard, demanding that the latter acknowledge his act and take responsibility for the two children. While Edouard admitted adultery with Maria, he refused to take any responsibility for the children. He feared that assuming responsibility would anger his wife and jeopardize his job as a preacher. Zacharie then told Elihu that he would take back his niece if Elihu wanted to divorce her, but he hoped that Elihu would reconcile with her. It was in this atmosphere of tension within the young couple's marriage and persistent conflict within the family that Maria's crisis took its dramatic turn, requiring the attention of a ritual specialist.

In later visits to Maria, months after the ritual for Hester, I found her much improved. Her symptoms had abated except for occasional headaches. Hester had become less demanding toward her. When I asked her if she thought the healers had cured her, she told me that no, it was because I had come to see her often. The people who lived near her, and those near Hester as well, had come to believe that I was a healer and diviner. My frequent visits to Maria had apparently given her a certain status. Hester, perhaps fearful of being deported to Europe and meeting an untimely end, had seen the advantage of making peace with Maria.

As for Beatrice, her situation did not seem to improve quite so dramatically, even though there had been a certain amelioration, a decrease in nightmare episodes. Edouard, however, had become hostile, telling me that he and Beatrice had already told me all that I needed to know. Although I had never admitted knowing about his affair with Maria, he may have surmised that I had learned of it. In previous interviews he had been pretentious but expansive, delighting in being able to display his knowledge of English and other subjects. In later interviews he became brusk and would interfere whenever I tried to talk to Beatrice.

THE CASE OF MARIA AND BEATRICE: COMMENTARY

The predisposing factors of Maria's illness were numerous: the ambiguous status of her birth (the illegitimate daughter of a Tutsi man and a Hutu woman), her quasi-orphan status as a child (the death of her mother, the absence of her father), her premarital pregnancy, the difficult relationship with her mother-in-law, the death of her second child, her problems of lactation, her husband's absence during all but two days of the month, her adultery, the children who closely resembled her former lover, her lover's pusillanimous disavowal of the consequences of his actions. All these factors combined to lead Maria to an untenable position. Her dilemma could be characterized in the following way: "How can I claim to be a good wife to my husband when I've given birth to two children that are not his? How can I claim to be Hester's victim when I've confirmed some of her suspicions of sexual misconduct?" Maria's illness reflected this ambiguous position of being both victim and persecutor, accuser and confessor, as well as the logic of someone caught between two standards of morality: one that condones sexual access to a wife on the part of real and classificatory brothers,[10] and another that defines adultery strictly and unambiguously. Maria's conflicts could be interpreted as reflecting a confusion that hinges on the disposition of the female body according to two different social logics: one, pre-Christian, precapitalist, and communally oriented; the other, Christian, capitalist, and individualistic.

As for Beatrice, the death of her mother and the instability of her childhood continued to haunt her adolescence and young adulthood. She would pass from one member of the family to another, from one guardian to another, often leaving a former guardian after a quarrel or misunderstanding. It was ironic that she was now living with Edouard and his family, the person so hypocritically involved in the problems of her co-patient. This fact only underlined the lability of her living situation. But the most important manifestation of the girl's affliction, according to Beatrice herself, was her failure to find a husband. Every time a potential suitor made overtures in this regard, he withdrew before marriage negotiations actually got underway. In other words, the symptom of her youth, the tragedy of not being able to find a real home, was repeating itself. She was failing to secure the only really solid position available to a rural Rwandan woman, marriage and child rearing.

In both their cases, there was a question concerning the disposition of the female body and its reproductive potential. In Maria's case her fertility had been attenuated by the illness. This was manifest in the death of her second child and in her persistent problems of lactation. In Beatrice's case, it was a question of completely arrested fertility consistent with the imagery of *kuzinga abakoobwa,* for Beatrice could find neither a husband nor a home.

Blaming Hester for all this had a certain logic to it. First to all, none of Simon's children except Hester's own two sons recounted anything favorable about her. Some spoke of her as a usurper, one who had forced Beatrice's mother, Talacia, out of the house. Others spoke of her as an *igishéegabo* (virago; see p. 31) who had seized the upper hand in the household by duping Simon through the use of an *uruzaratsi.* Others spoke unequivocally of her as an *umurozi* (witch, poisoner).

Only her two sons and her husband were capable of defending her, but Simon was too old and had obviously lost influence in family matters. He openly scorned Habimana, complained about the recalcitrance of his youngest son, Jano, and lamented that his own brothers no longer came to visit him. Jano was too young to defend Hester with any authority, and Elihu's divided loyalties were obviously more on the side of his wife than his mother. Some said that Hester drank too much and that she neglected Simon, failing to cook for him on some days. Simon's attachment to Hester, whom many other family members judged a poor and self-centered wife, made it seem plausible that she had indeed resorted to occult powers to ensnare him. Given this undercurrent of hostility toward her, she was the appropriate person to cast in the role of witch.

Beatrice's quarrel with her stepmother was longstanding. The onset of Beatrice's errant life coincided with Hester's arrival in Simon's household. Born into the household, Beatrice left it when her mother left, only to return a few years later when Simon came and took her back. After her mother's death, she became something of a Cinderella, an adolescent girl doomed to living with a capricious and unloving stepmother. From Simon's household, she moved to Habimana's, from his to yet others, until she moved in with Edouard. But the death of Talacia (poisoned by Hester according to Beatrice), was significant in another way, for it meant that she could no longer count on her mother for affective support in her eventually sexual and conjugal life.

Normally, it is the mother who gives a Rwandan girl her first indoctrination in sexual matters and encourages her to follow certain practices aimed at directing her nascent sexuality toward the socially positive goals of marriage and childbearing. For example, when a young girl first begins to menstruate (*kujya mu mihango*), there are a number of things that her mother tells her to do. First of all, she is told to lie on her back and to count the horizontal supports of the house. This action of counting is intended to prevent prolonged menstruation. In some areas of Rwanda, girls are told to count only to the third horizontal support, so that their periods will be only three days long in the future. More important, though, by the act of counting a girl situates herself in a sequential (temporal) matrix. The encompassing temporal sequence here is really the passage from childhood to nubility. It is also a sequence that implies the hastening demise of the parental generation's fertility, for by the time a young girl has become nubile, her mother has come that much closer to menopause.

Menstruation also situates the female body in space. Blood flows from the inside to outside, from up to down. This movement parallels the flow of another fertility element, rain, which moves from heaven to earth. Just as rain should be neither too sparse nor too abundant, so should a woman's menstrual flow be neither insufficient nor hemorrhagic. Menstrual blood should never be blocked within the body, it should always flow to the exterior. This symbolism is apparent in the spells termed *kumanikira amaráso* ("to suspend blood") and *umukoobwa utajya mu mihango* ("girl who cannot menstruate"), discussed in the previous chapter. The fear of arresting a woman's fertility by suspending blood between earth and sky is quite pervasive. When a woman gives birth at home, care is taken to remove any objects hanging from the rafters or the ceiling.

At menarche a girl's mother tells her to fetch leaves from several cultivated plants including gourds and courgettes, members of the Cucurbitaceae family. Plants of this family, when they are not consumed, are made into containing vessels. The butter churn (*igisaabo*), for example, is made from a gourd. The ritually important Rwandan plant, *umwishywa*, is also a member of the Cucurbitaceae family. Gourds contain liquids. Moreover, culinary transformations, such as making butter (a liquid congealing into a solid), are effected within their interiors. In the examination of the royal rituals in chapter 1, we have seen the association between churning butter and copulation/gestation (*gukúrakuza*) as well as the association between the king, womanhood, and the butter churn (*igisaabo*). The uterus is like a gourd. It can act as a repository for the gestation of new life or it can act as Death's shelter, just as a drinking gourd can contain a wholesome beverage or a poisonous mixture.

Women, cattle, and plants of the Cucurbitaceae family share the property of being potential containers of fluids. If the leaves of the plants gathered by the young girl wither quickly—an infrequent result—the girl is supposed to take care during her period to refrain from performing agricultural tasks. In other words, one must ascertain whether a girl's blood is compatible with the fertility of cultivated vegetables, and particularly that of vegetable containers. About cattle there is less ambiguity: menstruating women are enjoined in all cases to stay away from cattle. The flow of menstrual blood can arrest or vitiate the flow of cow's milk.

While menstrual blood is a common component in spells that can cause sterility, miscarriage, and other problems to the woman from whom the blood is taken, menstrual blood can also be used in spells against others, as in *kurotsa iruungu* (literally, "to swallow menstrual blood"), which causes the complexion of its victims to become redder and redder until they die, an illness called *bwaki*. During menstruation, a girl is not only potentially dangerous to her own fertility but also to the fertility of crops and cattle, as well as to the vitality of other people. When this power announces itself in her body for the first time, a girl must be correctly inserted into social time and social space—no longer a child, but a young woman capable of reproduction. A girl's mother must educate her to the possible constructive and destructive uses of this new power in her body.

Rwandan mothers encourage their daughters to go off to a secluded place on a hillside to practice *gukuna imishino*. This custom involves pubescent girls, who, together in small groups, manipulate their genitalia in order to elongate the labia minora. To do this, they use small twigs that have been stripped of their bark and smoothed, and sap from various plants. The twigs are used to pull gently against the labia minora, elongating them in the process. Through other manipulations a girl is supposed to enlarge her clitoris (cf. Kashamura 1973, 81). Sometimes another girl will insert her finger into a friend's vagina and the latter will be instructed in how to move her pelvis so as to facilitate reaching orgasm readily.

Although these customs are beginning to disappear with the influence of Christianity, many Rwandan women over the age of twenty, according to several that I interviewed, have practiced them. This fashioning of the genitalia is believed to enhance female sexual responsiveness and to prepare a woman's body for the insertion of a penis by opening the vaginal canal. A marriageable young girl should have an open body, ready to receive a man and to produce their progeny. By opening the female body, the possibility of its exchange to another family is also opened. Moreover, the marriage of a woman entails opening, or keeping open, avenues of exchange among affines, for when a woman is married, a new alliance is formed or an old one is reinforced. *Gusiba inzira,* for example, which literally means "to block the path," really means "to lose one's daughter before she can be married."

Relations between exchange partners should ideally be open and flowing, and so should a woman's body. Ensuring this is as much a social process as a biological one. A woman should not menstruate to excess, but her body should not be blocked either. It is the image of the blocked body that receives the most frequent expression in the context of pathology (e.g., *agakeécuru,* pp. 34–35; *igihama,* pp. 70–71). Most popular healers perceive this relation analogically; they administer herbal remedies whose symbolic properties, evinced in names or physical attributes, aim at opening the body and restoring its proper flow. Other healers perceive the relation between pathology, closure, and blockage quite literally. In cases of dysmenorrhea (painful or difficult menstruation) or sterility, they may attempt to force open the cervix by mechanical means. A Belgian gynecologist who practiced for several years in Kigali (Rwanda) noted: "Occasionellement, nous retrouvons dans l'anamnèse une dilatation instrumentale du col. La dilatation forcée du col pour la dysménorrhée ou la stérilité (!) devrait être abandonnée depuis longtemps, mais malheureusement elle est encore pratiquée"[11] (de Clercq 1982, 628).

The capacity of a woman's body to conform to the exigencies of openness and flow is essential to the maintenance of social life, hence the disposition of female fertility was once very closely surveyed. Unwed mothers were banished or killed. Young women who had attained childbearing age and had not developed breasts (*impenébeere*) or who had never menstruated (*impa*) were deemed abominations (d'Hertefelt and Coupez, 1964, 286) and met a similar fate. These punitive measures no longer exist. Furthermore, today many women leave the countryside temporarily or permanently to work in towns where they have more liberty to conduct their sexual lives as they wish. Although these new liberties are more accentuated in towns, they are not confined there. They have slowly and subtly permeated the hillside, at least to a degree; rural women are also asserting the right to choose. More and more women are finding ways to escape the scrutinizing eye of patrilineal morality. As a corollary to this, there is a widespread perception that premarital pregnancies, prostitution, and children born out of wedlock are becoming more common.

Many Rwandan males think this phenomenon is related to the lure of money and to the freedom of choice associated with Western commodity culture. One month before I departed for Rwanda there was an article in *Le Monde* entitled "Liaisons dangéreuses" ("Dangerous liaisons") and another reporting the same occurrence appeared in the French semiunderground newspaper *Libération* entitled "Touche pas à l'homme blanc" ("Don't touch the white man"). What these articles reported was that in the spring and summer of 1983, scores of young Rwandan women, virtually all residents of Kigali, Butare, and other cities in Rwanda, had been arrested and placed on "reeducation farms" outside of Kigali. All were accused of "vagabondage" or prostitution and some were indeed prostitutes. Others, however, were guilty of nothing more than having European boyfriends or consorting with Europeans socially. Some Rwandan authorities (discredited a year or so later) feared the unprecedented freedom of young urban women away from the scrutiny of their families; they were appalled by the choices these women were making about sex, romance, and marriage. Many Rwandan men whom I talked to maintained that Rwandan women were attracted to Europeans because of their wealth. Their resentment seemed to focus on the perception that a national reproductive resource was gradually being lured away by the blandishments of foreigners' money. In addition, they lamented the dissolution of patriarchal authority and the diminishing control that older women exercise over younger women.

Even before the influence of commodity culture, however, a potential for conflict inhered in the relation between older and younger Rwandan women. *Gukuna imishino* underlines the cooperation that ideally exists between a woman and her daughter in the preparation of the latter's fertility. It entails the gradual ceding of reproductive responsibility from one generation to the next. Although there is usually consent and cooperation in this transfer from mother to daughter, it also implies the evanescence of the reproductive powers of the parental generation. A woman who encourages her daughter to obtain sexual knowledge through *ugukuna* cannot do this without a trace of ambivalence, for the sexual birth of the daughter presages the reproductive death of the mother. For this reason, not so long ago, any usurpation of reproductive power on the part of the junior generation of females was punished very harshly. Unwed mothers with their babies were taken by boat out to the middle of Lake Kivu and abandoned on islands there. In other regions unwed mothers were hurled from high cliffs or thrown into rivers. Sometimes they were driven in front of advancing Rwandan armies so that their blood, with its impurity (*ishyano*), would be shed upon and thus vitiate the fertility of foreign soil. I was told by one woman, a healer and specialist in female reproductive problems, that the practice of killing unwed mothers persisted until the 1950s.

But it was not premarital sexual experimentation that was being punished in this way. It was the disorderly fashion by which a member of the younger generation had overstepped the prerogatives of the older one and "stolen" the right to reproduce. Every transfer of fertility operates according to a logic which insists that, between two adjacent generations, only one may exercise hegemony over reproduction. According to the same logic, however, no one in the ascending generation may rightfully impede the transfer of fertility to the following generation, for this could also cause reproductive difficulties among younger females and bring about the demise of the *inzu* (house, minor lineage).

The principal actresses in this transfer of the social capacity to reproduce are mother (*maáma*), daughter (*umukoobwa*), the girl's father's sister (*maaséenge*), and her husband's mother (*maabukwé*) when she marries. Between the mother-in-law and the wife of her son, there is the possibility of disputing the right to reproduce, for both women produce children to perpetuate the same *inzu*. The wife of the son thus steps in to replace the wife of the father. She takes away, in a sense, a power that the older one has enjoyed up until then. Between a stepmother and a stepdaughter, there is also potential disagreement over the right to reproduce because a woman tends to favor her own children, her own daughters, over the children of her husband's other spouses.

This theme of the jealous stepmother (*mukase*) is attested to in stories and legends. According to Pierre Smith (1975, 85):

> La marâtre est ainsi considérée comme la bénéficiarie de la mort de la mère de l'orphelin et sa malveillance le poursuit, car l'existence de cet enfant qui n'a plus de rapport direct qu'au père, fait pièce à sa propre progéniture. . . . Le personnage universellement décrié de la marâtre l'est d'autant plus au Rwanda qu'il se situe dans une culture où la fécondité et la reproduction sont affirmées sans cesse comme les valeurs suprêmes du triomphe de la vie. Le marâtre est donc le personnage humain négatif par excellence des contes merveilleux qui sont d'ailleurs les seuls à l'exploiter.[12]

The destructive potential of a stepdaughter's indignation toward a stepmother has already been demonstrated in the myth of the origin of cattle (see pp. 29–32). In that instance, Nyirarucyaba was seen to dispute with and then kill her father's Rundi wife through the use of a spear, an implement forbidden to women.

In Hester's case, she appears to have had a number of conflicts with certain members of her husband's family, but the fact that the most consequential of these disputes centered upon these two women, a stepdaughter and a daughter-in-law, should not be surprising. Hester, Beatrice, and Maria embodied three different modalities of fertility within the *inzu* whose realization could potentially conflict. In its evanescence, the fertility of Hester could be thought of as being replaced by that of her son's wife in ensuring descendants for Simon's *inzu*. It is thus logical that she have a say in the choice of Elihu's wife, and Maria had not been her choice. As for Beatrice, her generative powers would be ceded to another family in exchange for a cow. Simon would receive this cow and probably use it to obtain a wife for his unmarried son. Because of this, he would be quite concerned that she indeed find a husband. In order for Hester to be concerned, however, she would have to be the real mother of Beatrice and not a stepmother. In believing that her own reproductive destiny was intimately tied up with that of her mother, Beatrice might very well feel that this destiny was now being undermined by the same person who had ejected, even killed, her mother.

In order for the fertility of the younger woman to realize its full potential, an orderly transfer of reproductive power had to have occurred. The fact that it had not occurred, could be inferred from the fact that both women had lost their mothers before becoming marriageable and was also manifest in their symptoms. Maria did not produce enough breast milk (*amashéreka*), and one of her children had died. In addition, Hester had opposed Maria's entry into the family. In Hester's eyes, Maria had become pregnant in order to force Elihu and other members of the family into feeling that Elihu should marry her. According to Maria, other members of the family had allowed the marriage despite Hester's opposition, for they had observed that Elihu and Maria were very much in love. Elihu and Maria had chosen each other sentimentally. In Beatrice's case, she could not find a husband and Hester had, in the previous generation, usurped Beatrice's mother's reproductive role in Simon's household. This event prevented Beatrice from being able to live her adolescence in the company of her mother. In Beatrice's eyes, Hester was only repeating with Maria and her what she had done in the preceding generation with Talacia. It was no wonder that she attributed her frustrated attempts to find a husband to Hester's influence.

The substances (and symbols) that embody the movement of reproductive power—milk and blood—are especially important here. In order for there to be conception, white sperm must join with red blood. A single coitus alone is not sufficient, for conception is a process of building the child's body in the uterus. Sexual relations produce the child by the conjunction of the two liquid media of generation, the fusion of two *intáanga* ("gifts of self"). But if white semen nourishes the developing fetus in utero, it is white milk that will nourish the growing child. Maternal milk and male sperm are thus analogous in some instances. This notion is apparent in the belief, expressed to me by some healers, that sexual intercourse fortifies a woman, makes her more beautiful, and causes her breasts and buttocks to grow. In an indirect way, the female's vaginal ingestion of male semen helps to produce her milk.

Maria was lacking in the female analogue of the white male fertility principle—that is, maternal milk—because she had anticipated the right to fertility too quickly. She had failed to consider the consequences of exercising her fertility out of wedlock. Moreover, she had arrogated the right to exchange herself, by choosing Elihu sentimentally, rather than letting herself be exchanged through the normal manner: overtures from the man's family, visits between the families, relatively long negotiations and gift exchanges, and finally marriage. The right to conduct this process belongs to the families and not to the individuals. Although individual preference of spouse is often taken into account, there are other factors and procedures involved that lead cautiously to matrimony and these must be respected.

These constraints are more binding on women than on men. Male sexual development and behavior do not incite the social interest accorded to females: "En effet, si aucune rupture symbolique importante ne vient marquer les différentes étapes de la vie des garçons, une attention extrêmement sourcilleuse est portée aux différents stades et passages de la vie féminine, d'où par exemple l'opprobre liée à l'absence de seins chez l'adolescente, à la grossesse pré-nuptiale, à la stérilité"[13] (P. Smith 1975, 80). By ignoring these constraints, Maria had angered Hester, the *igishéegabo,* whose actions, like those of the mythical Nyirarucyaba, led to a diminished flow of milk.

Female sexuality is considered a desirable and even necessary precondition for ensuring fertility. However, in developing their sexuality, in enlarging their genitalia, women run the risk of having their genitals grow disproportionately large, or of having their sexual appetites become asocial and anomic. Hence the theme of the virago or *igishéegabo:* one who takes too much of an initiative, who usurps patrilineally controlled powers and disregards the possible consequences. Such a woman was Nyirarucyaba, who handled the artifacts of men and then sliced open a uterus. Such a woman was Hester, who gave her husband food impregnated with her vaginal fluids and then was able to control him. Maria, who assumed the right to make free choices in her sexual activity, comes close to being such a woman. Rwandan culture has always had an ambivalent stance about the sexuality of women, which on the one hand the culture encourages and on the other hand strives to control. Money and commodity culture have accentuated the ambivalence.

The initial fertility powers of a woman reside in her blood. Menstrual blood is the first sign of a girl's awakening reproductive capacity. But menarche does not make a young girl marriageable. This is contingent upon the transfer of the social capacity to reproduce, a transfer which occurs from mother (*maáma*) to daughter (*umukoobwa*), from HM (*maabukwé*) to female ego, from FZ (*maaséenge*) to female ego. It is because this transfer had not occurred in the correct fashion that Beatrice's fears, as evinced in her nightmares, concerned blood. In her dreams she saw a young girl named Giteega, who would approach her after taking blood from the objects and persons around her. Beatrice's fear was that she was losing her blood, and thus her fertility, because Giteega was taking it away from her at night. As blood is the fundamental female element of reproduction, its loss signified that Beatrice's reproductive potential might never be realized. Men, in courting her, could eventually learn this by consulting a diviner to see if the prospective match would be fertile; they would learn of this lack in her and end the courtship. It is clear that Giteega was Hester, a nocturnal Hester who diverted the flow of blood and inverted the flow of time. Hester had usurped Talacia's reproductive position, and then she had taken her life; now it was Beatrice's turn. Giteega was a rejuvenated Hester, one become young by drinking Beatrice's blood and impeding the transfer of fertility to the younger generation.

To many around her and certainly to these two young women, Hester resembled the mythical *agakeécuru* in the origin myth of Death. Postmenopausal, she was a blocked vessel capable only of transferring infertility to her quasidaughters, Maria and Beatrice, by commensality with them. Maria, in her treatment at Bare, spoke of an *urweeso,* the small pot used to stopper the larger cooking vessel, *inkóno,* which is placed on the fire. In making this accusation, Maria alluded both to the domain of culinary action (i.e., indirectly to sexuality) and to the modality of blockage, for an *urweeso* acts like a large cork, retaining the heat and steam of cooking within the *inkóno* as it is inserted into the neck of the larger vessel. Hester was a blocking being who arrested the flow of fertility fluids in her stepdaughter, Beatrice, and in her son's wife, Maria. It was in an *urweeso* that she retained the spirits enabling her to poison others and it was this *urweeso* that the healers had been unable to find during their exorcism. Maria may have been semidelirious during her treatment at Bare, but the metaphors chosen in her state of altered consciousness were quite cogent. Hester was the *urweeso* herself, she stopped up other vessels. Although Maria confessed to her adultery, she indirectly accused Hester of something much more serious, she denounced her as a blocking being.

This association between the *urweeso* cooking vessel and notions of fertility and blockage receives support from René Bourgeois's observation, based on fieldwork in Rwanda in the 1930s, that an *urweeso* vessel can be used by a young woman in love magic to attract a suitor and to thwart the actions of those who might oppose her desires:

> Urweso (vase en terre). La jeune fille urine dans un vase puis prend en mains deux chalumeaux, l'un troué et l'autre bouché; ce dernier est censé servir à changer les idées des ennemis qui s'opposent au

mariage de la fille, et celui qui est troué présage l'avenir et révèle ceux qui nourrissent le désir de l'épouser; quant au vase contenant l'urine, il est déposé sur le foyer de ménage et la jeune fille souffle dedans en disant : "Ce chalumeau est débouché; j'attends un fiancé avec patience; son chemin est ouvert," puis en s'adressant au chaluemeau bouché, elle dit: "Que ceux qui s'opposent à mon mariage soient confondus." (1956, 327)[14]

The symbolism underlying the above practice is clear. The urine represents the girl's sexual fluids, recalling the Rwandan fashion of making love, *kunyáaza*, "to make urinate." The *urweeso* suggests the girl's womb and at the same time, the possibility of its infertility. The two drinking straws (*umuhehá* sing., *imihehá* pl.) imply two different types of conduit, that is, two types of matrimonial partner or two types of phallus, one that will "churn" (*gukúrakuza*) the girl's sexual fluids because it is open and another that lacks this capacity because it is closed. The latter evokes all the girl's potential enemies, those who through witchcraft might "block the path" (*gusiba inzira*) between her and her future husband.

This practice reinforces the statement made earlier that the Rwandan conception of the human body incorporates both a notion of the body as conduit, through which things pass, and a notion of the body as container, in which things are retained and then transformed. Procreation as well involves the passage of a fluid through a conduit (penis) into a gourdlike object (uterus) that contains the "churning" process. This combination of conduit and container, straw (*umuhehá*) and gourd (*igicumá*), characterizes the utensil Rwandans most frequently use in their foremost social activity, the drinking of beer. It is also the first object a Rwandan is likely to put into a visiting ethnographer's hands.

This case demonstrates one of the possible permutations between the therapeutic modes of accusation and confession. The therapy used by Mutabazi and Frederick, which is often employed at Bare in spirit possession cases, permits, though does not necessarily require, both. The actions of Maria are interesting in this regard, because she confessed to her adultery while accusing Hester of witchcraft. Moreover, this confession/accusation allowed her to avert the worst consequences of her adultery. In accusing Hester she showed to others around her that she was capable of engaging the disruptive force of illness to combat the demanding situation of an unsympathetic mother-in-law and an absent husband. This accusation was all the more credible given the current of suspicion that had hovered around Hester for a long time and the obvious history of enmity between her and Beatrice.

In Hester, Maria found a convincing bête noire behind whom she could at least partly disculpate herself. She had touched on several issues of contention in the family, even though Hester may not have been guilty of one fourth of what was attributed to her. Perhaps Hester was partially a scapegoat and partially a villain. But more important, her social state of being a stepmother (*mukase*) and a mother-in-law (*maa-bukwé*), and her bodily state of blockage (postmenopause), predisposed her to serving as a catalyst to all the emotionally charged discourses that surround the disposition of the female body in rural Rwanda today—a social environment in which the body is becoming more a product of and for individual fulfillment and less a vessel of the group's capacity to reproduce itself.

Maria and Beatrice were both born shortly before the Rwandan Revolution (1959–61), which witnessed the demise of Tutsi hegemony, divine kingship, *ubuhake* (the patron-client relation), and the beginning of a new Rwandan society transformed in many ways beyond the change from Tutsi control to Hutu control. The young women are representative of the first Rwandan generation to have passed through these culturally and historically pivotal events and to have recently reached childbearing age. The fact that they should encounter difficulties in defining themselves in relation to the old and the new aspects of Rwandan culture is not surprising. Both were practicing Prostestants and yet had been afflicted by non-Christian spirits. Both were of rural origin and continued to do farmwork every day, but they were members of households where the males did salaried work—in Maria's case, her husband worked in Butare; in Beatrice's case, her guardian Edouard worked as a Protestant preacher.

Both women were also victims of misconducted exchange. The transfer from mother to daughter of the social capacity to reproduce had not occurred with either woman. In Maria's case several other exchanges had not occurred properly. She had exchanged herself by her romantic involvement with Elihu and not by allowing the normal process of long negotiations and frequent gift visits between the potential affines. She went even further in this regard in her adultery with Edouard. Moreover, the *inkwáano* (bridewealth cow) was being disputed between her father and maternal grandfather, and Simon had yet to receive the return cow, *indoongoranyo.* Though Maria performed a lot of work for Hester and Simon and offered them occasional gifts, she felt that her generosity was not appreciated.

Beatrice and Maria were partially the victims of gift logic's demise and partially the victims of its persistence. In her movements from household to household, Beatrice could not find a position as wife and mother in her own home. She could exercise her volition in the choice of guardian, but her volition was of no help in finding a husband. Hence she had been unable to assume the role of supreme gift—a wife given to another *inzu.* But then she had never really received the benefits of gift ideology either. Her mother had not been able to prepare her socially for reproduction. As for Maria, she seemed to act impulsively, making choices that ignored the patrilineal constraints that rein in a woman's behavior. Yet she was continually being reminded that the specter of gift logic still hovered over her head. Women, according to the patriarchal definition of this logic, are the objects of gift flow. They are not its agents, not are they the ones who control it. In this confusion between two contradictory sets of logic, spirit possession is neither election nor retribution. Instead it becomes an attempt to make sense of individual suffering against the backdrop of a changing world and a lingering ideology.

CHAPTER 5

Spirit Possession Therapies in Southern Rwanda

~~~~~~~

Although the imagery manifest in precolonial Rwandan symbolic forms appears to be more faithfully preserved in northern Rwanda, one also finds therapies of accusation among healers in the south and center. Misfortune-causing spirits are encountered in both regions as are many of the poisons discussed in chapter 3. Moreover, both northern and southern Rwandan healers tend to follow the fluid model of health and pathology outlined in the same chapter. Nevertheless, there are important differences between the south and the north.

In this chapter I will show that despite persisting image schemata in Rwandan symbolic thought, notions of misfortune and healing are beginning to transform in southern Rwanda. These changes are rather subtle. Healers here tend to confirm the persecutorial view of misfortune—the idea that agents external to the person cause suffering—but their therapies do not exclude the idea of internal causation. Furthermore, a number of spirit beliefs are encountered in the south that do not appear in Butaro. These will be examined and then several case histories will be provided to illustrate the manner in which they are mobilized in popular healing.

Many of the case histories pursue the major theme of the previous chapter—the idea that Rwandans are caught between two different social logics. This does not mean that the representations associated with Christianity, biomedicine, and world capitalism are uncontestedly assuming a hegemonic position. In some instances, Rwandans who have all but abandoned their premission practices are being pushed back in that direction, because Christianity and Western biomedicine have proven inadequate to resolve their problems.

MISFORTUNE-CAUSING SPIRITS IN CENTRAL AND SOUTHERN RWANDA

Not all Rwandan healers treat illnesses that are of spiritual origin. Many specialize in less perplexing maladies claiming that they are unable to treat spirit disorders. Almost all healers, however, would agree that certain misfortunes constitute a special category. When I presented a corpus of illness names to various healers, almost all of them grouped disorders of this type within a single category, which they called *ubwandu* (spirits) or *amashitáani* (devils or demons, from the Kinyarwanda word for Satan). Sicknesses not of spiritual origin were usually treated by healers in a straightforward symptomatic manner. For most of these illnesses, they claimed that a Rwandan remedy existed that could effectively treat the disorder. A healer need only determine and administer that remedy and then the situation could be corrected. Some healers were almost cynically pragmatic about the label they attributed to a sickness. "I give the sickness a name and then treat it accordingly. If the treatment works, then it means I was right. If not, then I give it another name and try the treatment for that."

In fact idiosyncrasy prevails from one healer to another and thus a wide variety of therapeutic styles and techniques are available to the average Rwandan. Although syncretism is notably absent from the religious domain—people either follow traditional religious practices or Christianity or both, depending upon the situation—the therapeutic realm seems almost promiscuously open to experimentation, combination, and variety. Nevertheless, most Rwandans, when they feel they require the attention of a therapeutic specialist, turn first to Western biomedicine. There are hospitals in towns such as Kigali, Butare, Ruhengeri, and Gisenyi, and numerous rural dispensaries where Western medicine is available. The cost of treatment in urban hospitals and rural dispensaries, operated partially by the state and partially by religious or charitable organizations, is nominal. Pharmacies, however, are run by private interests. The prices of medications there—most of which are of Western manufacture, though some are of Chinese or Indian origin—are comparable to those found in pharmacies in Western countries. Sometimes prices are higher in Rwanda. Because of an important Chinese presence in Rwanda,[1] treatment is also available from Chinese physicians and nurses who employ their own medications and acupuncture. This method of treatment was gaining popularity when I was in Rwanda, and I had even heard of a Catholic priest who practiced as an acupuncturist.

Nonetheless, for a wide variety of illnesses and for certain types of therapeutic demand, Rwandans resort to popular therapies, a type of medicine termed *ubuvuuzi bwa Kinyarwanda* (from the verb *kuvuura*, meaning "to care for, to cure"; thus "curing à la Kinyarwanda") or *ubuvuuzi bwa Gihanga* ("curing according to Gihanga," after the first king thought to have brought knowledge of various crafts to Rwanda). When illnesses do not improve with biomedical treatment obtained at a hospital or dispensary, when misfortunes strike a household in series, when illnesses strike suddenly, inexplicably, and with extraordinary symptoms, or when sufferers seek answers to questions that cannot be answered by biomedicine (such as why me? why now? and who or what is responsible for my illness?), chances are good that many Rwandans will find their way to a popular therapist, an *umuvuuzi* (curer) or an *umupfumu* (diviner). Bizarre, persistent symptoms or serial misfortunes lead sufferers to suspect a spiritual origin to their illness. Often they consult an *umupfumu* to affirm or deny this suspicion. If a spiritual or human origin (*uburozi* or poisoning) is confirmed, the patient will then consult an *umuvuuzi*.

The most basic spirit disorder is caused by *abazímu* or ancestor spirits. Rwandans use this term only when they refer to a pathological state induced by ancestor spirits; they do not refer to the ancestors whom they sometimes ritually venerate as *abazímu*. In ritual contexts, they refer to their ancestors as *ababyéeyi* (relatives) or *abakúraambere* (the ones that came first). The world occupied by the living is termed *buntu*.[2] The underworld, occupied by spirits of the dead, is called *buzímu*. Spirits of the dead, *abazímu*, are usually spoken of in contexts where they are behaving vindictively toward the living. In theory, ancestors are supposed to exert a protective influence over their descendants. Most descendants, though, feel that their predecessors would probably prefer to be alive if they could and thus their relation to the living is, at best, ambivalent. Rwandans think that the only link that binds the dead to the pleasures of life is their descendants. The living, therefore, have an obligation to share food and drink periodically with the dead. If the latter liked to eat certain things during their lives, their descendants should occasionally offer them small morsels. If they liked to drink *urwáagwá* (banana beer)[3] or *ikigaáge* (sorghum beer) during their lifetimes, their descendants should give them a few drops by sprinkling some on the ground during the ritual of ancestor worship called *gutérekeera*.

Problems are said to arise with ancestors when the living fail to heed their obligations to them. In such a case an ancestor spirit may strike back at the living, afflicting them with sickness. In other instances, someone other than a lineal descendant of an *umuzímu* (ancestor spirit) may entice the latter to relinquish his protection over a specific descendant, or he may induce the ancestor to attack his own descendant. The malevolence of *abazímu* reflects the hate and resentment that divide society's living members. The fickleness, the easily compromised loyalties of ancestors who would sell their descendants' well-being for a taste of beer, are often projections upon the *buzímu* (the underworld) of the problematic nature of social life in the *buntu* (world of the living). When Rwandans choose the idiom of spirit possession to articulate their perceptions of bodily or economic misfortune, they are usually pointing the finger of responsibility in the direction of those who are still alive: relatives, neighbors, rivals, associates, or friends. Nevertheless, the first battery of beliefs about spirit possession in both the north and the south concerns the *abazímu*.

Many healers in southern Rwanda maintain that *abazímu* involvement is required in all *amarozi* (poisonings, spells). If someone wishes to attack a relative by occult means, he must first placate his own lineal ancestors (through *gutérekeera*) and then solicit the complicity of his intended victim's ancestors. In this process he may engage the services of an *umupfumu*, asking the diviner to determine the ancestor(s) most likely to turn against a specified descendant. Then the *umurozi*[4] (poisoner) sacrifices a goat in honor of this *umuzímu*, promising to sacrifice a bull or sterile cow when the intended victim has been harmed. When an animal is sacrificed, those present at a *gutérekeera* ritual will consume it, but drops of the animal's blood and often small pieces of meat will be placed in a tiny shrine constructed to resemble a Rwandan hut (*indáaro*) as an offering to the spirit. Along with the bits of meat and blood from the goat, the sacrifier will give drops of *urwáagwá* (banana beer) or *ikigaáge* (sorghum beer) to the spirit by invoking his or her name and then sprinkling drops on the ground near the shrine.

Someone who intends to employ *abazímu* in poisoning may alter the *gutérekeera* ritual. He or she may burn a fire using wood from a stretcher that has been used to transport a cadaver (*umuhezayo*). The best time to accomplish rituals of nefarious intent is at night and during pivotal moments in the lunar cycle, during a full or new moon, or at pivotal moments in the solar calendar (e.g., at the beginning or end of the year). Spirits are thought to be more active at these moments.

Several other types of *amarozi* practiced in the central and southern part of Rwanda, including *amajini, ibiteega, nyabingi* (not the same as the Nyabingi cult practiced in northern Rwanda, though inspired by it), and *amaheémbe,* require alienating the protection of the victim's *abazímu* before these other spells can be employed. According to a central Rwandan healer named Matthieu, who worked in the Butare area of south-central Rwanda and whose information was corroborated by others, in order to inflict these spells upon someone who has no kinship relation to the poisoner, one must know the names of six lineal predecessors of the intended victim: F (*data*), FF (*sogo-kuru*), FFF (*sogo-kuru-za*), M (*maáma*), MM (*nyogo-kuru*), and MMM (*nyogo-kuru-za*). The poisoner must first make a sacrificial offering to his own ancestors. Once these ancestors have been placated, the *umurozi* takes branches from four plants employed in the *kubaandwa* cult: *umucyúuro, umukó, umukúundé,* and *ikibonobono.*

Umucyúuro (Cassia didymobotria, Erythrococca fisheri) is used in *kubaandwa* to sprinkle initiates with a white kaolin mixture. The cognate verb is *gucyúura,* which means "to bring something back to one's house that had been lent to someone else, to bring cattle back from the pasture, to bring a repudiated wife back into one's household, or to bring peace back into one's conjugal life" (Jacob 1984, 218).

Umukó (Erythrina abyssinica), probably the most widely employed tree in ritual contexts, was the tree beneath which Ryangombe died after having been impaled by a buffalo. While in agony, Ryangombe summoned the aid of the entire plant kingdom; the *umukó* tree was the only one to answer this plea. One of the few botanical specimens in Rwanda to evince pronounced seasonal changes, *umukó* blossoms toward the end of the long dry season, late August, at about the same time as *imvúra y'inká* (the "rain for the cows," one of the first rains announcing the end of the dry season). *Umukó* flowers are large, pointed upward, and are deep red in hue. Luc de Heusch and others consider the *umukó* tree to be a symbol of rebirth and resurrection. However, given the tree's colorful red flowers, its dramatic periodicity, and the skyward direction of its flowers, it is also accurate to think of the tree as a symbol of blood moving from earth to sky, perhaps reminiscent of king sacrifice. This association of the tree with blood and bodily fluids is reinforced by the fact that the tree's sap is milky white and therefore evocative of both milk and semen.

The name *umukúundé* (*Cajanus cajan;* Jacob 1987, 295) derives from the verb *gukúunda*, which means "to like or to love."

In southern and central Rwanda, many people occasionally honor the spirits of Ryangombe and his followers, the Abacwezi. Also known as kubaandwa, *initiation to the cult of Ryangombe occurs in two stages. First-stage initiates earn the right to attend celebrations of* kubaandwa; *second-stage initiates may incarnate either Ryangombe himself or one of the Abacwezi. Many people practice both Christianity and* kubaandwa.

The fourth plant's name, *ikibonobono* (*Chassalia subochreata, Psychotria* div. spp.; Jacob 1984, 127), comes from the verb *kubona,* which means "to see or to receive." Sometimes seeds of this plant were worn by unmarried women with the intention of "seeing" and "receiving," that is, finding and marrying, a husband.

The cult of Ryangombe addresses itself, among other things, to problems of sterility and fertility. This association is apparent from these plants. *Umucyúuro* is used to anoint cult celebrants with a white colored liquid, and its name implies the return of objects, cattle, wives, and peace to the domestic group, that is, good reciprocity relations with others. *Umukó* harnesses the symbolic powers associated with the colors white and red, the primary fertility colors in Rwanda and in many other parts of central Africa (cf. Turner 1967). The fertility associations of the other two plants, through the verbs *gukunda* and *kubona,* are clear.

The *umurozi* (poisoner) forms a bunch with these four tree branches and then goes to the entry of the victim's *urugó* (the space including the enclosure as well as the house of a Rwandan homestead). There he invokes the names of his victim's ancestors and then strikes the palisade of the *urugó* with the branches. He addresses the ancestors of his victim telling them that he will be more attentive, more generous in his ministrations to them than the victim has been. Next he invokes the names of his own ancestors, asking them to "invite" the ancestors of his victim to his house. After he has returned home, the *umurozi* asks his ancestors to welcome their "guests" (*abashyitsi*). He gives them food and drink (small quantities are sprinkled on the ground in a shrine dedicated to his own ancestors). He invokes his spirit guests by their names, promising them a bull, if they harm the intended victim. Poisoners are thought to attack a victim's health, the health of any member of the household, the reproductive capacity of wife or husband, the productivity of crops or livestock, or the victim's cash livelihood. Relatives that attack other relatives usually covet their victim's land or inheritance.

After the above spiritual preparations have been completed, an *uburozi* is prepared from various plant and animal substances, such as: *umukoma, umuhuta, umuhezayo, nyiragashiha,* a carcass of a scavenging bird known as *inkona,* bones of previous poisoning victims, or bones from the palm of a stillborn infant. These are all common ingredients, but other plant, animal, and human substances might be used as well. *Amarozi* vary widely and the people who prepare them, *abarozi,* know a great number of substances that work. Often poisons are introduced into the victim's food or drink; many of these contain pharmacologically active substances that can cause sickness or death. But there are also poisons that appear to work at a distance or that a victim need merely walk over (e.g., *imitáambikiro* or *amageza*), and no terminological distinction is made between those that act at a distance and those that have to be ingested. In fact, a commonly employed curative technique, *kurúka uburozi* (to vomit poison), applies to both types of aggression, confirming Pierre Smith's observation that Rwandan sorcery is usually thought to act through the alimentary tract (1975, 80).

Healers differ in their methods of counteracting poisons. Most employ substances derived from plants or animals. Some types of snake skin are thought to be particularly powerful antipoisons, as are elephant hairs, lion skin, and the bones and skin of a buffalo. Rwandan healers explain that the dangerous substances used in poisoning must be countered by dangerous substances used in the cure, a reasoning that closely follows homeopathic principles and that is encountered virtually everywhere in the world.

Many healers also recommend that the victim perform the ritual of *gutérekeera*, to honor his ancestors so that they will come to his defense, and *kubaandwa* rites, to honor Ryangombe and the *imaándwa* spirits, who are thought to exert a powerful magical protection over cult initiates. In northern Rwanda, sufferers would be likely to visit a Nyabingi priest (*umugirwá*) in order to offer something to the goddess in addition to performing *gutérekeera* for their ancestors.

The spell known as *amageza* involves placing poisons on a pathway frequented by the intended victim. This action is accomplished only after the necessary wooing of the victim's *abazímu*. Although it is expected that the victim and others will physically contact the poisonous substances with their feet, the poisons are not thought to act against anyone who has not been named during the poisoner's incantations. When the victim passes over the spot, the poisons enter his or her feet and legs, causing them to swell painfully. The poison rises in the body and usually affects the lower back and abdomen next. If the victim is not treated at this time, the poison will rise to the heart and cause death. One form of *amageza*, called *izayiko*, is thought to be particularly fast acting and dangerous. It is described by one healer as the *umutware w'amashitáani* (the chief of demons, of bad spells). Counteracting *amageza* entails ingesting a powder made from plant and animal substances, sacrificing to one's ancestors and to Ryangombe, if possible, and sometimes magically counter-aggressing the poisoner. This last measure is usually undertaken only when the first two methods bring no improvement, and it is only practiced by certain healers.

Another particularly virulent *uburozi* is *amaheémbe* (literally, "horns"; sing. *iheémbe*). Many healers say that *amaheémbe* spirits entered Rwanda from Uganda. These spirits are a special category of deceased persons like *abazímu*, although they are not necessarily related to the sufferer. They are either young men or young women who died affianced, but before marriage took place. When one of the partners to a prospective marriage dies before the wedding, the bridewealth cow, *inkwáano*, already presented to the bride's father, must be returned to the man's family. When one goes to the home of the wife's family to reclaim the *inkwáano*, a special opening in the palisade forming the perimeter of the *urugó* must be made and the cow brought out through it. If hoes are included in the bridewealth, these are thrown over the palisade. In neither case may the cow or hoes be brought out the same way they came in—through the principal entry (*iréembo*) to the enclosure (*urugó*). Once the bridewealth returns to the husband's family, similar arrangements are made to reintroduce the cow into that family's *urugó*. A special opening is made in the palisade, and hoes are unceremoniously thrown over the palisade. Ritual words are pronounced at the home of the deceased party, so that the spirit of the dead man or woman will remain at home, and not become a vindictive *iheémbe* spirit and follow the surviving party to do harm to him or her.

Amaheémbe spirits are thought to be particularly dangerous. They can rapidly attack the heart, causing blood to flow from the upper part of the body, through vomiting or nosebleeds, or from the lower parts, through bleeding from the vagina or anus. These spirits owe their viciousness to the fact that one of the most tragic fates that can befall either a man or a woman in Rwandan society, with its emphasis on fertility, is to leave this life without having fulfilled one's reproductive destiny. Dying just at the moment when one is about to accomplish the rite of passage that signifies society's acknowledgment of the formation of a new household unit is doubly tragic, for it may compromise the economic and reproductive futures of two *amazu* (houses) by annulling an alliance relationship between them.[5]

In order to preclude the possibility of the hapless partner's becoming a vindictive *amaheémbe* spirit, care must be taken to quickly, and unceremoniously, reverse the most significant gift exchanges (gifts of the means of production, i.e., cattle or hoes) that had occurred between the two families. Hence the somewhat expedient and shamefaced method of returning the bridewealth cow and hoes. When death aborts a marriage, peoples' hearts are affected. The heart is the central organ of consciousness, volition, and desire. Hence the rapidity of an *amaheémbe* spell to attack the heart, causing blood to flow from above or from below. In order to employ the *amaheémbe* spell, one first sacrifices to one's ancestors and then instructs them to find the spirit of a man or a woman who died in the above manner; then one makes a sacrifice to this spirit and entreats it to attack one's victim.

Other harmful spirits that appear similar in some respects to *amaheémbe* are those known as *ibiteega*. These spirits are said to have begun entering Rwanda from northwest Tanzania in the 1930s, although many healers say that, as an illness, *ibiteega* became important after 1960, especially in southern Rwanda (cf. Habimana 1986). According to healers whom I interviewed, *ibiteega* are the spirits of: deceased foreigners, prepubescent girls, adults of either sex who died without leaving any progeny, or women who died while pregnant. Like *amaheémbe*, *ibiteega* are the spirits of people who died before completely fulfilling some aspect of reproductive function, beings whose bodies were prematurely blocked by death. Young girls transformed into *ibiteega* spirits, are those who died before the onset of menstruation. Women who died while pregnant follow the same pattern. Although they may have given birth before, what is central to the belief is that at the moment of death their wombs were harboring new life, which was prevented from exiting their bodies.

Some healers say that *ibiteega* spirits attack tiny children, prepubescent girls or boys, and women. Others say that they can attack anyone, but are usually sent by poisoners who seek their victim's wealth. Symptoms include trembling, delirium (sometimes with convulsions), and the victim's making a lot of noise. Normally *ibiteega* can be reversed by administering a medicine, especially through the nostrils, that provokes the spirits into revealing who they are and who sent them. Sometimes the *ibiteega* are too strong and they prevent the victim from speaking, but this is rare. Usually this type of poisoning is not extremely dangerous; a healer administers a medication and the spirit leaves directly. Nonetheless, when a victim does not receive treatment quickly, this spell can cause death.

Amajini spirit affliction is more frequently seen among people who are Muslims or who live in proximity to Muslims. *Amajini* spirits are thought to be of Tanzanian origin. Islam is not as widely practiced in Rwanda as Catholicism and Protestantism, but Muslims form a visible minority in some places, especially in urban areas. The word *amajini* comes from the Arabic, *djinn*. Some healers claim that *amajini* attack thieves, rapists, cheats, and other wrongdoers who have escaped punishment (this judgment is, of course, in the eye of the one sending the spirit). In order to send them, one must read certain verses from the Koran, but no healer that I spoke with could tell me exactly which ones.

There are four types of *amajini*. The ones called *pao* are associated with the sea. *Pao* can stop the sea, or they can take a person from on board a vessel and hurl him or her into the water. Sometimes *pao* appear in the form of a white man or a white woman. *Jyabali* are another form of *amajini*, but these are associated with rocks. More frequently encountered in Tanzania than in Rwanda, they often appear in the form of a black person. *Korongo* are the *amajini* of cliffs. They attack pregnant women and babies. Hunters sometimes see them in the form of wild animals. Capricious, they can change rapidly from one form to another. When they strike a victim, they can take away his "heart" (his consciousness). *Mwitu* are yet another form of *amajini,* and they are found in bushes. A bush may appear foggy, or smoke may emanate from it. The bush may make a noise like a tree breaking. *Mwitu* can castrate a young man or render him impotent. They can make a young girl sterile, or if she conceives, cause her to miscarry. Symptoms of *amajini* poisonings include periods of silence and inactivity alternating with periods of extreme agitation and hallucinations. A victim may begin speaking in a language with which he has never been in contact, or he may speak frenetically and incoherently.

Amajini and the affliction called *nyabingi* have pronounced and similar symptoms. During the agitated state that characterizes certain phases of each affliction, a victim may fall on the ground, babbling incoherently, and he may bite his tongue. These symptoms resemble epilepsy, called *igicuri* in Kinyarwanda, but most healers can usually distinguish readily between them. One healer's treatment of *amajini* and *nyabingi* involves drawing up a bit of herbal concoction into a syringe (without a hypodermic needle), inserting the syringe into each nostril and then injecting the medicine while the head is tilted backward. The effect of this treatment is dramatic, causing violent sneezing, and its aim is to open the blood vessels in the head. After these injections of medicine into the nostrils, the healer usually gives the patient a bottle or gourd filled with another medicine to take home and drink at specified moments during the day.

Nyabingi affliction is rather frequently encountered in central and southern Rwanda. It is related, but not identical to the northern religious cult. In the north, Nyabingi (in Rukiga), or Nyabyinshi (in Kinyarwanda), is seen as a benevolent deity. In southern and central Rwanda, however, Nyabingi is not perceived as a goddess whom one may supplicate for health reasons, fertility, or material prosperity, but as one *ishitáani* (demon) among many. The reasons for this are cultural and historical. Northern Rwanda, because of its history of resistance to the expansionist tendencies of central Rwanda and its late integration into the Rwandan kingdom has always been perceived as "savage" by people from the southern and central regions.

According to one healer from central Rwanda, who had been married to a woman from northern Rwanda, *nyabingi* affliction comes from women who "possess" the goddess Nyabingi. These women are called *abaheko ba Nyabingi*. They form the Nyabingi elite. Women who are *abaheko* are usually chosen from among pubescent girls; their selection is manifested by possession symptoms. The girl falls on the ground and begins to tremble. Only when she seeks assistance from a Nyabingi priest can the possession sickness be cured. A girl chosen by Nyabingi in this manner, usually becomes a medium of the goddess and acquires formidable powers. Nyabingi mediums act as intermediaries between supplicants and Nyabingi, who in her turn acts as an intermediary to *imáana*. It is through Nyabingi, that *imáana* distributes wealth and beneficence to the entire population. Nyabingi had many female and male children; she has had many important priests. All of them may act as intermediaries between her and ordinary mortals.

Many of the beliefs associated with *nyabingi* affliction that this healer reported to me accorded in part with the actual practice of the Nyabingi cult in northern Rwanda. Where the healer's perceptions of *nyabingi* differed most radically from actual practice was in the domain of misfortune. According to him, someone wishing to do harm through Nyabingi can enlist the aid of a Nyabingi priest (*umugirwa*; pl. *abagirwa*) or one of the *abaheko ba Nyabingi*. If you have had a quarrel with a woman who possesses Nyabingi, she might very well send the spirit to afflict you. But the idea that Nyabingi can be solicited to do harm against someone else is not supported by the Nyabingi priests whom I interviewed in the north. Although there does exist a ritual procedure called *guhin-*

ziliza, in which a Nyabingi priest may pray for the goddess's help in pun-
ishing wrongdoers, many northern priests say that they will not employ
this ritual under any circumstances, and most say that it is only under
extraordinary conditions that it is ever employed—in particular, when
there is a perceived threat to a large group of people. According to many
abagirwá, Nyabingi can never be employed as, and never be equated
with, ordinary *amashitáani.* She is a goddess of fertility, of prosperity, of
health and well-being. To her cult followers, the southern and central
Rwandan view that Nyabingi is a bad spirit is a complete perversion of
their beliefs.

Yet people in the south and center persist in their conviction that
nyabingi frequently afflicts innocent people. According to healers in these
regions, Nyabingi followers possess small shrines at their homes built to
resemble traditional Rwandan houses. Occasionally sacrifices are made
to Nyabingi and pieces of meat and drops of beer are placed within this
shrine. These rites are private and familial. Rituals involving large
groups are also performed and these resemble the central and southern
Rwandan traditional religious ceremonies known as *kubaandwa.* This
depiction of Nyabingi ritual, however, is not entirely accurate.

Central Rwandan healers believe that group ceremonies involving
Nyabingi are responsible for spreading the *nyabingi* affliction. For example, Nyabingi cult celebrants in northern Rwanda may bring a bull to
sacrifice at a crossroads. On one side of the crossroads, people will sacrifice the bull, build a fire, and then cook and eat the meat. At the other
side of the crossroads, *urwáagwá* (banana beer) and *ikigaáge* (sorghum
beer) will be placed. Once enough meat has been eaten, people cross to
the other side and drink the beer. Neither the meat nor the beer is completely consumed; portions of both are left behind. Passersby who see the
meat and the beer are thus tempted to partake of it. Such travelers are
alleged to have been Rwandans from the southern part of the country
passing through the north on their way to jobs in Kenya and Uganda before these countries became independent. When these unsuspecting
people ate or drank anything from an abandoned Nyabingi feast, they
became afflicted by her and manifested symptoms much later. Often this
occurred on their journey back to southern and central Rwanda. Once
these hapless victims returned to their homes and became ill, they would
behave aberrantly. They would take bundles and place them on their
heads as if they were about to set out on a trip. Many would instinctively
try to return to the north, as if they had no control over their actions, yet

were involuntarily drawn back to the area where they had contracted their illness. Some were tied down to prevent them from moving about, but often these people would die. Many realized that they had to seek the help of Nyabingi priests and adepts in order to be cured. In doing so, however, they became Nyabingi adepts in their turn, and had to pay money or do work for a Nyabingi priest or priestess. By this means Nyabingi possession and worship spread to the south.

Nyabingi affliction is thus seen as a "foreign" intrusion into south-central Rwanda. Notice that *ibiteega, amajini, amaheémbe,* and *nyabingi* all share the quality of being spirits brought into the south and center from outside, spirits that are unknown and unrelated by kin ties to the sufferer. They are also more random in afflicting people than the ancestors one knows from one's own genealogy. Furthermore, in the case of Nyabingi, the spread of the affliction to southern Rwanda is directly linked to the demands of the colonial economy: migrant labor, the encountering of new behaviors and customs that threaten because they are different, and the close association between perceived spiritual power and the possibility of profiting commercially from this power. Although no true Nyabingi cult adept would ever maintain that an *umugirwá* could extract labor or wealth from an innocent passerby, as indicated in the healer's account above, it is interesting to note that the belief reflects a fear of exploitation based on spiritual domination. In that respect the belief resembles the notion of "zombi" in Haitian popular religion. Similar beliefs also exist among the Kaguru in Tanzania (cf. Beidelman 1986). The presence of these beliefs in southern Rwanda indicates that notions of alienation are beginning to penetrate this region's concepts of misfortune.

Such beliefs may very well be engendered in colonial and postcolonial economies, which are characterized by long-distance movements of people in search of wage employment, the crossing of cultural boundaries, the abstraction of human labor power, and the randomization of human suffering (cf. Taussig 1980). When the nature of domination changes in a political economy from one of "personal domination" to one of "abstracted domination,"[6] it appears that notions of misfortune, although they change more slowly, tend to move in the direction of abstraction as well. Misfortune-causing agents become beings unknown to oneself and one's family, beings who originate from outside the moral or national community. No longer are they ancestors who enforce respect for lineage and community morality, instead the newer spirits often appear to have no morality at all; they strike haphazardly, and those who employ them seek primarily to cause their victims' material loss. By depersonalizing the intentionality and efficacy of misfortune-causing spirits, patients and healers show that they are conceptualizing the newer forms of misfortune—unemployment, indebtedness, or other economic malaise—through the older idiom of spirit possession. The nature of the spirit beings, however, has adjusted to new exigencies in this "recognition" process. Such beings begin to acquire properties that resemble the character of current social relations.

Other spirits sometimes treated by central Rwandan healers are *ibiduma, ibivuga, imiyaga,* and *matimbya*.[7] In *ibiduma* possession, the victim begins to talk compulsively, but with his own voice, in contrast with *ibivuga,* where the spirits speak through him. In *imiyaga,* the victim attempts to bite himself. *Matimbya* possession is interesting because its treatment reveals something about how healers conceptualize the body. Characterized by uncontrollable trembling, *matimbya* is treated by having the patient sit over a hole in which a fire has been made. When subjected to this treatment, the spirits leave by the victim's mouth, indicating that the body is like an open conduit through which spiritual influences as well as aliments pass. Normally movement is downward, but under certain conditions, as in this treatment, this movement is reversed in order to evacuate the body. Fire is used because it operates in opposition to fluids; fire defies gravity, it moves up (cf. de Heusch 1982, pp. 65–72, on the dialectical relation of fire and water). This curing technique, although it does not superficially resemble *kurúka uburozi* (inducing regurgitation to eject a poison), follows the same pattern of movement from down to up, inside to outside.

Finally, healers in central and southern Rwanda also occasionally treat *imaandwa* possession. This spirit illness is related to the cult of Ryangombe and his disciples, the *Ibicwezi;* the cult is also referred to as *kubaandwa,* a verb which means "to allow oneself to be elevated."[8] Those that assume the identity of Ryangombe and his disciples during the celebration of this cult are called *imaandwa.* When someone has procrastinated in becoming a *kubaandwa* initiate, an *imaandwa* spirit, (i.e., an ancestor who was a *kubaandwa* initiate in the past or one of the *Ibicwezi* or even Ryangombe himself), may afflict the person with illness. This illness will disappear once the victim undergoes initiation into the cult. Today, many Christian Rwandans prefer not to become initiated into *kubaandwa* and merely seek the aid of a healer who will exorcise the spirit by administering medications. This was often the case with people who came to the clinic for popular medicine in Butare, because here the healers only administered remedies.

HEALERS OF THE BUTARE CLINIC FOR POPULAR MEDICINE

Several healers with whom I developed a close rapport worked at a clinic for popular medicine in Butare (*Ivuliro y'Ubuvuuzi bwa Gihanga*). The clinic had been set up by the Centre Universitaire de Recherche sur la Pharmacopée et la Médecine Traditionnelle (Curphametra), a multidisciplinary research group affiliated with the Université Nationale du Rwanda (UNR). It consisted of a simple one-story brick building with a cement floor and a corrugated iron roof. Every healer had his own stall within the building separated from others by a cloth curtain and illuminated by a fluorescent light. Unlike at the Bare dispensary, not all the Butare healers routinely wore lab coats. These healers practiced at the center two mornings per week and cared for patients who came from all parts of Rwanda, but mostly from the south and center. Patients usually arrived early, around 7:30 or 8:00 A.M., although the healers did not begin their work until about 9:00 A.M. Before receiving patients, the healers prepared the herbal medications they used by pulverizing plants with a mortar and pestle, and then extracting the medicinal fraction from the plants with water.

Once the healers were ready to receive patients, the latter formed a line in front of the small doorway to the clinic. As patients entered the dispensary, a secretary registered each one by writing his or her name in a book and then on a piece of paper returned to the patient. Once the patient paid the consultation fee of 500 francs (about $5), he or she was directed to the healer who specialized in the patient's affliction. Generally, healers interviewed patients for fifteen to thirty minutes, then made their diagnosis and administered the appropriate remedy. In cases of poisoning, the interview was usually longer. Each healer wrote the diagnosis on the patient's slip of paper and often instructed him or her to return the following week. Before leaving the dispensary, patients returned their slips of paper so that the healers' diagnoses could be compiled for statistical purposes.

The following case histories were elicited from patients who were treated at the clinic.

At the Center for Traditional Medicine in Butare, healers often prepare medications at the site itself. Here one of the healers is using a mortar and pestle to pulverize some plants. Later, he will use water to make an extract from the plants.

Matthieu treated a twenty-two-year-old man with pains in the upper abdominal region. These pains worsen when he drinks anything alcoholic. He's already been treated at the hospital, but his symptoms persist. He believes that he has been poisoned and that he needs an emetic to get the poison out.

Matthieu says that the man has contracted a poison passed to him in his food. Because one year has elapsed since his illness first began, Matthieu believes that the poison has already dispersed outward into his body. He gives him a medication in order to gather the poison together into a small ball in his stomach. Once this occurs, he will give him a medication to induce vomiting so that the poison can be ejected.

COMMENT: Matthieu's diagnosis is interesting because we can deduce from it how he conceptualizes the activity of poisons and antidotes. Poisons act centrifugally; they disperse outward into the body. This action can be reversed, however, for there are medicines that act centripetally. These gather the dispersed poisons together. Once the poison has coalesced, there are medicines that act as emetics or purgatives to evacuate the poison from the body.

In effect, the illness is transformed from an intangible consequence of social conflict into a tangible corporal "sign"—vomit or feces—that is ejected from the body.

Matthieu treated a twenty-four-year-old woman named Annunciata, who had been brought to the center by her father. Before coming to Butare, she and her father had consulted several other healers and had sought help at a psychiatric clinic staffed by biomedical doctors at Ndera, near Kigali. All to no avail.

At the age of sixteen, Annunciata began having strange dreams. She would see a man who would come to her and make love. She was afraid to speak of this to her mother. These dreams continued every month, but still the girl refused to speak of them to anyone. At twenty the possibility of the girl's obtaining an actual fiancé became a reality, but the man in her dream refused to let her do so, saying that he was her rightful husband. Young men who came to visit her would be contested by him. Now when she saw this man from her dreams, she would scream.

Finally, she became engaged, but as the day of her marriage approached, her intended became ill. His stomach swelled to the point where his testicles disappeared, and soon thereafter he died. The girl believes it was the dream man that killed him. Later another suitor became her fiancé. One day while going on a visit to his home and family, she began to tremble and subsequently fainted. She had seen the man from her dream. He was preventing her from reaching her second fiancé's house.

More recently, the dream man has threatened the girl herself, telling her that he could very easily kill her if he wished. She is worried that she will never find a husband, that every suitor will be attacked by this man and possibly be killed like the first suitor. Her sleep continues to be troubled by these nightmares, although she can usually work during the day.

On the basis of her symptoms—a man appearing to her either in her dreams or in daylight, her suitor's "castration," her fainting—Matthieu says that she has *amajini* affliction. This diagnosis is consistent with the description of *amajini* given earlier (pp. 148–150). In particular, it is worth recalling that the *mwitu* form of *amajini* can castrate, the *jyabali* form can appear as a person, and that the *korongo* form can cause loss of consciousness.

The girl's erotic dreams, which have been recurring for the past eight years, have taken on such a reality for her that now she cannot give herself as a wife. She appears to feel very guilty about the dreams, perhaps because she derived pleasure from them at the outset, perhaps also because she is Catholic. Matthieu's healing technique affords her the possibility of confessing her fantasy sins under the guise of accusing a spirit. The person who might have been able to help her most when the dreams first began was her mother (Rwandan mothers aid in socially channeling the nascent sexuality of their daughters), but she refused to talk to her mother about them.

Now it is the guilt and not the pleasure that is the reality of the dream man. He is ruining her life, making her feel responsible for her first fiancé's death. He is also preventing her from realizing her exchange and reproductive destiny as wife and mother. When she describes her first suitor and his symptoms, she describes him as blocked-up. Instead of leaving his body, fluids accumulated so that he swelled up to the point where his testicles disappeared. One might infer that the dream man caused the suitor's fluids to remain trapped within him to the point where it effectively castrated, then killed him.

The underlying symbolic imagery of her first suitor's death also characterizes Annunciata's relationship with her second suitor. She faints before she is able to reach his house. Just as the dream man blocked the body of her first suitor, he is now blocking the path to the second (*gusiba inzira*). The man from her dreams is "castrating" this young woman just as he "castrated" her first suitor. In doing this, he is preventing her from leading what remains the only meaningful life for most rural Rwandan women, marriage and child rearing. Even though Annunciata's case involves spirit possession, it is possibly more a confession of erotic guilt than it is an accusation.

It should be recalled that *gusiba inzira*, which literally means "to block the path," is used to describe the loss through death of a daughter before marriage. Exchange relations between families are sometimes compared to paths. Here similar imagery has been employed to signify the frustration of this girl's matrimonial hopes. In one instance, the possibility of marriage is precluded by death; in another, the path to the suitor's home is obstructed by the man from the girl's dreams.

Matthieu treated a forty-year-old woman named Verediana in December 1983. She had been sick for several months. Her primary symptom was prolonged, abundant menstruation, which she said had been caused by an *umurozi* (poisoner). She visited a hospital and received injections that stopped the hemorrhagic periods, but she still felt intensely afraid, and she often had trouble eating. Recently Verediana separated from her husband. Immediately afterward her symptoms improved, but then they became worse.

The patient accuses the older brother of her husband and his wife of being her *abarozi*. She thinks that her husband, a counselor in a Catholic church, is involved too. She also believes that the older brother possesses several spells—*igifaro, nyabingi, ibiteega,* and *abazímu*—which have affected her fertility in the past. For example, Verediana claims that her third pregnancy was interrupted at eight and a half months, shortly after her husband began sleeping with another wife. Somehow the child managed to survive, despite her diminished secretion of breast milk (*amashéreka*). Several years earlier, during the events of 1973 (when persistent tension between Hutu and Tutsi and the parliamentary government's inability to deal with the situation had led to a military coup), she was being transported to the hospital in labor. There were numerous roadblocks and barriers erected on the roads. The child was born alive at the hospital, but died the next day. Then her husband arrived and insisted that she leave the hospital.

Verediana states that another brother of her husband was once suspected of being an *umurozi* and was killed by a group of his neighbors. Her husband has had a total of eleven wives; now he has only two, but they do not all live together. She lives apart from them. Her husband occasionally comes to see her and they have been getting along better.

Matthieu diagnoses her illness as *amageza*, which it should be recalled, can cause blood to flow in excess from the vagina. He gives her a medication that he squirts into her nostrils.

COMMENT: Notice that this woman speaks at times of excessive flow from her body and then at other times of a physical or reproductive blockage. In 1983, she had hemorrhagic menses that she attributed to poisoning. Before that, a pregnancy had been interrupted, but the baby survived. Even before these two incidents, while she was en route to the hospital in labor, she encountered numerous roadblocks and barriers, and later her baby died. Although the roadblocks she encountered in this

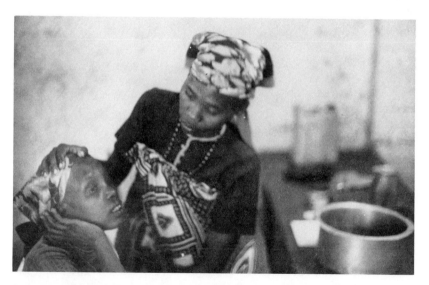

In spirit possession illnesses, medications are frequently introduced directly into the nostrils in order to facilitate the circulation of blood in the head. The healer shown here either inserts powdered medicines into the nostrils with her fingers or uses a needle-less syringe to squirt medicine into the nose.

incident were quite real, the degree to which they conform to the metaphoric imagery of the blocked path is noteworthy. It is also interesting to note that the background of this incident, the political events of 1973, constitute a moment when relations between the Tutsi and the Hutu had degenerated into violence. Other details she employs in her story are images of perturbed flow: her menstrual periods are prolonged and hemorrhagic, one baby was born prematurely (like the mythical Gafomo; see pp. 29–32); or images of blockage: trouble in eating, barriers on the roads, the death of a child soon after birth, and diminished lactation.

She implicates two classically problematic social relations, which merge together in her story. The first one concerns her affines, her husband's brother and his wife; the second, her polygynous household (when she sees her husband alone, they get along better).

Since relations with one's affines and with one's spouse in Rwandan society are the most crucial ones in matters of reproduction, it is no accident that this woman's symptoms have a strong gynecological focus. When Verediana's husband stopped sleeping with her, he arrested the process of regular flow of semen into her womb. He violated the ideal of *gukúrakuza*. It is not surprising that the baby was born prematurely, since he was, in effect, an unfinished product. Furthermore, notice that after the birth of the child she lacked maternal milk (becoming an *igihama*), which also may have been due to her husband's sexual neglect.

The choice of details used by this woman to describe her difficulties is not at all fortuitous. Perturbed bodily flow, and a consequent diminution of her fertility, is directly suggested by her symptoms and metaphorically implied by the contextual details of her story. Directly correlated with the symptomatic effect of perturbed bodily flow is the pathological cause of abrogated or problematic exchange: troubled relations with her husband in the context of a polygynous household; difficult social interaction with her affines; and suspended exchange relations between Tutsi and Hutu during the political troubles of 1973. This woman's story is remarkable in touching so many levels at once. While the symptomatic focus is her body, an analogy is continually being drawn between it and several domains of social life: domestic life between husband and wife, interaction with affines, and relations between ethnic groups on the national level.

Verediana's story is a web of concentric circles composed of progressively more encompassing relational dyads. A recurrent theme is the problematic nature of ensuring continuous and orderly exchange between the parties to the dyads. The first relational dyad is that of husband and wife; the second is the consanguine, affine dyad; the third is the Tutsi-Hutu dyad; a fourth, which is only implied, is that of spirits and humankind.

This case involves *abazímu* affliction. The man attacked by these spirits was the father of a healer named Alphonse, who frequently practiced at the Center for Traditional Medicine in Butare. Alphonse, thirty-six, married, and parent of three children, told me that his sixty-year-old father, Ephraim, had been attacked by *abazímu* for the first time in 1968. Occasionally, he still suffered from this affliction. Because Ephraim was a devout Christian, he resisted the usual popular methods of diagnosing and combating spirit possession. Alphonse convinced him, however, that by accomplishing the necessary ritual acts for him, his father would benefit without having to compromise his religious beliefs. Thus Alphonse was able to bring his father to accept the diagnosis of *abazímu* affliction and eventually to agree to his performing the *gutérekeera abazímu*.

A family head who does not celebrate this ritual to satisfy his ancestors with periodic offerings is vulnerable to spirit attack. Someone else in the family, or even outside of it, can make offerings to them and lure away their allegiance. One offers to the ancestors what they enjoyed during their lives. Negligence either causes them to relinquish their protection over descendants or provokes their anger. In either case, misfortune is the result.

Alphonse suspected that his father had been afflicted by spirits, because Ephraim's first symptoms were vomiting of blood[9] and profuse, incoherent speech. Ephraim's behavior had also been suspicious. Ephraim worked as a guardian at a Catholic convent, and he attended mass there every day. When he returned home in the evening, he often walked around inside the enclosure (*urugó*) imitating the gestures of a priest conducting Catholic ritual and mumbling bits of Catholic liturgy. Alphonse explained that the spirits acting against Ephraim were inducing him to behave badly at his job in order to get him fired.

After treatment at a nearby hospital did not yield a satisfactory result, Alphonse decided that his father needed the help of a popular specialist and took him to a healer. The latter gave him medicines to force the spirits to speak and determined that the person responsible for Ephraim's illness was his *mukase* (stepmother), Alphonse's FFW. This woman was angry at Ephraim over the division of land that had occurred before and after Ephraim's father's death. Ephraim's father had divided his lands among the children of his two wives. Ephraim's *mukase* thought that she and her children had been slighted. Because of this, she attacked Ephraim and other members of his side of the family with *abazímu* and *ibiteega* spirits, hoping to eliminate them and acquire their lands.

According to Alphonse, his father does not give offerings to his ancestors. Thus it was relatively easy for his *mukase* to induce the spirits to attack him. She might have done this by sacrificing in honor of her own deceased lineal relatives through the ritual of *gutérekeera,* and then to her deceased husband (Ephraim's father), entreating him to lure away Ephraim's ancestors. She might have told these spirits: "Ephraim doesn't give you anything. I'll honor you in place of your negligent descendant." Her deceased husband's assistance was essential in order to alienate Ephraim's other lineal predecessors, since both she and Ephraim were linked to him (see fig. 5).

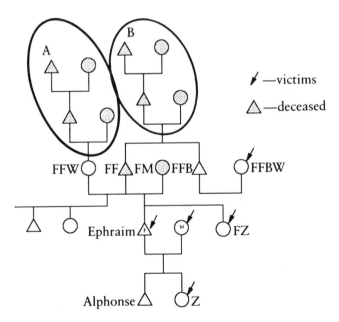

Figure 5. Relationships in the case of Ephraim. A = FFW's ancestors. B = FF's ancestors. FFW was believed to be the poisoner. She was thought to have used A and FF to lure B against F and other victims.

Several other relatives had also been afflicted by spirits in the past: Alphonse's FFBW (*nyogo-kuru wacu*), FZ (*maaséenge*), M (*maáma*), and Z (*mushiki*), who had all consulted doctors and healers without any significant amelioration of their symptoms. One healer told them that their situation would not change unless they united as a family and performed *gutérekeera*. Alphonse agreed to do this in place of his father to spare him the onus of contradicting his Christian principles. First though, he administered a medicinal inhalation to his father to make the spirits reveal themselves and communicate their desires. From this procedure he learned that they wanted meat and beer.[10] Then Alphonse set about learning how to perform *gutérekeera*.

Since Ephraim had never performed *gutérekeera*, Alphonse was forced to question older members of the family about the procedure. He had to learn an important aspect of non-Christian Rwandan religion, because he had never been instructed in how to accomplish the rituals of ancestor worship during his youth. Relatives told Alphonse that he needed to learn the names of several distant deceased relatives, including his FFF (*sogo-kuru-za*) and his FFFF (*sogo-kuru-za*). He also had to learn the names of key female ancestors, for one appeals to them as well in *gutérekeera* and *kubaandwa* rites. One's mother is the first female relative invoked (if she is dead); otherwise the first female relative is a FZ (*maaséenge*). Once he determined all of those to whom he should offer the sacrifice, and how to proceed, Alphonse obtained a goat and sacrificed it.

In *gutérekeera*, one ministers first to important lineal relatives, then to key collaterals, then to all the others. If an important relative is forgotten, the ritual must begin again. Usually male family heads perform *gutérekeera* rites, but sometimes women may perform them for the family, especially if they have already given birth to a son and a daughter. In *gutérekeera* it is important to give worthy offerings—good quality beer, even a bull or a cow in certain instances. The last time Alphonse performed the rites he used clay figurines to represent eight cows and a bull. (The group of cows were referred to in the royal rituals as *isibo*, i.e., "a flow"; see pp. 10–12.) One may use a substitute for cattle, but eventually one must give a real bull or cow, for it is best to acquit one's debt to the ancestors quickly. After acquiring the bull, as well as some beer, one presents the bull to the ancestors, asking for fortune, peace, and prosperity. Other members of the *umuryaango*, and perhaps some friends and neighbors, are invited to share the beef from the slaughtered bull. When everyone is present, one offers the bull again and names all the members of the *umuryaango* who could not come. Then the bull is slaughtered and the meat is divided.

The most important member of the household distributes a portion of the meat to everyone present. This person is often the eldest male, but if he is not a Ryangombe cult initiate, someone who is an initiate may take his place. The ritual performer then addresses the ancestors again and asks them to share what they have received with other *abazímu* that may be under their responsibility in the *buzímu*. Tidbits of cooked meat and drops of beer are then placed in small shrines (*indáaro*) intended for them. Some blood of the sacrificial animal is also destined for the *abazímu*, for it is an indispensable portion of the prestation that they receive.

Women present at a *gutérekeera* ritual receive portions from the anterior part of the sacrificial animal; they are forbidden to eat certain parts that are reserved for men. Women who have not yet given birth cannot eat the beast's heart, pancreas, udder, or testicles. But a woman who has already given birth to a child of either sex may eat the pancreas or the udder, if the sacrificial animal was a sterile cow. The herder who looked after the bull receives the testicles, and the one who cut the banana leaves on which the bull was slaughtered receives the diaphragm. The back of the neck goes to the person who butchered the animal.

Alphonse also explained to me that during *gutérekeera* one often promises to perform *kubaandwa* rites as well. These are thought to strengthen the effectiveness of *gutérekeera abazímu* and to please the ancestors. Although Alphonse had promised his ancestors to participate in *kubaandwa,* he admitted that he had not yet fulfilled this vow, because *kubaandwa* rites are very costly. He was waiting to see if the medicinal plants that his father and other members of the family had taken and the rituals already performed would suffice. Because they are characterized by prodigious drinking and the eating of beef, *kubaandwa* rites require large quantities of sorghum and banana beer, as well as a bull or cow. One has to know one's ancestors, especially those on the paternal side, in greater detail than is necessary for *gutérekeera abazímu* alone. One also has to know a long line of lineage heads (*abatware b'umuryaango*).[11]

Alphonse's sister, then age fifteen or sixteen, had been affected by the same spirits sent by Ephraim's *mukase* (her FFW). For an entire week the girl had done nothing but cry. An elderly female healer treated her, but had difficulty exorcising the spirits. Finally the woman gave Alphonse's sister a medication and sang. Through the singing, the spirits were cajoled into revealing themselves and could then be expelled. After exorcism, the spirits were collected in a stone. In the company of the healer, Alphonse's sister and mother walked to a nearby mountain and threw the stone from its summit. Alphonse was instructed to carry out *gutérekeera* rites for her as well. For this he used the beer alone; no goat or bull was sacrificed. The girl improved markedly after the ritual. Today she works as a nurse in a rural health dispensary not far from her family's home.

Ephraim's sister (*mushiki*) was also attacked by the same *umurozi*, her FW (*mukase*). The first attack occurred when she went out into the banana grove to harvest. When she returned to the house, she was trembling and screaming. Alphonse and his mother, who is also a healer, treated her without consulting another healer. After all, they were convinced that the sickness had originated from the same spell. To interrogate the spirits, they prepared a fumigation from bits of an old tire along with some medicinal plants. Under the influence of the smoke, the spirits revealed themselves as *abazímu* and *ibiteega* spirits. They had attacked this woman because she had supported Ephraim in litigation over the land disputed between her brother and their *mukase*. The court had decided in favor of Ephraim.

Four months after Ephraim's most recent episode of illness, the situation had moderately improved, but there had been other signs that the *uburozi* had not been completely neutralized. On one occasion, he developed a fear of the burgermeister (an elected official who heads the "commune"), and wanted to assault him. Ephraim's sister was also stricken again and went to Bujumbura, in Burundi, to seek treatment. In the banana grove belonging to Ephraim, family members found *indasaago* carved on the trunks of several banana plants.[12] On three separate occasions, Alphonse also found a tobacco pipe (*intúubá*) alleged to belong to Ephraim's *mukase* on paths leading to the family's enclosure (*urugó*). Placing a pipe on a path, as an *uburozi*, is intended to diminish a victim's strength, to make him smaller, since smoking a pipe reduces the contents of the bowl.

Ephraim's *mukase* (FW) was also noted to have asked Alphonse if his father had been initiated into *kubaandwa*. Alphonse offered this piece of evidence as proof that the woman was trying to estimate his father's mystical force in order to determine how to proceed in poisoning him. Since *kubaandwa* initiates enjoy the protection of Ryangombe and the *imaándwa* spirits, they are considered more resistant to *uburozi* than noninitiates. Of course, as a devout Catholic, there was little chance that Ephraim would be a *kubaandwa* initiate, thus a question of this type might well arouse suspicion. She had apparently not realized that Alphonse had assumed the role of ritualist for the entire family in order to perform *gutérekeera*, and possibly *kubaandwa*, and that it was really his mystical force that she needed to assess.

COMMENT: The victim's problems in this case included both a crisis of belief and a symptom involving the abnormal flow of a bodily humor, vomiting of blood. Furthermore, these two domains, symptom and belief, appear even more profoundly linked in Ephraim's incessant repetition of Catholic words and gestures. Through the iconic language of his body, Ephraim was expressing both the imagery of flow/blockage symbolism and the existential conundrum of what belief system to follow. The verbal and gestural language was a kind of logorrhea, an image of hemorrhagic flow. In seeking an instrumental rather than a transcendental goal in repeating these words and gestures, Ephraim manifested the symptoms of a consciousness adrift between two conflictual systems of signification: ancestor veneration and Catholicism.

Two other incidents in this case were characterized by images of perturbed flow: the cuts (*indasaago*) made on the trunks of the banana plants to "bleed" them of their sap and the pipe found three times on paths leading to the family's enclosure (*urugó*). Let us consider the cuts made on the banana plants. This action is similar to the inducing of hemorrhagic menstruation in a female victim. Both acts aim at draining away the vital fluids of a household's productive or reproductive capacity. Even though the cuts were not sufficiently deep to kill the plants by themselves, what was important in Alphonse's judgment was that an aggressive gesture against the plants had been made at all, and that this aggressive gesture had taken a form that suggested poisoning. He felt that the family's productivity was being attacked on two different levels at once; members of the household were becoming physically sick— Ephraim had even been vomiting blood—and the fluids of the most important cultivated plant in southern Rwanda were being symbolically drained away.

As for the pipe, or *intúubá* (from the verb *gutúubá* meaning "to reduce or to diminish"),[13] one must first explain that Rwandans conceptualize the smoking of tobacco as "drinking." The phrase meaning "to smoke," *kunywá itabi*, literally translates "to drink tobacco." One could imagine the process of smoking as fire transforming a solid into a liquid that can then be drunk; this conceptualization closely approximates the Rwandan idea. A pipe reduces by fire the contents that it contains. Used as a poison or spell, the pipe could be thought of as reducing, or siphoning away, the vital fluids of the people against whom it is directed and then rechanneling these fluids through a conduit to a witch or poisoner who imbibes them like a vampire.

Several prohibitions (*imiziro*) concerning pipe smoking reinforce this interpretation. For example, it is forbidden to smoke a pipe while milking a cow, to enter a corral where there are calves while holding a pipe, to set one's pipe on the same shelf where milk containers are stored, or to have cows drink from a watering trough into which a pipe has fallen (P. Smith 1979b, 15–16). Because Rwandans say that they "drink" tobacco, a pipe can legitimately be characterized as a conduit of flow. But this fluid movement is ambiguous in the sense that the "liquid" produced involves the destructive action of fire. Although these two properties—the production of a liquid and the destructiveness of fire—can be joined in smoking, they must be kept separate in other productive contexts. Fire is not compatible with things which produce or contain milk. Milk is never cooked in Rwanda, nor should drops of milk ever fall on a fire, for fear the cow will stop giving milk.

The image of a pipe is also of interest, for it combines two aspects that are analogous to Rwandan conceptualizations of the human body. Part of a pipe is a container like a gourd, a cooking vessel (note the pipe's more usual appellation, *inkóno*, "cooking pot"), a stomach, or a uterus, in which transformations occur. The other part is a hollow conduit, like an alimentary canal or a penis, through which fluids pass. Not only does a pipe embody male and female characteristics, penis and uterus, it also has traits common to human bodies in general. It contains substances, then transforms them, then passes along the products of this transformational process, as do human bodies. In the case of females, this containing process produces new life from the combining of blood and semen. The human body acts physiologically as a receptacle/conduit that receives, contains, and then passes on transformed products, and, analogously in social life, as a receptacle/conduit by and through which "gifts" move.

In sociological terms, this case hinges on two problematic kinship relations: that between a woman and her husband's child, and that between half siblings. Again productive resources and exchange relations were at issue. First of all, there was the relation between Ephraim's father and his two wives. One wife (Ephraim's *mukase*) was dissatisfied with the legacy of land that she and her children had received from her husband (Ephraim's father). Although she resented this inheritance, she had proven powerless to do anything about it through litigation. Two lines of collateral kin, therefore, the descendants of Ephraim's father's two wives, found themselves at odds. Then there is the question of exchange relations between the living and the dead. In effect, what occurs when a man becomes a Catholic and ceases to give sacrifices to his ancestors, neglects them to the point where he can no longer recall their names?

It is not mere coincidence that the spirit affliction here primarily involved *abazímu* (ancestor spirits), for this case was a family affair whose origin lay in the past. The key ancestor was, of course, the person whose gift had been the source of contention, Ephraim's father. In order for Ephraim, Alphonse, and other members of the family to begin to understand their problem, they had to come to grips with their past. They needed to deal with the consequences of actions that had transpired before them and over which they had had no control. This could not be done with the symbolic weapons offered them by Western biomedicine, Catholicism, and commodity logic, so they were forced into the ironic position of having to relearn their "traditions," of reorienting themselves to their own culture and history.

In endlessly repeating the gestures of a priest, attending mass daily, and obsessively chanting bits of liturgy, Ephraim might be depicted in Western psychological terms as acting out a "repetition compulsion." He may have reasoned that by repeating acts of Catholic devotion, he would eventually be able to harness the effectiveness of Catholic symbols and thus relieve his suffering. Ironically, however, he was being forced back in the direction of Rwandan religion. He was caught in the bind of either admitting the inefficacy of Catholic symbols in dealing with an archetypally Rwandan social problem or relying on the symbols of a belief system (*gutérekeera abazímu*) whose validity he could not support with a clear conscience. This dilemma was partially resolved when Alphonse agreed to relearn the names of the family's neglected ancestors and to recommence sacrificial offerings.

In sum, Ephraim's problems stemmed from conflict over a gift, the legacy of land left by his father. Western symbols (biomedicine, Catholic words and gestures) could neither correctly articulate nor cure his symptoms, because they reflect the history and symbolism of a commodity culture. In order both to articulate and to alleviate his sickness, Ephraim was temporarily forced to renounce Catholicism for ancestor veneration.

This solution is not atypical for many Christian Rwandans who, despite their devotion to Christianity, have found themselves or family members suffering from a mysterious affliction. No institutional framework, such as a "new religion" like Bwiti or Jamaa (Fernandez 1982; Fabian 1971), exists to aid sufferers caught in a similar bind. Instead families tend to make their compromises on an ad hoc, idiosyncratic basis. These solutions are seldom resolutions, though, for they leave undecided the fundamental question of whether to embrace fully the new ideological system.

GENTILLA, HEALER AND PATIENT

Familial relations are not the only source of conflicts leading to witchcraft suspicions and accusations, though it could be argued that in most cases exchange relations of one sort or another are at issue. Often, for example, Rwandans say that jealousy of someone else's wealth or professional status can provoke conflict that may lead to misfortune and subsequently to accusations of witchcraft.

One type of social conflict takes the form of a mystical battle between rival healers. Because healers are thought to possess the requisite occult knowledge and ability to engage in such battles, either for themselves or on behalf of their clients, they are often the first ones to be suspected of witchcraft. Furthermore, it is sometimes between healers that strength-testing contests occur, pitting the magical force of one against the other. Nevertheless, healers also acquire new knowledge and abilities by buying information or by serving as apprentices to other healers. Such knowledge is often passed down through the family, but not as frequently as one might think. Healers thus have a complex relationship with their colleagues, people whom they must both fear and emulate.

An interesting example in this regard was Gentilla. She was about fifty-five years old and a very successful healer, judging from the number of patients who came to her, but one who had resisted this calling when she was younger. Gentilla typified many Rwandan popular healers in that her vocation had come to her through an annunciatory illness. When Gentilla was an adolescent, she began behaving strangely. She would run about the hillside as if she were an animal. When she saw someone, she would say the first thing that came to her mind. Members of her family decided that she had a spirit possession illness, the only member of the family to be so touched. They took her to see a healer, but the healer's intervention did not bring about any improvement in her condition.

Later her situation improved a little by itself, although there were a few acute relapses. She also began having occasional premonitory dreams, which were proven out by subsequent events. Then, after she was married and had given birth to two children, her illness struck again. This time she went to a healer named Nanga y'ivuza (the "harp that plays by itself"), who practices a type of therapy based on interrogating the patient and encouraging him or her to confess "sins." Nanga told Gentilla that the only way that she could free herself of sickness was to become a healer herself. He proposed that she follow his therapy and also become a Nanga y'ivuza. Gentilla resisted this suggestion, because she did not want to become a healer. She merely returned home.

Her malady continued. One day in the course of aimless perambulations on the hillside, she paused to rest beneath an *umukó* tree.[14] While seated there, spirits came and told her that the only way she could prevent the sickness from killing her was to become a healer. Finally, she was ready to agree. Since then she has been receiving patients and healing them. Her reknown has spread and more patients come each year. Her vocation has become so much a part of her life, that her own health depends on it. When she abstains from healing for a few days, pains return to her body, her old illness begins to come back. This necessity to heal has made her acutely sensitive to the disorders of her patients. She says that she can almost immediately discern a person's illness. If it is caused by *abazímu,* she tells the person to return home and perform *gutérekeera* for his or her ancestors. When she sees it is a sickness that she cannot heal, she advises the patient to go to the hospital.

Although she had been exposed to Nanga y'ivuza's mode of therapy, which denies the existence of malevolent spirits, Gentilla employs all the common spirit names in diagnosing the sicknesses that afflict her patients: *ibiteega, amaheémbe, nyabingi, abazímu,* and others. According to Gentilla, *amaheémbe* poisoning causes symptoms very quickly. There is loss of blood and often one perspires profusely. *Nyabingi* possession is more progressive; one swells little by little or gradually becomes emaciated. *Ibiteega* possession is characterized by trembling, caused by a wind (*umuyaga*) rustling inside of one's body.[15]

Gentilla once became ill herself when a rival healer grew jealous of the size of her practice. He had come to her enclosure one day and accused her of having stolen his patients. Her rival declared that he was a stronger healer than she was, possessing the power to send spells such as *amaheémbe, ibiteega,* and *nyabingi.* It was therefore not right that she take his patients away from him. Gentilla complained of the man's brash action to the counselor of the sector, who fined the man two bottles of Primus (Rwanda's sole brand of bottled beer). They were given to Gentilla and drunk by her and a few others in her household.

But the matter did not end there. Several days later, she became ill and began vomiting blood. She also suffered from bloody diarrhea and pains in the vicinity of the heart. There was no question in her mind what had caused her illness. It was an *amaheémbe* spell sent by the rival healer. Gentilla treated herself by means of a powder prepared from herbs. After twelve hours of self-treatment, most of Gentilla's symptoms had been alleviated. She claims to know how to care for the *amaheémbe* affliction, but as a so-called healer of the day, she does not know how to return it to the person responsible for sending it. Her adversary, however, is a healer of the night, and so he knows how to employ *amarozi* (poisons, spells) as well as cure them. According to Gentilla, his professional activity is more oriented toward poisoning than curing. So far, he has not been pursued by the authorities. Gentilla adds that she will not bring a complaint against him. It would be almost impossible to prove that her rival had been responsible for her illness. Furthermore, she had already publicly charged that he was irresponsible and she had only received nominal compensation.

Since Gentilla does not counter-aggress bad spells, she fears that her rival may attempt to poison her again. She thinks that he first became jealous of her when she treated a woman who had been afflicted by a spell of *kumanikira amaráso* (to suspend blood). The child became turned transversally in the woman's womb. Gentilla gave this woman a medication that reoriented the fetus. Subsequently, the woman gave birth normally. Later, though, the rival healer came to Gentilla wanting to know which medicinal plants she had used. Although she told him the ingredients of the remedy, she also admonished him that no matter what medication he might use, it would not be effective without the talent to cure.

COMMENT: Gentilla's symptoms merit attention, particularly the vomiting of blood. As we saw in Ephraim's case, this symptom was frequently mentioned by Rwandans as proof that a particular illness had been caused by poisoning or spirit possession. Such a dramatic symptom, so rarely encountered in our own society, seems conspicuous by its presence among Rwandans, something like the instances of "brain fever" in Dostoyevsky's novels. When I first encountered the vomiting of blood in individuals' descriptions of their illnesses, I thought that the symptom must be anomalous.

Nevertheless, an earlier observer of Rwandan culture, René Bourgeois, mentions three cases where victims of *uburozi* manifested the symptom of vomiting blood (1956, 196–98). One case occurred to a woman in 1947. She was the victim of a spell sent by her husband, who had gone to work in the mines, probably in Katanga, and who had begun chasing women. Bourgeois also describes that "elle faisait ses besoins sur place" (196; "she accomplished her needs [urinated and defecated] wherever she happened to be"). Another case in 1952 involved a man embroiled in litigation with a neighbor over the boundaries of a field. Bourgeois notes that "il ne mangeait plus et faisait ses besoins d'une manière incoercible" (197; "he no longer ate and accomplished his needs in an unrelenting manner"). After treatment his symptoms disappeared. Later, however, his rival's daughter began to vomit blood, to jump in the air (it is forbidden for Rwandan women to jump into the air, for they are supposed to be "rooted" to the earth), and also to lose sphincter control (197). After the daughter died, her father set fire to the first man's hut, convinced that she had been the victim of a counterspell sent by the latter.

CONCLUSION

The incidents cited by Bourgeois all manifest the same underlying symbolic imagery. The sufferers in these cases had symptoms similar to that of Gentilla and Ephraim. Often, the victim of Rwandan sorcery becomes blocked and he or she loses those physiological capabilities that sustain the possibility of ordinary healthy life and productive social participation. This imagery of blockage occurs in the symptoms of impotence, inability to menstruate, inability to lactate, anorexia, constipation, incoherent speech, and catatonia. In other instances, however, the body instead of being afflicted with excessive closure, becomes afflicted with excessive openness. Blood, perspiration, feces, urine, or even words, appear to leave the body in a frightful deluge. These representations are really aspects of the same phenomenon, two sides of the same coin. They mirror the opposed but equally counterproductive situations of drought and inundation, calamities that were once the responsibility of the king to combat through his ritual actions. The flow of substances must be controlled by the correct social and ritual action.

Several of the cases discussed in this chapter occupy an intermediate position between "internal" and "external" causation. Their ambiguity should be considered in comparison with cases treated by Butaro healers (chapter 3), where external causation is clearly emphasized. Ephraim's case shows his oscillation between a popular Rwandan method of dealing with misfortune (ancestors) and a Western one (Catholicism and biomedicine). Gentilla's case exhibits a similar pattern. Although she was treated by a healer who emphasized internal causation—sin—eventually she became a healer in the more classical mode. In the next chapter, I discuss the healer who treated her, Nanga y'ivuza. Nanga's therapy is noteworthy for the degree to which it departs from the flow/blockage model discussed up to this point. It is also one of the most recent forms of Rwandan popular therapy and one that, in contrast to those already discussed, relies heavily on confession as its central therapeutic action.

CHAPTER 6

The Harp That Plays by Itself

~~~~~~~

A THERAPY OF CONFESSION IN SOUTHERN RWANDA

One very recent form of popular therapy in Rwanda is that practiced by a healer who calls himself Nanga y'ivuza, a name that comes from the words *inanga*, which means "harp," and *kwivuza*, which means "to play by itself"—hence, "the harp that plays by itself." Although the healer whom I met used this appellation as a personal name, the term was once applied to a group of healer-evangelists who practiced in Burundi until 1967.

The founder of this group, named Bashahu or Sebashahu, was born sometime before 1914 and was the son of Mibori, a Hutu client of a Tutsi chief named Ntarugera (Rodegem 1970, 547–50). Because of a quarrel between them, Ntarugera forced Mibori and his family to quit their land; the family's possessions and livestock were confiscated. Bashahu journeyed to Tanganyika, where he apprenticed himself to a healer named Mwiza. Upon returning to Burundi, Bashahu began his career as a healer in Gatara, where he tried to convince people that he possessed an immortality elixir. But few patients sought treatment from him. In

1948 he had to have a leg amputated because of a possibly syphilitic ulcer that would not heal.

In 1950 he began catechistic training to enter the Catholic Church. Several months later he became gravely ill and was transported to a dispensary. While in "articulo mortis," he was baptized Catholic (Rodegem 1970). Then, after a seemingly miraculous recovery, Bashahu claimed to have experienced beatific visions during his agony and to have received a book from heaven. He returned home, and his fortune as a healer changed dramatically: he now began to attract patients in large numbers. Because of his newfound popularity, though, he encountered opposition from the local Tutsi chief, who resented the fact that his followers were using health reasons and religious devotion as excuses for evading the tasks of corvée labor. Shortly thereafter, Bashahu was arrested for allegedly murdering and cannibalizing his niece. After a year and a half in jail, he was released for lack of evidence.

Following his release, he again attracted many adherents. Then in 1955, his health deteriorated once more. He was struck with blindness and partial paralysis; ulcers covered his entire body. Despite these infirmities, he continued to receive converts while seated behind a partitioning screen and to play the *inanga* (African 8-stringed harp) in his ministrations to them. Finally, in December 1955, he took his own life by throwing himself upon a spear (Rodegem 1970).

After their founder's death, Bashahu's followers set out to spread his revelations. They became, in effect, a syncretistic cult. Although the group opposed official Catholicism and its missionaries—"Christianity has brought us neither wealth, nor happiness, nor cure" (Rodegem 1970, 548)—the divinity of Christ was upheld. Popular Rwandan religious practices, however, were condemned; such activities as *kuraguza* (divination), *kubaandwa* (the cult of Ryangombe), and *gutérekeera* (ancestor veneration) were forbidden to cult members. Followers were told to raise sheep rather than goats and to eat mutton on ritual occasions.[1] Members of the cult, called *abananga*, dressed in white and were enjoined to observe mutual love and cooperation. *Abananga* were of two types: *abakijijwe*, "the saved ones," and *ab'imana zatoye*, "those chosen by God." The latter were the cult's leaders; a special second initiation was required to become one of them.

Members of the Nanga y'ivuza cult were not permitted to consult other Rwandan popular healers (*abavuuzi*), since *abananga* were healers in their own right. To be a member of the cult entailed observing its prescribed cures in the event of illness; other medicines and therapeutic procedures were deemed sinful. Special emphasis was placed on the use of *ubúuki* (honey) as a medication. Healing seances took place at night and consisted of insufflations, the laying-on of hands, and massage with or without honey.

In healing sessions adult members confessed their sins, because sickness, according to Nanga doctrine, was always punishment for sin. Serious sins included attempting to perform witchcraft, sacrificing to one's ancestors, and participating in any non-Christian religious cult. A cult adept could only confess sins of such gravity in private to an *umunanga* of the *ab'imana zatoye* grade, that is, a cult leader. Lesser sins could be confessed publicly. The status difference between the two types of *abananga*, however, was not necessarily permanent; an ordinary member who had demonstrated exceptional ability could choose to advance to the cult's next higher grade. Initiation to the second degree of membership in Nanga y'ivuza reputedly involved incest with a son or a daughter, eating human flesh, drinking human blood, including menstrual blood, then drinking and dancing until midnight. Those chosen for, but who refused the second level of initiation, were allegedly penalized by the murder of one of their children.

Although reports of their practices may have been exaggerated, *abananga* quickly earned the enmity of Catholic Church leaders and Tutsi authorities in Burundi. In 1963 a Nanga cult practitioner in the parish of Muhanga was excommunicated from the Catholic Church by the district's bishop.[2] The cult's existence in Burundi came to an abrupt end in 1967 when thirty members were hanged in the village of Gitega for crimes including the murder of children, incest, and cannibalism. Many other members were imprisoned on lesser charges.

The nature and veracity of the charges made against the Nanga y'ivuza cult must be considered in light of the ideological climate that prevailed in Burundi during the 1960s. First, however, we must understand the symbolic substrate underlying this ideology and, in particular, the relation of the charges to the general patterns outlined in chapter 1. The accusations leveled against the Nanga cult represent antitheses to gift logic, and they are also images of blockage or closed-circuit exchange, that is, of things that stay in, instead of being shared out. Incest, for example, is the sexual consumption of a consanguine, a category of kin that is normally destined to be sexually consumed by an alliance partner. Cannibalism is a form of endogamous consumption; it is eating within the species rather than outside of it. Drinking blood could also be thought of as endogamous consumption, for it means consuming a product of the human body. Drinking menstrual blood, according to the logic of poisoning, removes a fertility fluid from its normal circuit of flow and endangers the woman, her future progeny, and the drinker of the blood. To kill one's children is to refuse to give them to the next generation, to refuse to reproduce society.

Beneath the alleged illegality of the actions committed by the Nanga y'ivuza cult, there lurked the popular imagery of witchcraft and sorcery. It is uncertain whether *abananga* committed the crimes with which they were charged, but by insinuating that they were doing closed-circuit exchange, the cult's detractors were exploiting a set of negative images that had been culturally preestablished, images that were likely to resonate with popular fears and beliefs concerning poisoning (*uburozi*). These representations evoke the stereotype of the blocking being: one who wants to consume without sharing, who wants to produce himself but not others, who interrupts or closes rather than keeps open the conduits of flow.

However, some aspects of Nanga y'ivuza cult worship appear to be directly borrowed from positive flow/blockage imagery. For example, the cult's emphasis on honey as a propitious, medically effective substance is directly linked to the high value and importance accorded by Rwandan and Burundian culture to the production of honey. An entire Rwandan kingship ritual, *Inzira y'Inzuki,* was devoted to ensuring that the bees remain healthy, fertile, and productive. The most highly valued alcoholic beverages, mead and honeyed sorghum beer, required honey for their production. Furthermore, such beverages were more commonly consumed by the Tutsi elite and the king.

Certain traits of Nanga y'ivuza may have been influenced by elements of *kubaandwa* ritual, particularly the strong emphasis on fluid exchange and fluid imagery.[3] In procedural details as well, there is resemblance between the two cults. First of all, there is a two-stage process of becoming a full-fledged *kubaandwa* initiate, and only cult members who have undergone the second initiation may incarnate the *imaándwa* spirits. In like manner, one underwent a second initiation to become a Nanga cult leader (*ab'imana zatoye*). Just as with *kubaandwa*, this second initiation in Nanga y'ivuza required the gift of a substantial quantity of alcoholic beverages to the congregation, revelry, and possibly the drinking of a bodily fluid. In *kubaandwa,* one imbibed a mixture that contained, among other things, the urine of the chief initiator. In Nanga y'ivuza, one allegedly drank blood. Another significant parallel between the two ritual systems is the element of confession. Although virtually absent from most other popular healing or religious rituals, confession plays a small role in *kubaandwa*. In Nanga y'ivuza, however, confession assumes central importance; it becomes the sine qua non of cure.[4]

In addition to the fact that certain Nanga y'ivuza beliefs and practices may have predisposed the group to negative caricature, the political atmosphere in Burundi during the late 1960s was unfavorable to the *abananga*. Just a few years earlier, in 1961, Hutu had succeeded in overthrowing Tutsi domination in Rwanda. Tutsi in Burundi feared a similar course of events, for in this country, they had been able to retain their privileged position. No strong Hutu political movement had yet taken root. Fears that such a movement might yet gain élan were ever present. Eventually these fears resulted in the massacre of at least two hundred thousand Hutu "intellectuals," i.e., those Hutu who had at least an elementary school education.

Nanga y'ivuza members, all of whom were Hutu, were perceived to be hostile to both the Tutsi patron class and the Catholic Church. Tutsi authorities could only mistrust an organization that seemed to reject both the religious and the political status quo. Anti-Catholicism on the part of *abananga* might have been pardonable, for the Catholic Church in Burundi was already beginning to be viewed as responsible for the Tutsi downfall in Rwanda. However, by appearing to encourage the disrespect of patron-client labor arrangements, *abananga* were pitting themselves against the privileged Tutsi minority as well. Simultaneously offending both the Church and the dominant ethnic group in Burundi was a perilous course of action. Its result was the cult's elimination as a syncretistic movement.

The Nanga y'ivuza healer whom I met in Rwanda became involved with the cult after an illness that he describes as an attack of madness. Several voices were speaking within him at once, voices that the healer now identifies as being those of the *abatagatifu* (saints). The illness came upon him one evening and lasted an entire week. It did not abate until he underwent initiation into the Nanga y'ivuza cult and began healing in his turn. (He is somewhat vague about the extent of his involvement with the cult.)

He did not attempt to revive the cult as an evangelistic organization and win new converts. Nevertheless, in the beginning of his career as a healer, some Rwandan authorities were suspicious of him. The prefect of Gikongoro forbade him to settle there, so he decided to move to Butare Prefecture, where I met him in the summer of 1984. He had been practicing there since the late 1960s, using Nanga y'ivuza, or simply Nanga, as his name. He had five wives, all of whom practiced as healers in their own right following their husband's method. Each wife lived in a different part of south-central Rwanda, and each one operated a separate healing establishment. All had been his former patients. Nanga spent a great deal of his time traveling from one wife's residence to another, where he would participate in healing sessions with the patients as well as attend to household, business, and personal affairs.

I worked most closely with Nanga's youngest wife, Delphine, who lived in the southernmost part of Rwanda, just a few miles north of the border with Burundi. At least a dozen people, who were patients or relatives of patients, lived with Delphine. A five-room dormitory of daub and wattle construction had been built for these long-term guests, since some of them might stay for several months during the course of their treatment. Delphine had been instructed in the same method of healing that Nanga practiced, but she was also a commercial brewer of several qualities of urwáagwa (banana beer). She sold the best to a restaurant in Butare, and the lesser grades she sold in the public market not far from where she lived. A banana plantation surrounded her compound. Occasionally when Nanga came to visit Delphine and treat the patients there, he spent a few hours tending the banana plants and doing other farm work, for Nanga had a financial interest in the success of Delphine's urwáagwá business.

Nanga seemed to enjoy farmwork almost as much as he relished treating patients. At another wife's healing establishment, he had a sizable coffee plantation and a hand-operated machine to hull the raw coffee beans, which he proudly demonstrated to me. Nanga was quite serious about antierosion measures; drainage ditches crisscrossed the mountainside on which the coffee trees grew. An avid planter, Nanga had received citations for having implemented the latest farming techniques recommended by agricultural extension service agents; he lamented the fact that few young people seemed interested in winning these prizes. Nanga also cut trees into planks to be sold as construction lumber. He complained about the apparent lack of incentive among some of today's youth, who preferred to pass their time drinking beer or smoking marijuana rather than working. He would warn that soon Rwandan roads might fall into total disrepair, that the soil might erode away completely, that potable water might become scarce. Nanga was quite proud of his involvement in so many economic activities at once, for he believed fervently in the virtues of free enterprise and hard work.

Although these other activities occupied much of his time, Nanga's vocation, in the true sense of the word, was healing. Nanga believed that the immediate cause of illness was *"ubwoba"* (fear), but that the ultimate cause was sin. Sin abrogates the normal relation of protection that personal saints, *abatagatifu,* exercise over someone. Usually one's own sins breach the relation of protection, but sometimes it is the sins of one's parents whose consequences are visited upon the children. Chief among sins was doing harm to others: betraying a friend, sowing quarrels among neighbors and friends, cheating, stealing, lying, taking or giving bribes, divulging a secret left by a deceased relative, and attempting to do witchcraft. Another major offense was the practice of non-Christian religious rites, such as the veneration of one's ancestors, participation in the popular cults of Ryangombe or Nyabingi, the use of love potions (*inzaratsi*), and the wearing of protective talismans (*impigi*).

Jealousy was also considered to be a sin, for jealousy almost inevitably led to suspicions of *uburozi* (poisoning, witchcraft). Belief in *uburozi*, Nanga maintained, dates from the time of *guhákwa*, which means "to become someone's client, to work for someone else under the cattle agreement known as *ubuhake*." Some people became wealthy under this agreement (abolished in 1954), and those who did were often suspected of being *abarozi* (poisoners, witches). To Nanga such suspicions were, and continue to be, morally wrong. His opinion is quite telling. It means that although he traces the origin of poisoning and witchcraft back to the time when *ubuhake* was first enacted—a moment when the process of social and economic differentiation already underway in Rwandan society became accentuated and concretized in the form of an apparently voluntary agreement—Nanga does not condemn the process itself. Instead, he condemns the improper social emotion, jealousy, that *ubuhake* engendered among those who did not prosper by it. Today the same principle holds: if someone becomes rich, it is wrong to resent him. Instead, one should concentrate upon improving one's own lot.

Jealousy—resenting what another has received—comes close to being the obverse of naïveté—failing to resent what one has given (to an unworthy recipient). Although naïveté is not considered a sin, according to Nanga it can also bring on suffering. If the saints perceive that someone is often taken advantage of, they will make that person ill, so that he will consult a Nanga y'ivuza healer to divine the cause. The healer will instruct the patient in how to go about ceasing his naïveté. The person must be made aware that he should take responsibility for his actions, as well as for his misfortunes. In contrast to popular belief, Nanga denies that *abarozi* can harm others through nonempirical means. Belief in a spell such as *kumanikira amaráso* (discussed in chapter 3) was to Nanga the height of credulity.

Although the saints can punish someone for sin or naïveté, they demand nothing for their normal state of benevolence except that their descendants practice only Christian rites.[5] They prefer to speak to their descendants directly through healers like Nanga, rather than through the intermediary of non-Christian ritual, such as *gutérekeera*. Each person is born with a particular saint (a deceased predecessor), who watches over him or her. As long as one does not sin, this saint will offer protection. Whether one sins or not, though, is a personal decision; a saint cannot prevent someone from sinning. If a transgression is committed, that person's saint denounces him or her to the other saints. They decide on the appropriate punishment, which may take the form of illness, bad luck, unemployment, or virtually any other type of misfortune. When someone dies, that person in turn becomes a saint, one who must first become more "specialized,"[6] but who will then become a guardian saint for a newborn member of the family.

Given this emphasis on sin, it is not surprising that Nanga's treatment centered on confession. He would interview patients individually, asking each one if he or she knew such and such a person, such and such another. Often he would go through a long list of Rwandan names in this way, with most patients responding, "Ndamuzi" (I know him/her). Then he might mention an incident or something else very specific about the person being spoken to and discuss this briefly. Occasionally he would lapse into glossolalic speech, which seemed like a mixture of bits of French, Kiswahili, Kinyarwanda, Kirundi, and other less intelligible sounds—the language of the *abatagatifu*. Sometimes Nanga played a thumb piano while he spoke in the language of the saints, but in most instances that I witnessed, he did not use a musical instrument. Nanga claimed to be able to heal because he understood the saints' language, in which they would reveal everything about the patient to Nanga, including the patient's sins. In the face of such omniscience, patients would be encouraged to thoroughly confess their sins, for it was only by confession that they could reopen the channels to their *abatagatifu*. Often a patient's parents were encouraged to attend a healing session, so that by their confession, their child would recover.

The following is a sample interview between Nanga and one of his patients, which took place during a healing session attended by about twenty patients. In these large gatherings, he would interrogate each patient in turn, while the others listened attentively.

Much of Nanga y'ivuza's therapy involves interrogating patients and engaging them in brief question-response dialogues. By demonstrating knowledge of his patients' "sins," Nanga hopes to encourage them to confess.

Nanga (pointing): That man there, what is your name?
Patient: Sebinego.
N: What is your child's name?
P: Kayumba.
N: Do you know Adèle?
P: Yes.
N: Busigana?
P: Yes.
N: Sekabwa?
P: Yes.
N: Miriamo? Rugire? Sempabuka? Bucyana? Gashagasa?
P: Yes [to all].
N: To how many healers have you brought your child?
P: Two.
N: What did they tell you?
P: They said he had demons [*amashitáani*].
N: What is your relation to Mubandori?
P: He is a distant relative.
N: (Another list of names.)
P: Yes. . . . , etc.
N: Did your child fall on the ground or did he have pains?
P: The child did not fall, but in the beginning he would want to vomit and he wouldn't be able to.
N: [Another list of names.]
P: Yes. . . . , etc.
N: Have you had litigation with someone recently?
P: Yes, with the older brother of my brother [i.e., parallel cousin].
N: Do you know Kurukeli?
P: Yes.
N: Is there a member of your family [*umuryaango*] that lives there (i.e., near Kurukeli)?
P: Yes.
N: Do you know Semutwa?
P: Yes.
N: Is there any [kinship] relationship between you and him?
P: No.
N: Between you and Segatwa?
P: Yes, Segatwa was a relative, but now he is dead.
N: Did the other healers tell you where the demons came from?
P: They said that a poisoner had sent them. One day the child was watching over cattle, when he was returning home, someone gave him something to drink. Now he walks around and says, "I'm afraid. I want to vomit."

N: Do you remember recently when you wanted to go on a journey?

P: Yes.

N: What were you planning to do?

P: I was going to look for a job.

N: Have you had a toothache lately?

P: A tooth hurt and I had it pulled.

N: [More names.]

P: Yes. . . . , etc.

N: Did you recently hear the cries of people attacked by thieves?

P: The thief was caught and killed.

N: Recently a girl's hand was solicited in marriage, do you know her?

P: Yes.

N: Do you know Garwaya?

P: Yes.

N: Do you know someone who had a mouth infection recently?

P: Just a little while ago, one of my children had a toothache.

N: Yes, that's it. Do you know Karegeya?

P: Yes.

N: Is there any relation between you and Karegeya?

P: No.

N: You're not telling the truth!

P: No relation, besides the fact that my sister got married to a man from the family of Sundegeya.

N: There! That's a relation.

P: It's not direct.

N: It's a relation nonetheless. Do you know Sebugabo?

P: Yes.

N: Is there any relation between you and Sebugabo?

P: No.

N: Kagabo?

P: Yes.

N: Do you know Bagenzi?

P: I know Nyirabagenzi.

N: Is there any relation between you and Nyirabagenzi?

P: We belong to the same *umuryaango*.

N: And I suppose that his relatives performed *kubaandwa* rites for you and other members of your family?

P: [No response.]

N: Do you know Kamageli?

P: Yes.

N: Is there any relation between you and Kamageli?

P: No.

N: I don't agree.

P: The person with whom I have a relation is Nyiramageli, because she is my uncle's mother-in-law.

N: Did lightning strike near your house recently?

P: Yes.

COMMENT: Nanga's therapy comes close to a popular Rwandan form of divination called *kuragura umutwe* (divination by the head, i.e., by mental processes alone, without the aid of any auxiliary paraphernalia). Nanga would deny this judgment, but not as vehemently as he denies the existence of spirits such as *nyabingi, amaheémbe,* and *ibiteega.* To Nanga, non-Christian spirits are unable to aid in divination, whereas the *abatagatifu* are capable of revealing hidden things about patients, though they are unable to predict the future. The saints reveal the reasons for the patient's illness; they reveal the patient's sins. By using the Swahili word *abatagatifu,* Nanga was clearly indicating that the saints are of Christian inspiration, for it is the word used by Catholic missionaries to translate the concept of "saint" into Swahili and Kinyarwanda. However, Nanga's understanding of the saints was that they were once living members of one's *umuryaango.* In this respect, they are not unlike *abazímu,* who are also the spirits of deceased ancestors.

Nanga would agree with this conclusion, but with certain qualifications. He would point out that the traditional Rwandan concept of *abazímu* includes the idea that these spirits commonly attack neglectful descendants for the slight of having forgotten to offer them food and drink by means of the *gutérekeera* ritual. The concept also includes the belief that *abazímu,* at their worst, may attack innocent people, because their loyalty has been suborned by a poisoner. But ancestor spirits cannot really do this, Nanga maintained; they can only withdraw their protection from the living or punish them for their sins. Furthermore, they only desire their descendants' adherence to a certain standard of morality; they do not demand occasional gifts through sacrifice. Thus it is more correct to call them *abatagatifu* than to apply the more traditional term *abazímu.*

An important characteristic of Nanga's therapy is that he does not doggedly pursue any single line of questioning with his patient. Instead, he seems to touch on a theme, pursue it briefly, then drop it and move back into the mode of citing names. He thus encourages the patient to reflect on his or her social relations. Occasionally, Nanga, or more often the patient, comments on the nature of those relations, but usually the matter is not dwelt on unless the patient goes into detail.

In a public healing session, such as the one from which the interview was excerpted, Nanga tends to follow a strategy of indirection. He prefers that the patient arrive at his or her own assessment concerning the nature of the sins and their consequences. Here, his strongest insinuation that the patient has sinned comes with his half question–half accusation that the patient and other members of his *umuryaango* might have participated recently in *kubaandwa* rites. The patient's silence after this insinuation is telling. Another leitmotif, which weaves in and out of Nanga's persistent citing of names, concerns the symptoms of illness, both the patient's and those of his children. Nanga does not directly offer any reason for them, but he may be subtly coaxing the patient into perceiving a connection between his sins, the breaches and conflicts that he may have had with others, and the symptoms of his illness or that of his child. That there might be a divine origin to these symptoms—that the saints might be displeased with the patient—is also implied in Nanga's question concerning lightning. A bolt that strikes near the house could be construed as a warning from the spiritual world to the living. Again, Nanga offers no explanation either for the question or for the phenomenon. He lets his interlocutor formulate his own judgments.

In a private session with Nanga, however, when a patient is ready to confess in full his or her most intimate sins, Nanga is more direct and less equivocal. He advises his patient to repent and to change his or her behavior. Certain sins are less grave for some people than for others. The sin of adultery, for example, can be overlooked for men, but it is very serious for women. Nanga advises adulterous women to never commit adultery again. But when a man commits adultery, Nanga advises his wife to be forgiving, for as Nanga often said, "A man is like a bull; it is his nature to attempt to mount as many cows as he can."

Nanga was clear about the cause of illness. Other people cannot poison you, unless they put something with known pharmacological properties into your food or drink. People bring illness on themselves through their sins. The only qualification to this general precept in Nanga y'ivuza therapy, which situates individual responsibility in the foreground of misfortune explanation,[7] is the diminished responsibility of children. They are virtually the only ones whose illnesses can be brought on by others. The range of responsibility, however, is quite small, for it is their parents who cause their sicknesses. If the father or mother of a child sins, chances are good that the child will suffer. The saints afflict the child so that the parent will reflect upon his or her actions and repent. Although Christian influence is discernible in this idea, Nanga therapy also resembles Freudian psychiatric theory, which situates the origin of psychopathology in early childhood experience, which centers on the child's interaction with its mother, father, and siblings.

In other Rwandan theories of misfortune it is taken for granted that a parent desires the health and survival of his children. Nanga's views differ on the causes of children's illnesses. A wife may bewitch the child of a co-wife, a collateral kinsman may bewitch the children of his brother or classificatory brother, but a mother or father would never compromise the survival of one of their own offspring, even inadvertently. Nanga's theory is not found in *kubaandwa*, nor in any other form of popular healing. It must be seen as an independent invention. The appearance of this theory in Nanga therapy correlates with the increasing importance of commodity logic, a system of signification that might be expected to divide older Rwandans, still accustomed to the gift logic of domestic production and patron-client relations, from younger, better-educated Rwandans beginning to enter the cash economy. Nanga's therapy has attracted a wide following, because it is adept at curing the disorders of people who are living increasingly according to commodity logic, but who still feel subject to the moral constraints of gift logic. This dilemma, though more pronounced in southern Rwanda, is the entire society's problem. The following case histories illustrate aspects of this conflict.

FELICITY

Many of Nanga's patients suffered from illnesses that other popular healers would have probably labeled poisoning. Some patients just came for the day to be treated, but others lived with one of Nanga's wives for weeks or months. One patient, Felicity, had come to see Nanga because she was twenty-eight and not yet married. Being unmarried at this age is a cause of serious consternation for a Rwandan woman. Felicity had given birth to two children from previous affairs, but had not married either child's father. She worked as a secretary in Butare and lived there in a two-room apartment with her young son and a cousin who had come to live with her to attend school in the town. Despite the fact that she just barely made ends meet, many of her relatives perceived her as rich, because she had a salaried job. One day an "aunt" (*maaséenge*, FZ) showed up with her baby, expecting to be sheltered and fed for an indefinite period of time. Felicity did not know how to deal with this woman, nor with any of her other demanding relatives.

Nanga treated Felicity, advising her that her problem was not one of sin as much as naïveté. She should be firmer about saying "no" to people, even if it meant that relatives might accuse her of being selfish. It was not her fault, but theirs, if they became jealous of her because she had a job and they did not. People need not feel they are doing wrong by trying to earn money, Nanga maintained; instead it was wrong to be jealous of someone who had a job or who was earning a good living. People should be responsible for themselves.

MAGDALENA

Another patient of Nanga's who had a salaried job, Magdalena, worked as a medical assistant in a neighborhood health center in Kigali. She was married and had one daughter and three sons. Her sons lived with her in Kigali, and her daughter, the eldest child, lived with a friend in another town. Magdalena was a longtime friend of Delphine; they had grown up on the same hillside.

At first Magdalena thought that her symptoms were due to malaria. She took the usual medication, Nivaquine (chloroquine sulfate), but without result. Then she thought that it might be exhaustion, because she had been working very hard. She decided that she needed some rest. After a fifteen-day medical leave from her job, however, her illness persisted. Sometimes she would faint and fall to the ground without knowing why. She underwent medical examinations, but these only revealed a mild case of hypertension, which could not have caused all her symptoms. She was prescribed medication, but every pharmaceutical preparation given to her made her nauseous. It was for this reason that she thought about consulting a popular healer.

Her husband took her to a female healer, where she stayed for two weeks. This healer gave her herbal potions and powders, but Magdalena was dissatisfied with the result. A second healer, a man, gave her medicines to be drunk at home. Again, however, there was no amelioration of her symptoms. Later a third healer in Ruhengeri brought about some improvement, but her headaches continued. Furthermore, she had trouble eating anything other than boiled, unseasoned beans. Food with sugar would make her sleepy, salt would irritate her mouth, and alcoholic beverages caused her nausea.

After these three popular healers, she went to the psychiatric hospital at Ndera just outside of Kigali. There she was given an EEG and prescribed medicines to take at home. She took these for two days, had a bad reaction, and then decided to abandon them. Finally, she went to see Delphine and Nanga in May 1982. Her illness had already lasted a year.

Magdalena stayed at Delphine's home for three months, where she was treated daily with medicines and words. She returned home, but after one week, came back to Nanga and Delphine, because she was feeling ill once again. This time she stayed two months. Then she came home for two weeks, but returned to Delphine's after this period. This pattern of alternating between therapeutic stays with Delphine and Nanga and periods at home continued until May 1983. Finally, in June 1983, Magdalena decided she was well enough to begin working again. Before this time she had been unable to look at people at her job, for she would be disturbed by the vision of flies buzzing around them. Now, though she still has headaches on occasion, most of her symptoms have subsided appreciably. She can eat everything except goat, chicken, fish, eggs, and alcohol. She is able to work and to take care of her children.

Magdalena recounted that her treatment with Delphine and Nanga consisted of daily sessions with either healer and the other patients. Sometimes these were interviews similar to the one given above; sometimes they took the form of more open-ended discussions. In the latter, Magdalena was encouraged to talk about incidents that had occurred during her childhood—in particular, all the illnesses with which she had become affected since then. Nanga told Magdalena that her saints communicated to him that her sickness had begun at age four. It began when, as a child, she would become nervous and get angry very easily. Magdalena could not venture an opinion as to the reality of the saints, but she affirmed that as a child she had experienced many difficult moments. She also insisted that among all the healers she had consulted, only Nanga and Delphine's treatment had been effective. Another aspect of their treatment of her involved the taking of remedies. Nanga used only two: a sudorific medication and a purgative. Magdalena explained that the sweat-producing medicine was supposed to dilate and to unblock the blood vessels, and the purgative was intended to rid the body of invading foreign bodies.

Although Magdalena's husband accompanied her to Nanga and Delphine's a few times, he began to tire of his wife's mysterious and seemingly endless sickness. Eventually he separated from her. Despite this, the people who were paying for Magdalena's stay at Delphine's were from his side of the family. At the time I talked with her, Magdalena was preparing to bring him to court, either to force him to return home or to give her money to aid in the rearing of their children. Previously the court had given the couple six months to reconcile, for divorce is not granted when one member of the couple is ill, but this six-month period had now elapsed.

Magdalena's illness had not completely disappeared when I met her. Although she was working again, occasionally she could not sleep well and sometimes she suffered from headaches. Part of her illness could probably be attributed to the fact that she worked very hard: five days per week from 7 A.M. until noon and then from 2 P.M. until 5 P.M., and a half day on Saturdays. The understaffed dispensary treated an average of five hundred patients per day, and sometimes as many as six hundred, so her seven-hour day tended to be hectic. Although the center was considering adding to its staff or sending some patients elsewhere for treatment, neither measure had yet been taken. Added to her employment, she also had the responsibility of caring for her three young sons. Her salary only permitted her to live in a two-room dwelling. An adolescent girl helped with some of the housework, but Magdalena clearly seemed overworked.

COMMENT: The similarity of Nanga's therapy to Western psychiatric practices and theories is clear from this example. Nanga places great importance on childhood experiences, and he encouraged Magdalena to talk about all the incidents in her past when she felt malaise. Then he claimed that her illness really began at age four. These statements alone are quite remarkable. No other popular Rwandan therapy attempts to probe so deeply into the etiology of the patient's condition, nor makes so bold a statement concerning the moment of its origin. Notice also that Magdalena passed months in residence with Delphine and that she underwent treatment by words and medicines every day. Contrary to other Rwandan popular therapies that seem to offer (and from which patients expect) overnight success, Nanga realized that some illnesses—we would call them neurotic, psychotic, or psychosomatic disorders—take a great deal of time and patience to treat.

Nevertheless, some of Nanga's healing techniques do resemble those of other popular therapies. For example, Nanga employs procedures that exploit flow imagery, namely the use of purgatives and sudorifics. He explains the action of purgatives as aiding the expulsion of foreign bodies that have invaded the body, and he views the action of sudorifics as aiding in the "opening up" of the blood vessels. This imagery, however, is confined to the context of the individual human body; it does not involve other persons or elements from the wider cosmos. Furthermore, when Nanga mentions invading foreign bodies, he is speaking of abstract entities, such as germs, rather than willful beings such as spirits. When Nanga speaks of the desirability of enhanced blood flow, he means this only within the confines of a single body. In contrast to other popular healers, he never cuts the skin to allow blood to flow outside the body or to introduce medicines into it. Blood must be conserved; it must never be let.

This representation of the body differs from other popular therapies where the pathological status of the body is seen as causally and directly related to the actions of others (e.g., *abarozi* [poisoners, witches]), and where the body is perceived as part of a macrocosm in which it is inserted. Whereas in most Rwandan therapies the person is perceived as concretely a part of both a social and a cosmological whole, in Nanga therapy the person is to a large extent abstracted from both his social nexus and the cosmos. This does not mean that Nanga discounts social causality as a factor in illness. On the contrary, Nanga emphasizes the importance of the patient's relationship to others. But where other popular therapies postulate a direct and immediate relationship between illness and social factors, Nanga therapy postulates an indirect relationship. In the former, external factors of improper exchange relations with others, the absence of gift exchange, of hospitality, or even of ordinary conversation, can lead to illness. In the latter, the internal state of improper social emotions is sinful and as such, subject to the punitive action of the ever-watchful saints. In Nanga therapy, it is the witchcraft in one's own heart that is dangerous, not the witchcraft out there in the world.

Freudian psychology similarly attributes an important role to social factors in the causation of neurosis, but these social factors are important only to the degree to which they influence the internal mechanisms of the personality: the id, the superego, and the ego. A Freudian therapist cannot arm the patient with the necessary counterpoison to neutralize a hated and feared superior. He or she can only bring the individual to the realization that emotions and the inability to deal with them are a function of an internalized imago, for example, the representation of an experientially more primordial authority figure, such as a father. In both Nanga and Freudian therapies, patients must discover the cure that is inside them.

Many of Nanga's patients seemed to have problems similar to those of Felicity and Magdalena. Many were young and had salaried jobs, whereas their parents were peasants. Often they appeared trapped in the same kind of bind, where relatives and friends perceived them as rich, even though they had little disposable income beyond their living expenses. They were now living and working in a cash economy, but their origins were in a gift economy of domestic production. Their crises were rooted in a dilemma: whether to act according to gift logic and risk impoverishment or to act according to commodity logic and risk being accused of selfishness, perhaps even witchcraft, by friends and relatives.

Nanga was able to treat patients whose problems stemmed in part from the gift/commodity dilemma because he had been able to find a solution to this for himself. Through personal experience with illness, he had internalized his culture's most salient conflict. Then he had found a means of resolving it by discovering in the Nanga y'ivuza cult a restructured version of the flow/blockage dialectic—one that apparently favored blockage over flow. As a consequence, Nanga could then morally choose commodity logic over gift logic and thus resolve his personal crisis. Furthermore, he could eventually apply this revelation to this method and theory of therapy. Just as blockage could come to eclipse flow, so could the commodity eclipse the gift. This shift of emphasis formed the symbolic basis of Nanga therapy. In conceptual terms, Nanga could assume the role of "culture broker" for commodity logic by offering a moral system based on the concept of sin, but that integrated elements of flow/blockage symbolism. In this respect, he provided patients with an ideological structure that would not appear radically new to them, even though it implied significant rejection of gift logic. Nanga's therapy could bridge the gap between gift logic and commodity logic by offering a symbolic system that was cognitively intermediary between the old system of ritual and myth and the new symbols of the marketplace.

Nanga's life provided his patients with an example of what could be gained by assuming this new destiny, one intimately linked to the possibilities afforded by the cash economy. Besides healing, Nanga grew coffee, raised bananas that were brewed into commercially sold banana beer (urwáagwá), and occasionally cut trees to sell as construction lumber. Because of these activities and the fact that he had numerous patients (who paid relatively high fees), Nanga was quite well off by local standards. He was a model African small-capitalist farmer, as well as a healer and an entrepreneur, and he was very successful.

Nanga implicitly understood that the therapeutic problem under commodity logic was guilt, caused by excessive retentiveness or accumulation, and concomitant social isolation through failure to observe reciprocity. Nanga's healing function was partly one of disculpation. According to gift logic, to accumulate and not share is to be a witch. According to commodity logic, on the other hand, to make a profit and yet share too much is to misuse one's capital. When one chooses commodity logic, one is forced to be retentive. Using a restructured version of Rwandan symbolic imagery, Nanga could treat patients confronted with choosing blockage over flow, profit motive over reciprocity. Nanga's answer to those faced with this dilemma is thus understandable: witches do not exist, and jealousy of those who are wealthier than oneself is wrong. This reasoning may also explain why he perceived a conflict between the older and younger generation even to the point of attributing the latter's illnesses to the former's sins. The older generation was more likely to adhere to traditional practices and to gift logic. Hence, as in Freudian therapy, parents "cause" their children's illnesses.

The transition to commodity logic also implies a different notion of the person, someone more individualized and autonomous, but in danger of becoming isolated from others by being retentive or acquisitive to excess. Hence there were two major strategies to Nanga's therapeutic interventions. First, in response to guilt and retentiveness, Nanga offered purgation in the form of confession, which reduces the burden of accumulated sins. Moreover, Nanga used only two medications: a purgative and a sudorific, and these could be seen as analogous to confession in that they evacuate the body, just as confession evacuates the soul. Nanga often used these two medications, but he preferred to believe that the key to cure resided within the patient. "Each patient comes with his own medicine and he leaves with it," he was fond of saying. Instead of external causes—i.e., *abarozi* (poisoners) and spirits—the patient should look within for the source of the cure.

This idea is also expressed in Nanga's name, "the harp that plays by itself," which is clearly an image of autonomy. In Nanga therapy, the body is represented in a similar way, for instead of a body metonymically and metaphorically connected to the things and persons that it touches— the idea that underlies the therapy of the Butaro healers—the principle of Nanga's therapy is the self-afflicting, self-restoring body. The body is thus an instrument that, like Milton Friedman's idealized free market economy, regulates itself. Furthermore, Nanga passionately disagreed with traditional healing practices intended to cause blood to flow through cupping (*kurúmika*) or through small incisions (*indasaago*) made on the skin. Blood must not be shed in this way, Nanga would say; it must be kept within the body. Nanga continued to treat sweat and feces according to flow imagery, but he refused to shed blood as a therapeutic measure. In his therapy, blood is the body's capital humor. It must not be diminished.

Nanga's therapy also incorporates a different notion of debt than that implicit in accusation therapy. In the latter, debt implies the expectation of continued exchange with others; there is no moral stigma attached to it provided people reciprocate as well as receive. Gift debts are never completely paid off, they merely invite a return; and, a return gift does not cancel the relation, it merely elicits another return. In confession therapy, debt implies a burden upon the soul that must be relieved in relation to transcendental beings—saints. Debt may also imply sin.[8]

The second aspect of Nanga's therapeutic strategy, the reduction of social isolation, was achieved in several ways. First of all, patients often lived with one of Nanga's wives for several weeks or months, they interacted and participated in cooking meals, cleaning the compound and their living quarters, brewing *urwáagwá* (banana wine), and sometimes working in the field. Once or twice during the day, they gathered together and Nanga's wife treated them. They talked about themselves, their illnesses, and all the incidents in the past when they had had similar feelings of malaise. Sometimes they received massage from Nanga's wife or from each other. All these techniques served to reestablish feelings of connectedness to others. Furthermore, part of Nanga's therapy seemed to be aimed at educating people to the possibility that they could form meaningful social ties outside the constraints of traditional morality and gift logic. These group therapy sessions allowed Nanga's patients to experiment with this possibility.

The therapeutic strategies of the Butaro healers and Nanga are virtually antithetical: where the Butaro healers seek out the witch in one's social nexus, Nanga healers seek out and purge the witch in one's self (i.e., sin and guilt). This may be why Nanga y'ivuza cult members in Burundi were perceived as people who advocated blockage instead of flow, and were charged with crimes that were images of closed-circuit exchange. Nanga healers have attempted to resolve the psychosocial contradictions associated with accumulating wealth in a society that, until recently, has emphasized the conversion of wealth into social relationships through the giving of gifts. The problem that they confront could be formulated, How can one accumulate wealth and not be considered someone who blocks the flow of gifts (i.e., a witch)? They have resolved this contradiction by reducing the pertinence of flow imagery from the social group to the individual body. Given this shift, the therapeutic problem becomes one of seeking out and expunging blockage within the self, rather than blockage within the group. Thus their therapy is one of confession, rather than of accusation.

Nanga's focus on confession is also interesting because in Western history confession was not codified as a sacrament in the Catholic Church until the Lateran Council of 1215 (Foucault 1980, 58). Moreover, as the importance of confession as a means of establishing guilt increased, the importance of accusatory techniques declined. Interrogation and inquest gradually supplanted "ordeals" and testing rituals such as duels and "judgments of God." This trend, Foucault argues, was associated with the rise of individualism in the West: "For a long time, the individual was vouched for by the reference of others and the demonstration of his ties to the commonweal (family, allegiance, protection); then he was authenticated by the discourse of truth he was able or obliged to pronounce concerning himself. The truthful confession was inscribed at the heart of the procedures of individualization by power" (58–59). Although Foucault does not make this correlation, recent scholarship situates many of the cultural features associated with capitalism—alienability of land, private ownership of the means of production, wage labor, and individualism—as early as the thirteenth century (Macfarlane 1979).

Confession as a psychological and social technique presupposes a relationship to authority. "The confession is a ritual of discourse in which the speaking subject is also the subject of the statement; it is also a ritual that unfolds within a power relationship, for one does not confess without the presence (or virtual presence) of a partner who is not simply the interlocutor but the authority who requires the confession, prescribes and appreciates it, and intervenes in order to judge, punish, forgive, console, and reconcile" (Foucault 1980, 61–62). Thus it is not surprising to find confession sometimes wielded as a hegemonic tool, where the subject becomes the object of his or her own condemnation, which merely apes the precepts and beliefs of the authority extracting the confession. Consider, for example, the efflorescence of confession ritual in Europe during the witchcraft craze of the sixteenth to eighteenth centuries, a period that also witnessed the "take-off" of capitalism in Europe (Wallerstein 1976) and the decline of holistic theories of pathology (Thomas 1971).

Confession has become institutionalized as a central activity and as a "core symbol" in modern rituals of political repression. In these rituals—that is, in torture—bodily pain and disfigurement become the primary means of inscribing the "verity" of a particular ideology on the subject's own words (cf. Scarry 1985). Confession has also thrived as a therapeutic technique. An entire branch of the medical industry has grown up around its use. When a patient consults a psychiatrist, the success of therapy depends on his or her progressively more profound disclosure of all that has been repressed. But confession could also be viewed in another light: as the manifestation in the therapeutic and religious domain of a society's transition to capitalism, for part of this transition involves a "monadization" of the person (Augé 1975).

Certain categorical distinctions are peculiar to capitalist culture, for example, the difference between the home and the workplace, between who a person "is," as a member of a familial group, and what he or she "does" to earn a living. In Sir Henry Maine's terms the transition from traditional to modern society involves the movement from "status" to "contract." In Marx's terms the transition from precapitalist to capitalist society involves the combination and tension between "use value" and "exchange value" in the core artifact of capitalism, the commodity. Under capitalism, this combination comes to imply the separability of use value from exchange values, as the home becomes the locus of the realization of use values, and the marketplace becomes the locus for the realization of exchange values. Under capitalism exchange value predominates. It is doubtful, however, that a society based purely on status or purely on use value ever existed.

In like fashion, in my discussion of precolonial Rwandan symbolic thought (see chapter 1), I attempted to show that the values associated with flow tended to be positive, whereas those associated with blockage tended to be negative. Despite this, the imagery of flow was inseparable from that of blockage; Rwandan verbal categories and the rituals of kingship seem tacitly to acknowledge their conjoined nature. What appears to be occurring today, however, as evinced in Nanga's therapy, is that flow imagery has begun to separate from blockage imagery. Nanga can still nominally uphold the validity of the flow model in conceptualizing some therapeutic measures—as in his use of purgatives and sudorifics and before him, in the Nanga y'ivuza cult's valorization of honey—but beyond the body the modality of blockage prevails, for in social life one should attempt to make a profit and accumulate wealth. The circle of relations to which the individual applies the social analogue of flow imagery has begun to diminish, becoming restricted to the household. For this reason, Nanga therapy continues to underline the causal relatedness of parental actions to children's sicknesses. The household is becoming the last social sphere in which market ideology does not govern interaction, and where flow/blockage ideology can persist. Beyond the household, as Nanga therapy leads its patients to acknowledge, the model of flow as a social principle is gradually losing its significance. This is indicative of the historical process occurring in Rwanda, its incorporation into the world economy.

Confessional therapies are a corollary to this historical process, because they reflect and reinforce the dichotomization of the person into who one is (i.e., "substance") versus what one does (i.e., "code of conduct" or "contract") (Barnett and Silverman 1979; Schneider 1968). Nanga's therapy mirrors this cultural distinction in that it purports to act only on phenomena located within a person (substance). This idea is evinced in Nanga's remark, "Each patient comes with his own medicine and he leaves with it." In like fashion, such therapies deemphasize pathological causes external to the person, a notion exemplified in another of Nanga's assertions, "Witches and evil spirits do not exist."

When misfortune becomes a question of internal qualities—that is, judgments of substance—it becomes difficult to sustain therapeutic notions and procedures that implicate the person in wider schemes of causality. At their most encompassing level, these schemes include representations of the cosmos. At their least encompassing level, they concern moral representations of human bodily organs—for example, the heart is the locus of volition, the liver is the seat of passion—where a model of social emotions becomes transposed to the realm of physiology. Between the level of the body and that of the cosmos, one encounters representations of social life in its relation to health and well-being. These representations include beliefs about the motives of others, as in witchcraft and sorcery. Although holistic theories of the body and of the cosmos may persist in capitalist culture, such theories are inevitably marginalized by the dominant discourse on the nature of pathology, a discourse that privileges microscopic, particulate reality, as in the germ theory of illness, over cosmogonic, relational reality. Whereas the germ theory separates and excludes, holistic theories conjoin. When "substantialized" theories of the person and of pathology come to predominate over holistic ones, which appears to be occurring with Nanga y'ivuza, the separation between persons and things, family and work, mind and body comes that much closer to appearing like a natural property of the universe.

Nanga's therapy takes the conjoined symbolism of the flow/blockage dialectic and separates it into spheres of pertinence. Although Nanga affirms the desirability of a flowing, or at least, unblocked body and a harmonious household, he does not advocate "open-circuit" exchange in everyday social life. On the contrary, he affirms the virtues of profit making and capital accumulation (i.e., "closed-circuit exchange"), a principle that runs counter to precolonial and pre-Christian Rwandan values. This shift of emphasis could be compared with the Marxian observation that, under capitalism, use value and exchange value become separated between the home and the marketplace. Marx describes this historical transition in terms that make sense in the context of Western culture; Nanga makes this separation comprehensible through symbols that derive from Rwandan culture. Moreover, by tacitly supporting the principle of blockage in social life, Nanga, in a sense, makes it all the more probable that there will be blocked souls and bodies in need of confession and purgation. Nanga's therapy reflects and reproduces both the ideology of commodity logic, and the pathologies that it engenders. However, by culling from popular Rwandan flow/blockage imagery while limiting its pertinence, Nanga therapy provides an intermediate zone where people caught in the agony of the transition between gift logic and commodity logic can articulate and sometimes alleviate their suffering.

Yet Nanga's therapy constitutes an extreme. He encourages his patients to choose commodity logic and then to get on with their lives. As we have seen with other forms of therapy, such as that practiced by healers at the Center for Traditional Medicine in Bare, healers and patients deal with the same dilemma without having to choose between the two systems of logic. In these forms of healing, people may be trying to preserve aspects of gift logic while reserving the option to participate in the material advantages of the commodity world.

Conclusion

~~~~~~

The great challenge to an historical anthropology is
not merely to know how events are ordered by
culture, but how, in that process, the culture is
reordered. How does the reproduction of a structure
become its transformation?"

MARSHALL SAHLINS

During the course of this work, I have analyzed Rwandan popular concepts of misfortune in light of the society's transformation from a gift
economy to a commodity economy. I have not dealt with economic issues
as these are usually defined in classical or formalist studies. Instead I
have followed a substantivist approach (Sahlins 1972, xii), considering
not the individual choices of people who act according to presumed uni-
versal canons of rationality, but rather the productive life of society conceived as a "system of signification" or totalizing system of meanings
(Benoist 1975, 17). I have treated both the gift and the commodity as
"total social phenomena," following Mauss, Marx, and Gregory. This

study differs from other substantivist studies, though, in its focus. Rather than the usual concern with production and exchange, I have attempted to expand analysis to include the symbolic constructs mobilized by Rwandan popular healers and their patients in the course of therapy.

Although it may seem problematic to attempt to encompass what are obviously "micro" phenomena—the discourse of patients and healers—within an explanatory framework that is clearly oriented toward the analysis of "macro" phenomena—Rwandan society's economy as a whole—I do not believe that this difficulty is insurmountable if one begins from the vantage point of indigenous cultural constructs. Cultures are redundant; similar themes and organizing principles permeate apparently distinct domains of social action. Homologies, analogies, and tropes that operate in one sphere of thought and action are likely to be encountered in others. Lévi-Strauss shows in "The Story of Asdiwal" that, for the Tsimshian, similar structures of meaning underlie social, economic, and cosmological concerns (1976, 146–97). In the same vein, but much closer to my own ethnographic material, Françoise Heritier illustrates that, for the Samo in Burkina Faso, theories of the person, which focus on semen and blood, present an "ordered and coherent vision of the world" (1985, 111). These theories explain observable phenomena in terms of this coherent vision, while they tend to justify the existence and reproduction of the social order. In a later discussion of sterility and aridity, Heritier demonstrates that relations of homology obtain between the society's view of the world, its view of how society should work, and its view of the healthy individual body (1984, 126).

In reconstructing aspects of precolonial Rwandan symbolic thought, my findings support Heritier's observation; flow/blockage imagery suffused representations of the body, of society, and of the cosmos. This imagery lay at the base of a Rwandan theory of kingship and the polity, a Rwandan theory of production and exchange, and a Rwandan theory of physiology. It was both a structure of meaning and an ideology in which social action was grounded. As ideology, it subtended the matrimonial strategies of Rwandan divine kings in their mythico-historical oscillation between marrying "in" and marrying "out." As structure, flow/blockage imagery permeated myth and ritual, such as in the origin myth of Death or in the "Path of the Watering." As a psychological and physiological construct, it persists as a principle in the conceptualization of health, fertility, and sexuality.

If analogies act as mediating devices between cultural realms and that mediation can be demonstrated, it must also be emphasized that the underlying symbolic processes occur within the individual psyche. Culture does not exist outside the confines of the individual mind. I have consistently employed the terms *gift logic* and *commodity logic* to stress the cognitive and psychological dimensions of this historical transition. The gift-to-commodity transformation is as much a change in the way people conceive of themselves and social relations as it is a historical phenomenon involving international trade. I have attempted to illustrate some of the ways in which these two different systems of signification interact and then are articulated in sickness and therapy. In part, I examined what becomes of flow/blockage symbolism under the influence of world capitalist culture. If Rwandan gift logic is characterized by the flow/blockage dialectic, capitalist culture appears to reverse the relation between flow and blockage. Blockage (profit making, accumulation) becomes positively valued.

For this reason it was necessary to describe the history of Rwandan contact with the West, particularly with the most influential of Western "culture brokers," Catholic missionaries. By the time Europeans reached the kingdom of Rwanda, central Rwandan society was already characterized by social asymmetry between Tutsi cattle owners and Hutu cultivators. The Tutsi had been able to assume political control in central Rwanda and, through ritual, to dominate the symbolic apparatus of Rwandan culture. They defined the terms of Rwandan gift logic. Hence they usually represented themselves in mythology and through the institution of kingship as the ones most able to uphold the positive social aspects of flow. But their own mythical reconstruction of the past belies the fact that their position in this regard was more ambiguous. They were aware that flow (or open-circuit exchange) carried to its logical extreme in the realm of matrimony and alliance could only lead to a dilution of royal blood, a dissolution of the difference between "celestials" and "autochthones," and a concomitant reduction in their privileged status. They realized, however, that complete renunciation of flow for the mode of blockage (closed-circuit exchange) would alienate the agricultural majority from the source of mystical beneficence.

Although Tutsi kings had to strike a balance between the polar options of flow and blockage, they appear never to have arrived at a permanent solution to this dilemma. We observe this in the semimythical extremes of hyperendogamous (B-Z marriage) and hyperexogamous marriage (e.g., Gihanga and his Rundi wife). It is not surprising, therefore, to find Rwandan kings depicted as the enemies of blocking beings, and yet becoming the epitome of blocking beings in myth by marrying their sisters. This seeming contradiction within the institution of kingship was mirrored by a contradiction between Rwandan social and Rwandan cultural constructs. On one hand, we observe the hierarchical rigidity of precolonial Rwandan social organization (Maquet 1954); on the other hand, Rwandan symbolic thought shows a pronounced emphasis on fluidity and movement. This apparent antinomy cannot simply be construed as Tutsi mystification. In a cosmology that emphasizes fluidity as a life principle, power arises from the ability to control or interdict flow; one manifests power over flow by the ability to either open or close the conduits of the body politic. The king displayed the power of flow/blockage by embodying both principles within his person at once.

But the blockage aspect of Rwandan symbolic pragmatics could sometimes be overstressed by the Tutsi elite. This tendency can be discerned in the patron-client relationship known as *ubuhake,* because the indebtedness resulting from the original bovine gift from Tutsi to Hutu could never be fully acquitted. With female offspring of *ubuhake* cattle always being returned to Tutsi patrons, Hutu found themselves in the position of surrendering control over the means of reproducing bovine products in exchange for the means of consuming them. Many Hutu, aware that this exchange relationship kept them in a state of subjugation, were ready to experiment with alternative systems. When Catholic missionaries first entered Rwanda, they encountered resistance to their original intention of evangelizing the Tutsi elite. Instead, they found Hutu cultivators, especially the most impoverished among them, apparently eager to accept Christianity.

Missionary success in the early stages of evangelization grew out of a "working misunderstanding" (Bohannan and Curtin 1964, 11). Hutu gravitated toward Catholic missionaries as a way of securing the protection of non-Tutsi (and thus more equitable) patrons. Missionaries, for their part, usually related to their Hutu converts in ways consistent with exchange notions that were part of their Western cultural heritage. Unbeknownst to many of the missionaries, they were converting their Rwandan followers as much to commodity logic as to belief in Christ. Later, missionaries were more conscious of their multifaceted influence on Rwandan society. They encouraged their Hutu followers to acquire private land and to enter the cash economy as a means of evading Tutsi exactions. In accepting commodity logic as well as Christ, Hutu Christians learned that they could avoid many of the most onerous aspects of Tutsi domination and obtain material and social benefits.

Politically, however, the reformist, pro-Hutu faction within the Church was unable to gain ascendancy until the 1950s. Before then, Western influence and missionization exacerbated the one-sided relationship between Tutsi and Hutu. It allowed the Tutsi to accentuate the blockage aspect of Rwandan symbolic pragmatics. They came to occupy most of the positions in the indirect-rule state apparatus. Only Tutsi had access to the missionary-directed administrative school at Nyanza. Furthermore, the king became estranged from the masses as he began to neglect the ritual prescriptions incumbent on Rwandan kings, and as Hutu were centrifugally pushed away from the seat of power. Western influence and missionization solidified the hold that Tutsi enjoyed over the land, but it motivated Hutu to sidestep the Tutsi gift system. This divisive process could be summarized as the more the Tutsi constricted the conduits of exchange, the more the Hutu sought the advantages of the commodity system.

The Catholic Church was not always cognizant of the reasons or the mechanism for its success with the Hutu in Rwanda. This explains its perennial tergiversation, its apparent inability until the years just before the Rwandan Revolution to renounce its avowed intention of supporting the Tutsi elite. Finally, though, the Church unequivocally backed Hutu emancipation when social justice priests, who began entering Rwanda in the 1940s and 1950s, shifted the balance from elitist to populist priests. The Church reaped the benefit of its support of the Hutu revolution, and today its temporal and spiritual influence remains considerable.

Because of this influence, the Rwandan Catholic Church has been able to discourage heterodoxy and, in particular, the growth of syncretistic movements. Elsewhere in Africa, the clash between precolonial modes of thought and capitalist culture has often been addressed in the context of new religions. New theories of the person and of misfortune have emerged. Once viewed as arising primarily from external causes, sickness has come to be seen as originating from internal causes. Accusatory therapeutic techniques have begun to give way to confessional ones. Although the growth of syncretistic movements has been stifled in Rwanda, issues similar to those found in new religions have become implicit themes in Rwandan popular healing. One also witnesses a similar shift toward confessional techniques.

Accusatory therapies, such as the one described in the northern Rwandan commune of Butaro, preserve the flow/blockage symbolism of precolonial Rwandan gift logic. In both the symbolic language of symptoms and the procedures and remedies prescribed by popular healers, we find the body conceptualized as causally implicated in the encompassing macrocosm. Flow/blockage imagery connects the body metonymically and metaphorically to the cosmos and to the wider social nexus in which it participates. A theory of the person and of the social whole, it is a relational concept whose analogies "flow" from one domain of social concern to another (Wagner 1986, 50). Sicknesses of the body are seen to be connected to perturbations in social relations. Blockage or interruption in the exchange relations that link members of the group to one another can cause misfortune. First and foremost in accusatory therapy, the individual suffers because poisoners within his or her social matrix have failed to uphold the imperatives of reciprocity. Therapy takes the form of restoring flow to the body by identifying and removing the source of blockage within the group—by neutralizing or eliminating the poisoner, or by fortifying the sufferer against a mystical assailant by providing the sufferer with symbolically appropriate remedies.

Typically, poisoning manifests itself through the perturbed flow of bodily humors, which either become blocked or begin to flow anomically. This symptomatology is central to Rwandan popular medicine, because liquids are important both as substances and as symbols in exchanges of all types. Fertility arises when separation is overcome and where mediating fluids traverse the boundaries between categorically distinct realms of being. The earth becomes fertile when the sky sends rain. Humanity reproduces itself when the separation between male and female is overcome by the passage of fluids between sexual partners. The fetus is produced in the uterus from the "gifts" (*intáanga*) of its father's semen and its mother's blood. The baby's body is produced from its mother's milk, whose production is indirectly stimulated by the husband's sperm, as well as by the exchange of gifts between the child's matrilateral and patrilateral kin. Men and women marry and form new productive units from the exchange of gifts (cows and beer) between the husband's family and the wife's family (see appendix A). Men become "brothers" by mutually exchanging and imbibing each other's blood. Neighbors remain on good terms with each other through the gifts of hospitality and beer.

Maintaining the orderly flow of gifts was a prime concern of social life in precolonial Rwanda and it depended on the complementary interaction between distinct social categories: king and subjects; Tutsi, Hutu, and Twa; patron and client; male and female; affines and consanguines. Rwandan culture once possessed something that resembled the Maori concept of *hau* (Mauss 1925, 8–10), which I would call the spirit of the liquid gift. Today this spirit lives on in Rwandan culture, though less brilliantly than in the past, and particularly in the therapy practiced by Butaro healers.

At first glance it may seem ironic that the symbolic patterns associated with Rwandan kingship should be most well preserved in northern Rwanda, which until the 1920s was only peripherally implicated in the life of the central Rwandan kingdom and where the Tutsi population was always small. In precolonial Rwanda, blocking beings could arrest the flow of beneficence from sky to earth and cause misfortune of a general nature. In Butaro today, blocking beings can arrest the flow of generative fluids in men and women. The similarity of the symbolic structures of the precolonial center and those of its once recalcitrant periphery indicates that flow/blockage symbolism was not confined to the central Rwandan Tutsi elite. Furthermore, evidence from other areas suggests that this symbolism is found widely among central African Bantu.

Although there is considerable variation in the imagery concerning flow/blockage among these peoples, this conclusion is supported by evidence to the north of Rwanda reported by Beatty (1960) for the Bunyoro. The Bunyoro king was called *mukama*, "the one who milks," and his death was equated with disordered flow—"The milk is spilt; the king has been taken away!"(28). Among the Komo of Zaire (de Mahieu 1985), the central preoccupation of male circumcision is the removal of impediments to substance movement. This concern is partially made literal—objects are actually inserted into the urethra in order to unblock it—but it is also metaphorized: Komo ritual songs query, "Who obstructed the waterfall?" (132). Similar themes emerge among the Yaka of Zaire on the conceptualization of female fertility problems and human reproduction in general (Devisch 1984). Incest for the Yaka is like moving against a river's current (26). Witches act analogously to those who commit incest; they act at countercurrent, taking blood from their descendants rather than giving it to them. Among the Kaguru of Tanzania, "kinship is compared to streams, which represent fertility, continuity, and connectedness" (Beidelman 1986, 14); a matri-clan (*lukolo*) is defined by some Kaguru as a "place where water flows" (34). These observations lend support to one of the themes of this study: that flow/blockage symbolism has an ethno-epistemology that encompasses but yet cannot be adequately described solely by the oppositions open versus closed and continuity versus discontinuity.

Evidence from these other ethnographic areas also supports what has long been a working hypothesis for Luc de Heusch (1966, 1972, 1982): that the mythical structures of southern and central African Bantu cultures are transformationally related. Although I am in agreement with this hypothesis, I believe that the pursuit of this objective could be advanced by direct systematic examination of flow/blockage imagery in other Bantu areas. This imagery, for example, more specifically explains the symbolic pragmatics of the Luba king's incest with his mother and sisters in a closed hut than does de Heusch's general hypothesis concerning the violation of social norms. This study also differs from those of de Heusch in paying closer attention to the diachronic mutability of structures. In popular healing in southern and central Rwanda, significant changes have occurred to flow/blockage imagery. For example, although some accusatory therapies in southern Rwanda continue to admit the role of poisoners and spirits in causing misfortune, these therapies have begun to incorporate spirit beliefs that manifest "abstraction." According to healers who combat them, these newer spirits entered southern Rwanda from outside the area; many have Swahili names and appear to act randomly. Vaguely defined persecutors afflict victims with the intention of diminishing their wealth or extracting their labor. In employing these newer beliefs to explain illness, healers and patients manifest their awareness, or perhaps anxiety, that Rwanda has become implicated in a wider production and exchange matrix—the world economy—whose laws of motion are more arbitrary and capricious than the vicissitudes of social life with one's kin and neighbors. In this respect, these newer beliefs deviate from the earlier representation of spirits as beings whose identities can be learned through divination and whose role in misfortune is more personalized. Despite this abstraction, the imprint of flow/blockage is still discernible. For example, although *ibiteega* spirits are abstracted in the sense that they are the spirits of deceased foreigners and thus unknown to their victims, *ibiteega* are foreigners whose reproductive lives were blocked before reaching fruition (girls who died before the onset of menstruation, women or men who died unmarried or without progeny).

Confessional therapies deviate even further from the precolonial flow/blockage model. Although flow/blockage imagery persists in Nanga y'ivuza therapy, its relevance is limited to notions of physiology. No longer is it a relational model whose analogies flow between notions of physiology and notions of society and the cosmos. Furthermore, whereas in precolonial Rwandan symbolic thought, flow/blockage symbolism is conjoined (Barnett and Silverman 1979, 70–71), in Nanga therapy it becomes separated. Flow/blockage retains its value as a model for the body alone; profit making and accumulation become a model for social life. Confession and purgation figure importantly in this type of therapy, because blockage continues to be perceived as a physiological principle governing symptom formation. But the less this therapy concerns itself with macrocosmic blockage, the more it concentrates on microcosmic blockage. One evacuates the internal witch (i.e., sin) and ceases to worry about external witches, because they no longer exist. The model of the person in Nanga therapy becomes analogous to free market dynamics— the person is self-afflicting—through retentiveness and guilt, yet self-restoring—through confession and purgation. Nanga therapy disculpates people who, through necessity or desire, have had to become retentive and renounce gift logic.

Yet a third strategy in Rwandan popular therapy indicates that there is a spectrum of possible resolutions to the contradiction posed by the ideology of the gift and the ideology of the commodity. This form of therapy, practiced by some southern Rwandan healers, incorporates both confession and accusation. Here a sufficiently open-ended therapeutic paradigm allows patients and healers to combine aspects of the earlier theory of misfortune—"there are witches out there"—and the new theory of misfortune—"the witch is in me"—without apparent contradiction. Such therapies, as the example of Frederick and Mutabazi would indicate, may in fact externally concretize the patient's split internal state, his or her oscillation between ideas of persecution and feelings of guilt, between belief in and doubt of witchcraft. Furthermore, by externalizing the internal schizoid state of its patients, this therapy may allow them to more adequately understand the contradictions that they embody and that in turn embody them. This cognitive function may in itself be therapeutic, even if it is not always curative in the ordinary sense of complete symptom remission.

In the case history involving these healers and their patients, Maria and Beatrice, we witness one of the central conflicts in present-day Rwandan society: the question of the female body's disposition according to the opposed moralities of gift logic and commodity logic. Women were once foci of flow/blockage symbolism as well as subjects of its actualization.[1] Today expanded notions of choice are beginning to influence how women behave in romance, sexuality, and marriage. Women such as Maria are exercising the right to make sentimental and sexual choices much more so than they did in the past. But this shift is problematic, for if women are becoming free and independent transactors, what is to replace the former cultural imperative of ordered succession in attaining the social capacity to reproduce? Beatrice cannot give herself as a wife, because she cannot accede to fertility as an autonomous being. The older generation must prepare the younger for fertility; it must transfer its knowledge to the junior generation and Hester impeded this transfer by poisoning Beatrice's mother. The paradox of Beatrice and Maria is their own and their society's affliction, for neither can create an identity for herself in the present without resorting to organizing symbols that derive from the Rwandan cultural past.

These organizing symbols take the form of an "image schema," a corporally enracinated mental structure or model that enables the mind to cognize the world around it and that imprints itself on language through tropes (M. Johnson 1987). The oppositional structure of flow-blockage resembles an image schema, for it derives ultimately from bodily experience while it continues to motivate cognition even in the face of historical change. The afflictions of Maria, Beatrice, and others discussed in this study show that Rwandans live the present through the active participation of the past. Ephraim cannot calm his hemorrhagic vomiting, nor keep the *abazímu* at bay, with Catholic ritual; someone in his family must relearn "tradition" in order to negotiate the present. Annunciata cannot "open" the path to a husband without first "opening" her body, but Catholicism equates *gukuna imishino* with masturbation, making it a sin. When she has erotic dreams, guilt assumes human form and "blocks the path" to her suitors. The past with its dialectical imagery of flow and blockage hovers like a specter over today's participants in Rwandan medicine. It provides patients with a model that allows them to understand their bodies in the present; but the present, with its commodity logic, often impugns the model.

Progressively, there has been erosion of the model's capacity to organize the entirety of social existence. No longer is the Rwandan polity conceptualized in these terms; less and less is social life being conducted according to its dictates. The last cultural redoubt where the flow/blockage imagery of Rwandan gift logic survives, and where it confronts the ideology of capitalist culture, is in the minds and bodies of individual Rwandans. Nanga y'ivuza therapy comes closest to acknowledging this fact. Whereas Freud views the unconscious as a battleground of conflicting individual desires, Nanga therapy implicitly assumes that the conflicting elements may be alternate modes of sociality. The sufferings of Rwandans are as much the symptoms of one culture's absorption by another as they are the signs of psychosomatic illness. They illuminate the paradox that while a specifically Rwandan cultural dialectic has managed to endure profound historical changes and to reveal itself in "forward-moving implication" (Wagner 1986, 77–78),[2] yet another dialectic, the dialectic between gifts and commodities, has begun to supercede and to obviate that of flow and blockage. Some types of Rwandan popular therapy continue to ground their imagery in flow/blockage symbolism, but Nanga therapy appears bent upon curing patients of their lingering adherence to this symbolism.

This study touches the intersection of three spheres of thought and action: the body, cultural symbolism, and history. Rwandan symbolic thought is not a "closed system" in Horton's sense (1967), nor is diachrony here merely the recapitulation over time of the same or similar structures of thought. Meaning in Rwandan healing, as elsewhere in the developing world, is the product of conflictual forces. For this reason, anthropologists have been forced to deal with the issue of process and symbolic transformation and to integrate a diachronic view of symbolism into the analysis itself. They have had to add a pragmatic dimension to the study of cultural symbolism. Cultural categories are not automatically reproduced in the same structural configurations; they can be transformed during the course of their reproduction. Continuity and difference cannot be separated (Wagner 1975). New meanings grow out of the ways people use old symbols to "re-cognize" new social situations. This process may occur in two ways: "signs can acquire new conceptual values (1) insofar as they are placed in novel relationships with objects in the referential process; and (2) insofar as they are placed in novel relationships with other signs in the instrumental process" (Sahlins 1981, 70).

In the face of Western contact, the flow/blockage dialectic has encountered a system that emphasizes profit and capital accumulation. Whereas the precolonial culture emphasized the positive value of flow over blockage, the new culture appears to invert this relationship. In precolonial Rwandan symbolic thought:

health : body :: flow : social relations
poison : body :: blocking beings : society
blockage : body :: calamity : society.

As long as the tendency toward flow predominated over blockage, Rwandan society could reproduce itself. But these symbolic parameters have encountered the following principles of capitalist culture:

profit (or wage) : capitalism :: health : body
accumulation : capitalism :: reproduction : society.

This new set of values reverses those implicit in Rwandan culture, for profit and accumulation closely resemble precolonial antireciprocity notions of blockage. The imagery of flow/blockage, in order to accommodate capitalist culture, has to be divorced from notions of macrocosmic (sociological and cosmological) causality. This has been achieved by substituting the afflicting principle of "sin" for that of "poison." The notion of sin partially salvages the validity of flow/blockage symbolism, yet it reduces its pertinence. Sin can produce both moral blockage (countered by confession) and physiological blockage (countered by purgation) and thus appear intermediary between the old concepts of pathology and the newer ones.

With the concept of sin, however, a new analogy can be extrapolated:

sin : individual :: unproductive members : society.

This analogy is both the product of transformation and the condition for reproducing social relations in accordance with commodity logic. Following this analogy we see that the body can be compared to market relations:

internal cause : body :: supply (or demand) : market
autonomy : person :: market : society.

The blockage of accusatory therapy (failure to observe reciprocity notions) can logically shift to something with positive connotations, allowing the "Invisible Hand" of the marketplace to operate and regulate itself (A. Smith 1776, 477). An ailing economy cures itself through the market.

An analogous transformational process has characterized Rwandan popular medicine, if we accept the assertion that Nanga y'ivuza therapy is the most recent expression of this medicine. For this reason, the study of Rwandan culture and its indigenous medicine cannot be separated from its history. And history implies both structure and event.

Appendixes
Glossary of Kinyarwanda Terms
Notes
Bibliography
Index

APPENDIX A

Matrimonial Gift Exchanges in Precolonial Rwanda

The following chart lists the matrimonial prestations and counter-prestations that were once habitually exchanged in central Rwanda. This chart, which I have translated from the French, comes from Jacques Maquet, *Le système des relations sociales dans le Ruanda ancien* (1954), 88–89. Maquet did his fieldwork during 1950–51. According to him, the institutions and customs described here derive from the late precolonial (late nineteenth century) and early colonial period up to about 1910 (p. 13). European contact had no appreciable influence on Rwandan social relations until 1910. Maquet's description and analysis are based upon his informants' recollections of these social arrangements.

HUTU

Husband's *inzu*   Wife's *inzu*

1.   One hoe, one large container of beer after the [marriage] agreement.

     Father ——————————————▶ Father

2. one female calf or 12 to 14 goats (bride price) given 1 to 3 weeks after gift #1 (*gutenbutsa*).

Father ——————————▶ Father

3. household utensils given the day of the wedding (*ibirongoranywa*).

Husband ◀—————————— Father

4. one hoe, or a sheep, or a goat, plus containers of beer at the end of wife's seclusion period.

Husband ◀—————————— Father

5. one hoe, or a sheep, or a goat (sometimes a female calf) given one week after each birth.

Husband ◀—————————— Patrilineage

6. counter-brideprice (the "growth" of the bride price) given 2 to 3 years after the marriage.

Father ◀—————————— Father

TUTSI

Husband's *inzu*   Wife's *inzu*

1. one large container of mead, one hoe, and a forked branch from a special tree (*isando*).

Father ——————————▶ Father

2. one cow (bride price) *inkwáano* a few days later.

Father ——————————▶ Father

3. one cow (counter–bride price—*indoongoranyo*) when the wife leaves her father's household.

Father ◀—————————— Father

4. household utensils given the day of the wedding.

Husband ◀—————————— Father

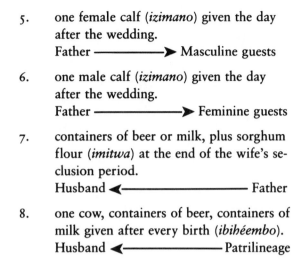

5.   one female calf (*izimano*) given the day after the wedding.

    Father ⎯⎯⎯⎯⟶ Masculine guests

6.   one male calf (*izimano*) given the day after the wedding.

    Father ⎯⎯⎯⎯⟶ Feminine guests

7.   containers of beer or milk, plus sorghum flour (*imitwa*) at the end of the wife's seclusion period.

    Husband ⟵⎯⎯⎯⎯ Father

8.   one cow, containers of beer, containers of milk given after every birth (*ibihéembo*).

    Husband ⟵⎯⎯⎯⎯ Patrilineage

Today, there are no longer appreciable differences in the gifts given by Tutsi and Hutu. In both cases, one cow or two constitutes the bride price (*inkwáano*). The custom of giving a return bride price (*indoongoranyo*) seems to be disappearing. Sometimes, the *inkwáano* is a once and for all bride payment, which does not necessarily establish a continuous exchange relationship between the two families. Moreover, often a simple cash payment to the bride's father is made in lieu of a cow. The practice of "recompensing" (*guhéemba* - *ibihéembo*) the wife and her husband after each birth, continues to be followed by the wife's family (though not the entire patrilineage as shown above), neighbors, and friends of the family. The gifts given in *guhéemba,* however, are not likely to include a calf or a cow.

APPENDIX B

Gifts of Beer Made in Rwanda before Independence (1961)

This passage is quoted from Pierre Bettez Gravel, *Remera: A Community in Eastern Ruanda* (1968, 142–44). Gravel did his fieldwork from April 1960 until July 1961, a time marked by widespread political upheaval pitting Hutu cultivators against Tutsi cattle owners.

"Beer, as a highly perishable commodity, is ideally suited to rapid redistribution. It would be futile to point out, one by one, all of the occasions that prompt a gift of beer. Most of them will come under a few general headings, and a few others will serve as illustrations.

Firstly, beer is distributed at home by a man, who upon making his beer, invites his close neighbors and close relatives in for a chat. Or, he may hold a beerfest for a working-party, as described above.

Secondly, there are the more formal gifts of calabashes of beer. (In Central Ruanda these gifts are made in earthen pots rather than in calabashes.) Some of these gifts of beer have special names:

    1. *Ibiyagano.* A gift of beer made to a man who has lost a member of his family. This is always accompanied by a bundle of firewood.

    2. *Ibihéembo.* A gift of beer to a woman who has given birth. This is also always accompanied by a bundle of firewood.

    3. *Inzogá zogusaba.* (The literal translation is "the beer for betrothal.") Of the many calabashes of beer that are given for betrothal, three have special names:

    a. *Gufatirembo*. ("To pass the door," i.e., "to open the door.") This gift of beer is given to initiate the betrothal proceedings.

    b. *Nyina w'umwana*. ("For the mother of the girl.") This beer accompanies the bride-price.

    c. *Ugutebutsa*. ("To accelerate the proceedings.") This gift of beer is made when, after many gifts of beer, the parents of the bride have not yet indicated that they are ready for the marriage ceremony to take place.

4. *Ibitwikurura*. ("To uncover.") The gift of beer brought by the bride's father to indicate that the bride could come out of her husband's house after the period of seclusion that followed the wedding. A rich man might bring up to twelve calabashes of beer on this occasion, and everyone brings an accompanying minimum gift of two pots of butter. These pots of butter are obligatory. If one has no cows, one asks a herder or cow owner for the milk required to produce the butter; they may not refuse this request.

5. *Ibica mwiréembo*. ("To pass through the door.") This is the beer brought on the visit made by a young man to his parents-in-law following his marriage. The calabashes might number up to eight or nine, and must be accompanied by a minimum of two wooden containers of milk. Fulfillment of the request for milk in order to make this gift is also obligatory for the herder or cow owner.

Other gifts of beer fall into the same category of formal gifts as those listed above. However, their names simply describe the occasion of the gift. One such gift is *inzogá yogucyura*. This is beer given by a husband to make a wife return from her father's home, if she has left with intent of divorce. A woman might also bring beer home to her father and accompany this with small gifts of foodstuffs for her mother. Or, a man is obligated by custom to bring beer on his frequent visits to his wife's father. The wife's father brings beer when he reciprocates the visits of the young husband. Beer is also used "to thank" someone (*inzogá yokwitura*), or to thank one's patron upon receipt of a cow (*gukora ubgatsi*: literally, "to pull up the grass," as a gesture of thanks).

Because of the necessity "to be seen" by the chieftain there is a constant flow of visitors bringing beer at the house of the chieftain. The beer is promptly redistributed among those present. This flow stopped after the elections of July 1960, because visits to the ex-chieftain were forbidden by the new burgomaster. Nevertheless, they indicate the chieftain's past role as a pivot for redistribution.

Evidence secured from old timers and the ex-chieftain himself, as well as from the official documents of the administration, shows that the chieftain had rights to first fruits and he received various gifts from those who wanted "to be seen" by him. If he was a "good" chieftain, he would redistribute these gifts after taking his share. If he was a "bad" chieftain and did not do so, he would lose his constituents to a neighboring "good" one. In any case, first fruits and *redevances* were eventually replaced by a salary, which could also be redistributed."

Today these gifts of beer continue to be given, although perhaps somewhat less systematically than in the past. It is interesting to note the characterization of a good chieftain. Clearly he had to take the function of redistribution seriously. Liquid gifts flowing into his house had to flow out in virtually equal measure. Moreover, the movement of such things could be considered to resemble the movement of persons. Notice that Gravel unconsciously makes use of a liquid metaphor to describe the movement of visitors to the chieftain's house, just as I have quite consciously done in analyzing Rwandan notions of production and exchange and their analogical correlates in representations of the body. A good chieftain had to act in consistency with the imagery of an "open conduit" in his exchange relations. Most of what he received, he had to give away quickly; things had to pass "through" him. The Rwandan king (*umwaámi*) was constrained by the popular image of a good chieftain. For this reason, it is not surprising to find instances in Rwandan folklore where the *umwaámi*'s person, and its role in ensuring prosperity, is metaphorically referred to with "conduit" imagery.

The system Gravel describes changed radically after July 1960, when the new burgomaster (who was in all likelihood Hutu) forbade people to visit the ex-chieftain (who was probably Tutsi). Gift logic quite clearly received a setback with the success of the Hutu revolution. It should be noted, however, that some aspects of the old system have lingered into the present. Burgomasters in today's Rwanda are also somewhat constrained by the imagery of the good chieftain. In the evening, it is not unusual to find constituents at a burgomaster's house discussing important matters and drinking bottles of Primus (a brand of beer) that he has provided.

Glossary of Kinyarwanda Terms

~~~~~~~

The spellings here closely follow the orthography of the Kinyarwanda dictionary put together by the Institut National du Recherche Scientifique in Butare, Rwanda. The entries are arranged alphabetically by root word. Each root is followed by one or two prefixes. Verbs have only one prefix: *ku-*, *kw-*, or *gu-* (e.g., the first verb on the list, when written out, is *kwáama*). Nouns often have two prefixes, indicating the singular and plural forms (e.g., *umwáana* [child] and *abáana* [children]). In many cases, there are subentries giving other examples of the word's usage.

-áagwá, urw	banana beer or wine.
-áama, kw	to bear fruit, to fructify, to be fertile; to be famous, to be known by everyone; to have done something for a long time and to continue to do it, to have a certain habitual comportment; to be prosperous or to live a long time.
-aámi, umw, ab	king(s).
-aámikazi, umw, ab	king's wife, wives.
-aambika, kw	to wear, to put on.

kwaambika	to adorn the bride with *umwishywa*
umwishywa	(*Momoridca foetida*) (a former marriage practice).
-áana, umw, ab	child, children.
-baandwa, ku	to participate in the cult of Ryangombe.
-boró, im	penis.
-búto, im	seed.
-byáara, ku	to engender.
-byáara, umu, aba	cross-cousin(s); for male ego: MDB, FZD; for female ego: FZS, MBS.
-byéeyi, umu, aba	parent(s), relative(s).
-caáca, ga	informal body brought together to settle disputes.
-cáandwé, ama	saliva.
-cíira, gu	to spit.
gucíira imbazi	to spit milk mixed with herbs on the bride (former marriage practice).
-cumá, igi, ibi	calabash(es) or gourd(s) to drink from.
-cúna, gu	to perform the ritual acts necessary to cure someone of infertility or other misfortune.
-cúnyi, umu, aba	one(s) who does the above.
-cyúuragura, gu	to "dance at night," to perform ritual acts intended to harm others.
-dáaro, in	small hut, often built for ritual reasons.
daatá	father (F).
daátabukwé	father-in-law, wife's father (WF).
daatá-wáacu	father's brother (FB).
-doongoranyo, in	return bridewealth cow or prestations.
-éera, kw	to be or become white; to perform the ritual acts associated with the termination of mourning.
-eeso, urw	small earthenware pot, often inserted into the neck of the larger pot (*inkóno*) used in cooking.
-fuungura, gu	to dilute a drink so that more people can drink it; to eat.
-gaba, ku	to give a gift.
-gabo, umu, aba	man, men; husband, husbands.
-gabo, ubu	generosity; courage; virility.
-gabékazi, umu, aba	mother of the king.
-gaáge, iki, ibi	sorghum beer.
-garágu, umu, aba	client(s) (under the former patronage system).
-gega, iki, ibi	granary, granaries.
-girwá, umu, aba	Nyabingi priest(s) or priestess(es).
-gó, uru, in	household enclosure(s).

-gobyi, in	placenta; sheepskin used by mothers to carry their infant children on their backs; stretcher to carry the sick or injured.
-goma, in	drum; reign or exercise of sovereignty.
-goro, in	residence of the king; temple.
-guunga, in	small gourd or horn used in the popular medical procedure known as "cupping."
-há, gu	to give to, to offer to.
guhána ingo	(literal) to exchange houses, to agree to sleep with each other's wife(ves).
-hákwa, gu	to become the client of someone, to work for someone as his client.
-hake, ubu	former patron-client relation (abolished in 1954).
-haama, gu	to cultivate sun-hardened land; to have intercourse with a woman lacking in vaginal secretions.
-hama, igi, ibi	woman (women) who lacks milk after giving birth or who lacks vaginal secretions during intercourse.
-hehá, umu, imi	straw used to drink from an *igicuma*.
-héemba, gu	to recompense.
-héembo, ibi	gifts given to a woman who has recently given birth.
-heémbe, i, ama	animal horn(s).
-héembera, gu	to be filled with milk (mammary gland).
-híinga, gu	to cultivate.
-híinzi, umu, aba	cultivator(s).
-híinza, umu, aba	"chief(s) of the fields," title given to some Hutu notables before the consolidation of Rwanda under a Tutsi king.
-huunda, gu	to acclaim.
-huúngu, umu, aba	boy(s), son(s).
-íima, kw	to refuse someone something.
kwíima inzoga	to refuse drink to someone.
-íirabura, kw	to be or become black; to enter mourning.
-íiru, umw, ab	court ritualist(s).
-íita, kw	to name.
-jya, ku	to go.
kujya mu mihango	to have one's period, to menstruate.
-ká, in	cow, cattle.
-káma, gu	to milk; to dry up.
-káma, umu, aba	milker(s); lord(s), king(s).
-keécuru, umu, aba	old woman, women.
aga, udu	small old woman, women.

-kó, umu, imi	erythrine tree (*Erythrina abyssinica*).
-koobwa, umu, aba	girl(s), daughter(s).
-kóma, igi	porridge made from sorghum or other cereal.
-kóno, in	cauldron.
inkóno y'itabi	tobacco pipe.
-kubá, in	thunder.
-kuna, gu	
gukuna imishino	to lengthen the labia minora by manipulation in preparation for marriage.
-kúrakuza, gu	to turn over incubating eggs (hen); to separate out butter from milk that one has churned; to have sex with a woman who is pregnant with one's child.
-kúraambere, umu, aba	spirit(s) of a patrilineal ancestor(s).
-kuri, in	remedy given to pregnant women to assure the fetus's health.
-kúza, gu	to make something or someone grow, to raise.
-kwáano, in	bridewealth, usually bovine.
-kwé, ubu, ama	marriage(s).
-léetwá, ubu	corvée, unremunerated labor time that one gives one's patron.
-lili, iki	after parturition, a several-day period of seclusion for both mother and infant.
-maáma	mother (M).
maabukwé	mother-in-law, wife's mother (WM).
maáma-wáacu	mother's sister (MZ).
maaséenge	paternal aunt, father's sister (FZ).
-máana, i	supreme being, God.
-maándwa, i	deities; followers of Ryangombe.
-manura, ku	to make something descend.
maarúme	maternal uncle, mother's brother (MB).
-meré, ka	character, manner of being.
kameré muntu	essence of a person, said to be contained in the saliva.
mubyáara	cross cousin (see *kubyáara*).
mukase	stepmother, father's wife.
mushiki	sister, female parallel cousin.
-naanga, i	Rwandan harp or sitar.
-naáni, umu, imi	number eight; legacy given by a father to his son, especially when the latter marries.
-ntu, umu, aba	person, people.
-ntu, bu	world of the living.
-ntu, iki, ibi	thing(s).
-ntu, aha	place, location.
-nnyano, ubu	food given to children who have accomplished ritual actions of planting for a newborn

	(this food is said to be mixed with a small quantity of the baby's feces).
-*nyáara, ku*	to urinate.
-*káli, in*	urine.
-*nyáaré, ama*	vaginal secretions during intercourse.
-*nyáaza, ku*	to cause "urination" in the woman, to make love in the Rwandan fashion.
-*nywá, ku*	to drink.
kunywá itabi	to drink tobacco, to smoke.
-*óoba, ubw*	fear.
-*óoko, ubw, am*	group(s) defined by common traits, such as a clan, a race, or an ethnic group.
-*oónko, ubw*	brain.
-*pa, im*	girl of childbearing age who has never menstruated.
-*penébeere, im*	girl of childbearing age without breasts.
-*pfumu, umu, aba*	diviner(s).
-*pigi, im*	talisman.
-*ragura, ku*	to divine.
-*raguza, ku*	to consult a diviner, to have divination done.
kuragura amaheémbe	to divine by horns.
kuraguza amaheémbe	to have a diviner divine by horns.
kuragura umutwe	to divine by "head" (mental processes alone).
kuraguza umutwe	to have a diviner divine by his head.
-*rásaaga, ku*	to make small incisions in the skin as a popular medical procedure, to scarify.
-*dásaago, in*	small incisions, scarifications.
-*ráso, ama*	blood.
-*rebé, i, ama*	the entry to a Rwandan house.
mu irebé	to be at the entry.
-*rebé, i, ama*	water lily, lilies.
-*reémba, ubu*	impotence.
-*réembo, i*	the principal entryway to a Rwandan home's enclosure.
-*roga, ku*	to poison, to ensorcell.
-*rozi, umu, aba*	one(s) who ensorcells or poisons.
-*rozi, ubu, ama*	poison(s), harmful charms.
-*rúka, ku*	to vomit.
kurúka uburozi	to vomit poison.
-*rúmika, ku*	to perform "cupping" in popular medicine.
-*ruungu, i*	menstrual blood (especially in the context of poisoning).
-*rya, ku*	to eat.
-*ryaango, umu, imi*	patrilineally based descent group.
umutware w'umuryaango	head male of the descent group.

-ryáango, umu, imi	doorjamb.
-saabo, igi, ibi	large calabash used to churn butter.
-saangwabutaka, umu, aba	(member[s] of) clans considered to be the first to occupy the land, autochthones.
-saanza, igi	liquid that exudes from the vagina after parturition.
-sazi, ibi	psychosis, madness.
-se, ubu	links of ritual interdependence between clans, especially between autochthonous and nonautochthonous clans (see -saangwabutaka).
-se, umu, aba	person(s) linked to another (others) by the relation of *ubuse*.
-shéebuja, umu, aba	patron(s) in patron-client relation.
-shéegabo, igi, ibi	authoritarian woman (women), virago.
-shéreka, ama	breastmilk.
-shika, gu	to capture the voice of a sorcerer in order to interrogate it.
-shitáani, i, ama	devil(s) (from the word "Satan"), bad spirits.
-shyano, i, -hano, ama	catastrophe(s), misfortune(s), ritual impurity.
-shyitsi, umu, aba	guest(s), visitor(s).
-shuúhe, ubu	heat, warmth.
-siba, gu	to block, to obstruct, to fill up.
-sibo, i	a "flow" of cattle, of soldiers; force, élan.
guca isibo	to "cut the flow," to jump very high while dancing.
gusiba inkarú	to do grave harm to someone.
gusiba inzira	to "block the path," to lose one's daughter before she can marry.
-siibya, gu	to impede.
gusiibya urugendo	to prevent or impede someone's journey.
-sohora, gu	to exit, come out, bring out.
gusohora umwáana	to bring out a newborn child after the seclusion period (*ikilili*) in order to introduce him or her to members of the community.
-sohoro, ama	semen.
-soongero, aga, udu	spire(s) that projects from the roof of a traditional Rwandan house(s).
-súbyo, i, ama	medicinal powder(s) inhaled through the nostrils or drunk in a liquid in order to conjure away *ishyano*.
-ta, ama	milk.
-tagatifu, umu, aba	Swahili and Catholic word for "saint(s)".
-táambikiro, umu, imi	malevolent charm or poison concealed beneath the surface of a footpath.
-táambiko, umu, imi	piece of wood used as a barrier.

-táanga, gu	to give, to accord, to give a gift.
-taanga, in	"gift of self," male or female reproductive contribution.
-teega, gu	to place in peril, to expose to danger.
-teega, igi, ibi	spirit(s) of deceased foreigner(s), bad spirit(s).
-térekeera, gu	to venerate one's ancestors with offerings of beer, milk, blood, and meat, singly or in combination.
-tí, umu, imi	medication(s), remedy (remedies).
-tíma, umu, imi	heart(s).
-toóre, in	Tutsi warrior(s).
-tsírika, gu	to prevent an ensorcellment, to conjure it away at its source.
-túubá, gu	to reduce, to diminish.
-túubá, in	tobacco pipe (in contexts where one emphasizes the reductive and possibly nefarious action of a pipe).
-úuki, ub, am	honey, mead.
-vubyi, umu, aba	rainmaker(s).
-vuuliro, i, ama	dispensary (dispensaries), place(s) where the sick are cared for.
-vúra, im	rain.
-vuura, ku	to care for, to treat.
-vuuzi, umu, aba	healer(s).
-vuuzi, ubu	art of healing.
ubuvuuzi bwa Gihanga, ubuvuuzi bwa Kinyarwanda	popular medicine.
-zaratsi, uru, in	medicine used to gain power over someone, usually (but not always) of the opposite sex; love potion.
-zímu, umu, aba	ancestral spirits.
-zimu, bu	· underworld, place where the deceased reside.
-zína, i, ama	name(s).
-zira, in	path, way.
-zogá, in	alcoholic beverage.
inzoga y'inturire	sorghum or banana beer fortified with honey.
-zu, in, ama	house(s), household(s), minor lineage segment.
-zúungu, umu, aba	white person(s).

Notes

———————

INTRODUCTION

1. I am grateful to Michelle Wagner for this information.

2. Marx's insight has been used by M. Taussig (1977, 1980) to analyze the actions of Bolivian peasants undergoing incorporation into the global economy. My objection against applying it to Rwanda it that it posits too strict a separation between "use value" and "exchange value." The gift/commodity distinction has the advantage of implying a spectrum of intermediate forms.

3. At least most classical economists from Adam Smith to Paul Samuelson begin their analysis with an assumption about the nature of economic man, "homo economicus," who is, according to these economists, a "maximizing" individual.

4. The Rwandan kingdom emerged about the fifteenth century A.D. (Vansina 1962, 15).

CHAPTER 1. THE DYNAMICS OF FLOW

1. "Rwandan cultural symbolism does not refer to any explicit code, nor to any system of preconceived correspondences. Traditional Rwanda had neither figurative art, nor fixed religious places, nor a fixed cycle of festivals, nor a fixed capital, nor even a village despite one of the highest [population] densities in Africa. We are dealing here with a culture whose symbolism, like its settlement pattern, is omnipresent yet diffuse and mobile. A thing is almost never there to represent another thing in an automatic or permanent way; the most that one can say is that something may recall, suggest, or evoke something else in a habitual fashion only in certain contexts." (All translations from French are my own.)

2. "A powerful quality, the dynamic principle of life and fecundity, which traditional Rwandans sought to appropriate by ritual techniques. In some cosmogonic tales, this same force is conceived of as a conscious volitional entity, which one could term Divinity. But no religion addresses itself to this anthropomorphic hypostasis precisely because the term *imáana* does not refer primarily to a personal being whom one must honor and supplicate, but a diffuse fluid that must be captured. . . . The quality of *imáana* is associated with a vast category of persons and objects through whose mediation traditional Rwandans thought they could tap its effects."

3. "But, according to the concepts held by Rwandans, it is the king who is the supreme possessor of the fecundating fluid, *imáana;* the royal ritual is nothing else than the description of techniques that allow him to direct its benefits to the entire country."

4. "In order to increase the number of cattle, *imáana* began by creating kings."

5. "The wife that Gihanga had brought back from Burundi became pregnant in her turn. During her pregnancy, a quarrel broke out between the wives; they were arguing over the skin of an animal killed by Gihanga. Nyirarucyaba, the eldest daughter of the latter, mortally wounded the Rundi wife by striking her in the stomach with a boar; she died but the child she was bearing, although born prematurely, was safe and sound. Gihanga named him Gafomo ["product of a Cesarean section" (P. Smith 1975, 286; noted by de Heusch)]. Nyirarucyaba fled and took refuge in the forest. There she was welcomed by a certain Kazigaba [eponymous ancestor of the Zigaba clan]. She married him and they had children. One day, though, upon learning that her father was ill, she became sad. Just then she saw cows emerging from a lake. One of the beasts came over and gave birth before her doorway, then the calf became entangled in forest vines. Though its mother stayed with it, the other cattle began making their way back to the lake. Nyirarucyaba molded a clay pot and went to milk the cow. Noticing that the liquid had a pleasant taste, she brought the calf close to the entry of her hut and tethered it there. The cow followed. Then Nyirarucyaba sent some of the precious brew she had just discovered to her father through the intermediary of her mother. Gihanga, agreeably surprised, had his daughter brought to him and accorded her his forgiveness. Nyirarucyaba brought other jugs with her. The milk cured Gihanga of his illness. Then he demanded that his son-in-law send him the cow. The latter refused at first, so Gihanga grew angry. Finally, Nyirarucyaba brought the animal herself.

Then once again the wild cattle began to emerge from the lake so Gihanga decided to take possession of them. But Gafomo, who had perched on top of a tree, screamed out in fright when he saw the immense herd. The cattle ran back to take refuge in the lake and it closed in upon them. The narrator concludes 'Only a few cows remain. These are the ones that Rwandans have husbanded; if cattle had come in greater numbers, no man would be the ruler of another.' "

6. The two principal autochthonous clans were the Singa and the Zigaba. Originally, the latter were completely Hutu clans whose settlement preceded that of the Tutsi. The first queen mothers came from these clans, but later both were prohibited from participating in the royal institution (P. Smith 1970, 7).

7. "The King is not a man,
   O men that he has enriched with his cattle . . .
   He is a man before his designation to the throne . . .
   Ah yes! That is certain:
   But the one who becomes king ceases to be a man!

The King, it is he *Imáana*
And he dominates over humans . . .
I believe that he is the *Imáana* who hears our pleas!
The other *Imáana*, it's the King who knows him,
As for us, we see only this defender! . . .
Here is the sovereign who drinks the milk milked by *Imáana*
And we drink that which he in turn milks for us!"

8. The "most representative symbol of feminine beauty and fecundity."

9. The tale dissimulates the contradiction that *imáana* is both the Creator, the father of four brothers, and *imáana* the life force, one of the brothers, by using the term *Rurema* for "Creator" here.

10. Witchcraft in Rwanda is more frequently what Edward Evans-Pritchard has termed "sorcery," involving the introduction of harmful substances into food or drink, rather than an innate, congenital potentiality (cf. 1937). Although witchcraft of the second variety does exist, both are called *uburozi*.

    According to Pierre Smith, only sorcery exists in Rwanda: "Les Rwandais sont obsédés par les effets néfastes de l'alimentation qui exige mille précautions, d'autant plus que la sorcellerie est toujours conçue comme un empoisonnement" (1975, 133n). (Rwandans are obsessed by the possible harmful effects of eating, which demands the observation of a thousand precautions, even more so because witchcraft is always conceived of as poisoning.)

11. Luc de Heusch (*Rois nés d'un coeur de vache*) has commented at length on the dialectical interaction between fire and water in ensuring fertility and productivity.

12. The first mythical Rwandan king, Kigwa, fell to the earth from the sky. Later he married his sister, Nyampundu, whose name comes from *guhuunda*. (When the consonant *p* follows an *m* in Kinyarwanda, it is pronounced like *mh*. Kinyarwanda orthography, a relic of German and Belgian colonialism, is not 100 percent consistent.)

13. "The Luba sovereign assumes the ambiguous status of heir to this celestial hero with refined manners as well as to an autochthonous king who commits incest and abuses his power. At the moment of his coronation, he copulates secretly with his mother and his sisters in a hut with neither a door nor a window, called 'house of misfortune.' This closed edifice, without opening to the outside world, is symbolically cut off from the circuit of exogamous marriage. This is the supreme locus of accursed transcendance, where the sacredness of power is acquired as an element that is foreign to society."

CHAPTER 2. RELIGION AND THE BODY POLITIC

1. Although *ubuhake* was quite widespread in central Rwanda, it was much rarer in the peripheral regions of north and south.

2. Ndorwa was the name of the defunct kingdom to the north of Rwanda consisting of parts of present-day northern Rwanda and southwestern Uganda.

3. This hierarchy consisted of land chiefs, cattle chiefs, and army chiefs whose functions and duties were more or less distinct, but also to a large extent competitive, especially about control over Hutu labor (Maquet 1954, 163). Moreover, some of the chiefs

within this hierarchy were Hutu and Twa, which afforded the latter some possibility for advancement within the system. Although the older system was characterized by Tutsi domination as well, it was certainly more flexible than the newer system.

CHAPTER 3. ACCUSATORY THERAPY IN NORTHERN RWANDA

1. "To poison" is the closest approximation to the Kinyarwanda verb *kuroga*, even though a Rwandan *uburozi* (poisoning) does not always have to be introduced into the body by ordinary empirical means.

2. This dual meaning also demonstrates an implicit connection among fluidless women, the sun, and cultivation during the dry season.

3. Recently C. Darling et al. (1990) reported that a female homologue of the male prostrate gland may be responsible for fluid ejaculation by many women at the moment of orgasm. Rwandans appear to have been aware of this phenomenon long before Western science.

4. Many Rwandan politicians use the services of popular healers and diviners, but political affairs constitute a domain where healers are the least likely to reveal information to nosy ethnographers. Whereas I was frequently present when healers consulted their patients and allowed to ask questions, when local politicians consulted healers—for medicine to assure good luck, protection against a rival, or information about a rival—no healer would permit me to eavesdrop.

5. Writers such as Iris Berger tend to lump the cults of Nyabingi and Ryangombe together, along with other cults encountered in the interlacustrine region of Africa (1981). Berger uses the term *kubaandwa* to characterize all of them. This classification obscures the fact that the cults of Ryangombe and Nyabingi differ in several fundamental ways. The cult of Ryangombe is much older and, in terms of its symbolism, is probably related to that of divine kingship. Cults similar to Ryangombe are also found in eastern Tanzania and Burundi (cf. de Heusch 1966).

6. Some *abagirwá* may use their influence among their followers predominantly for personal gain, but such priests usually do not enjoy their influence for long. There are in fact a few self-styled Nyabingi priests who engender people's skepticism, but the frequently encountered portrait of the Nyabingi priest as charlatan is grossly exaggerated, as many central Rwandans and Christians today would admit.

7. The literal meaning of *gushika* is "to attract by force" (Jacob 1985, 98).

8. *Amaheémbe* is the plural form of *iheémbe* (horn). When healers speak of this form of divination and therapy as a procedure, they tend to use the plural form. When referring specifically to the "horn" used, they usually speak of it in the singular.

9. These spirits are related to Ryangombe and his disciples in the *kubaandwa* cult in central Rwanda, who are also referred to as *imaándwa*. In this instance, however, they do not serve as the basis for collective cult practices.

10. This bodily fluid, employed metonymically here to represent the entire person, is quite obviously associated in other contexts with fertility, as its other meanings suggest. (See p. 28 for a discussion of *imáana*'s saliva.)

11. "*Uracyúuragura?*" (in Kinyarwanda). *Gucyúuragura,* which could be translated as "to dance at night," refers to the practice of coming to one's victim's house at night, dancing nearby, and throwing poisonous substances on or near the house.

12. This is less true today than it was before independence in 1960. In preindependent Rwanda, the hairstyles of unmarried women were demonstrably different from those of married women.

13. In some instances, the rainmaker was called *umuvubyi;* in other instances, *umuhiínza,* from the verb *guhiínga* (to cultivate). In yet other cases, he was called *umwaámi* from the verb *kwaáma,* or *umwaámi w'imvúra* (king of the rain). *Abahiínza* and *abaámi* were the politically most important notables in precolonial Rwanda. The Rwandan king, called *umwaámi,* eventually subsumed most of the ritual functions of the *abavubyi, abahiínza,* and other *abaámi* whom he deposed, including the centrally important task of ensuring regular rainfall.

CHAPTER 4. THE CASE OF MARIA AND BEATRICE

1. The Curphametra or Centre Universitaire de Recherches sur la Pharmacopée et la Médecine Traditionelle directs pharmacological research into the therapeutic properties of medicinal plants used in popular medicine. Based in Butare at the Université Nationale du Rwanda, it operates a small dispensary where several popular healers ply their trade.

2. Unfortunately, Father Kayinamura passed away before the publication of this book.

3. "who employ rites or magic, or who work at night. If they are true healers, why can't they work in the full light of day. . . . but I admit that some are effective in certain cases."

4. The pangolin plays an important role in the ritual life of many central African peoples and a central role in the symbolic theories of some anthropologists (cf. Douglas 1966).

5. The cow that is given as bridewealth from the husband to the wife's father is called *inkwáano.* The first female offspring of this cow is usually given as a return present from wife's father to husband's father; the calf is called *indoongoranyo.* Although this custom is not always followed in present-day Rwanda, it is significant in this case because of Maria's relation to her husband's family. Another reason for the custom's pertinency is that the cow given for Maria must not "jump the gun" and reproduce before the cow given for a sister who has preceded her in marriage. At any rate, even if the cow calves before the one given for her sister, that calf must be withheld until the sister's *indoongoranyo* has been given. The reason for this will become apparent later in this text. For the moment, it should be noted that the fertility of successive generations, and even age gradations within a single generation, should follow a socially ordered pattern. They should not become mixed up. The younger should not anticipate the elder, nor should the elder unduly retard the younger. To do so could mean compromising the fertility of one or more of the persons involved; sterility and miscarriage are possible results.

6. "Giteega," which might be rendered *igiteega* with the augmentative prefix, is the singular form of *ibiteega,* a type of bad spirit. *Ibiteega* appear to be spirits of the dead,

somewhat like *abazímu,* but with the notable exception that they are spirits of deceased foreigners, unrelated and usually unknown to their victims, rather than spirits of ancestors, who are discoverable to their victims through divination. The origin of this belief appears to be recent (the 1940s, according to Habimana 1986) and its source possibly Tanzanian. It is true that the belief in *ibiteega* is more frequently encountered in southern than in northern Rwanda. The verb *guteega* means "to expose to danger or damage, to place in peril." "One says that the bad spirit *igiteega* eats and drinks at the home of the one who possesses it and that it speaks through the mouth of the one it possesses" (Jacob 1984, 302).

7. *Umuzúungu* means "white person."

8. *Amashitáani* are bad spirits, but the term is general and is usually used in a Christian context. From "Satan" comes "shitan," *ishitáani* (singular), and *amashitáani* (plural). This word is used especially in contexts where more specific spirit names exist but are not used because they are of non-Christian origin. Christian Rwandans are often embarrassed to attribute any credence to non-Christian beliefs and especially where these concern spirits capable of afflicting human beings. A word like *amashitáani* permits them to have their cake and eat it too, as it were; it reduces all spirit beliefs to the derogatory catch-all category of demons and devils, but it does not assert that these do not exist and cannot cause harm. Once the maternal grandfather of Maria showed me an instance of the word *amashitáani* in the Kinyarwanda version of the Bible. This seemed to assuage his discomfort with being Christian and yet being unable to deny the reality of the forces afflicting his granddaughter.

9. The belief that Nyabingi can act as a bad spirit, capable of blindly attacking innocent people, is an idea that one commonly encounters in the south of Rwanda but never hears among the practitioners of the Nyabingi cult in the north.

10. In former times it was permissable for a married woman to have sexual relations with her husband's brothers, half-brothers, and parallel cousins. She might also have sex with her own male cross-cousins. (Today this tends not to be the case.) Women were thought to be more eager for sex than men. Perhaps because of this belief, their sexual behavior was more closely scrutinized than that of men (cf. Maquet 1954, 95–97).

11. "Occasionally, we find in the patient's medical history evidence of instrumental dilation of the cervix. The forced dilation of the cervix for dysmennorrhea and sterility (!) should have been abandoned a long time ago, but unfortunately it is still practiced" (i.e., by some traditional healers).

12. "The stepmother is thus considered as the one who benefits most from the death of the mother of an orphan, and her [the stepmother's] malevolence continues to pursue the orphan, for the existence of this child, who has only a direct relation to the father now, interferes between the father and her own children. . . . The universally disparaged character of the stepmother is even more discredited in Rwanda because here the culture unceasingly affirms fecundity and reproduction as the supreme values of triumphant life. The stepmother is thus the archetypal negative human character in Rwandan folktales, which are, moreover, the only stories that make use of her."

13. "In effect, whereas no important symbolic boundary marks the various stages of a boy's life, very close attention is paid to the different stages and passages of feminine development, hence the disgrace linked to the absence of breasts in the adolescent female, to premarital pregnancy, and to sterility."

14. "*Urweso* (earthenware pot). The young girl urinates into a pot, then takes two drinking straws into her hands, one open and the other blocked; this latter is thought to frustrate the intentions of enemies who oppose the girl's marriage, and the one that is open is thought to presage the future and reveal those who want to marry her; as for the pot containing the urine, it is placed on the hearth and the young girl blows into it [with the open straw] and says, 'This straw is open; I patiently await a suitor; his path is clear," then speaking to the blocked straw, she says, 'May those who oppose my marriage be thwarted.' "

CHAPTER 5. SPIRIT POSSESSION THERAPIES IN SOUTHERN RWANDA

1. Engineers and skilled laborers from the People's Republic of China were involved in road construction in several areas of Rwanda during 1983–85 and also in 1987.

2. This word is related to several words in other Kinyarwanda noun classes, such as *umuntu* (person), *ikintu* (thing), and *ahantu* (place). The plural of *umuntu, abantu* (people), identifies Kinyarwanda as a Bantu language.

3. Bananas are the most important cultivated crop in southern Rwanda and are grown wherever possible in northern Rwanda as well (higher altitudes and cooler temperatures limit this). Virtually every household has banana trees growing around it. Social activity focuses on the drinking of banana beer.

4. *Umurozi* (pl. *abarozi*) is derived from the verb *kuroga*, which means "to poison" or "to send a bad spell against someone." The prefix *umu-* designates the noun class (in the singular) referring to persons. Thus *umurozi* means "one who poisons"; *abarozi* means "those who poison"; *uburozi,* "a poison, a spell"; and *amarozi,* "poisons."

5. Remarks made earlier (pp. 10–12) about *gusiba inzira* (to block the path) should be kept in mind here.

6. Barnett and Silverman (1979, 41) describe "personal domination" as the domination of persons by others (rather than by some abstract entity like the "market"). "Abstracted domination" (55) is the domination of things separable from the person by something else that is also seen as apart from the person. In its most direct form, the latter characterizes capitalist class domination, where people are dominated not by people such as feudal landlords, but by factors such as time, work, and money.

   Precolonial Rwanda was characterized by "personal domination." Since the elimination of *ubuhake*, Rwandans have become more involved in the cash economy through wage labor, cash-cropping, taxes, and the consumption of imported manufactured goods. Individual actors thus have to deal with the "abstract" forces of the marketplace and the world economy. In that sense the idea of "abstracted domination" more appropriately characterizes present-day Rwanda.

7. These spirits all involve the mouth. Catatonia and compulsive speech are symptoms frequently cited by Rwandan healers that someone has been poisoned.

8. Variants of *kubaandwa* are found throughout the interlacustrine area (cf. de Heusch 1966; Berger 1981).

9. This symptom was often cited as "proof" that a sickness was of extraordinary, i.e., spiritual or magical, origin. René Bourgeois mentions it as a symptom of *uburozi* (1956, 196–97). Few symptoms exemplify the concept of abnormal flow as dramatically as this one.

10. These things, along with the blood of the sacrificial animal, are the usual gifts to one's ancestors.

11. Not all healers instruct their clients in how to conduct the rituals of *gutérekeera* and *kubaandwa*. At the Center for Traditional Medicine in Butare, for example, this is not done.

12. *Indasaago,* from the verb *kurasaaga* (to scarify), usually refers to the tiny cuts that are made on a person's skin as a therapeutic procedure to induce bleeding or to permit the introduction of medicines into the blood.

13. A pipe is more frequently called *inkóno y'itabi* (cooking pot of tobacco), but in instances where one wishes to insist on the reductive (and therefore nefarious) action of pipe smoking, the word *intúubá* is sometimes used.

14. This tree, it should be recalled, plays a central role in the *kubaandwa* cult.

15. These symptoms are not necessarily the same ones reported by other healers for these spirits.

CHAPTER 6. THE HARP THAT PLAYS BY ITSELF

1. To this day, many Hutu and Tutsi in Rwanda and Burundi have spurned mutton, because sheep are believed too noble to be slaughtered for food. Only the Twa consume mutton. Sheep are respected for their pacific quality and especially for their apparent ability to keep cattle herds calm. Rwandan and Burundian women use sheepskins to carry babies on their backs.

2. While in Belgium in the summer of 1985, I spoke with Father François Rodegem, a former Catholic missionary who had worked in Burundi and the author of the short article from which all of the above information is extracted. Although he could neither directly confirm nor deny any of the above allegations, he tended to support the generally negative cast given to the Nanga y'ivuza sect.

3. I am grateful to Jan Vansina for his suggestion concerning the possible influence of *kubaandwa* on Nanga y'ivuza.

4. Whether the central role of confession in Nanga y'ivuza is due more to indigenous influence, i.e., *kubaandwa*, than to the influence of Catholicism, Westernization, and capitalist culture is a moot point, one which will be more fully developed later. Furthermore, whether confession in *kubaandwa* was of the same type as that in Nanga y'ivuza, where one confesses to voluntary acts of moral turpitude, is also debatable.

5. Attendance at a Christian church is also desirable. Nanga did not attempt to assume a sacerdotal function for his patients. His own teenage daughter attended a nearby Catholic church where she had been baptized.

6. Nanga's explanation of this "specialization" process was vague.

7. Notice that although Nanga's therapeutic theory emphasizes individual responsibility, it does not deny the role of social causes. It differs from accusatory therapies, however, in the degree of importance attributed to the individual.

8. It is interesting to note that in certain versions of the Lord's Prayer the word "debt" is used instead of "trespass": "forgive us our debts, as we forgive our debtors." To be in debt in a commodity economy implies something different from the obligation to reciprocate; it can mean defective moral citizenship. Debtors were once imprisoned.

CONCLUSION

1. The following mythical figures should be recalled: the *agakeecuru* (small, old, menopaused woman), who contains and propagates Death; Nyirarucyaba, who ultimately impedes the flow of milk onto the land; the unwed mother without breasts (*impa* and *igishéegabo*), who impales Ryangombe; as well as females considered to be abominations in early Rwandan society, such as *impenébeere* (breastless women of childbearing age), *impa* (menseless women), and unwed mothers.

2. In contrast to the Western view of the past as "relic," only minimally influencing our cognition of life in the present, Wagner emphasizes the past's active role in modeling our perceptions of the present, "constraining the actor to carry forward each new stage in compliance with the stages already completed" (77–78).

Bibliography

Althusser, L., and E. Balibar
1979   *Reading Capital.* London: Verso Editions.
Appadurai A.
1986   "Introduction." In *The Social Life of Things,* edited by A. Appadurai,
            3–63. Cambridge: Cambridge University Press.
Atterbury, M.
1970   "Revolution in Rwanda." Madison: Department of African Studies, University of Wisconsin, occasional paper 2.
Augé, M.
1975   "Logique lignagère et logique de Bregbo." In *Prophétisme et thérapeutique,* 219–38. Paris: Hermann.
Augé, M.
1979   "Towards a Rejection of the Meaning-Function Alternative." *Critique of Anthropology* 4, nos. 13–14:61–75.
Augé, M.
1984   "Ordre biologique, ordre social: La maladie forme élémentaire de l'événement." In *Le sens du mal,* edited by M. Augé and C. Herzlich, 35–92. Paris: Editions des Archives Contemporaines.
Augé, M., and C. Herzlich
1984   "Introduction." In *Le sens du mal,* edited by M. Augé and C. Herzlich, 9–34. Paris: Editions des Archives Contemporaines.
Barnett, S., and M. Silverman
1979   *Ideology and Everyday Life.* Ann Arbor: University of Michigan Press.
Bastien, J.
1985   "Qollalhuaya-Andean Body Concepts: A Topographical-Hydraulic Model of Physiology." *American Anthropologist* 87, no. 3:595–611.

Bateson, G.
1958   *Naven.* Stanford: Stanford University Press.
Beatty, J.
1960   *Bunyoro.* New York: Holt, Rinehart & Winston.
Beidelman, T.
1982   *Colonial Evangelism.* Bloomington: Indiana University Press.
Beidelman, T.
1986   *Moral Imagination in Kaguru Modes of Thought.* Bloomington: Indiana
            University Press.
Benoist, J. M.
1975   *La révolution structurale.* Paris: Grasset.
Berger, I.
1981   *Religion and Resistance: East African Kingdoms in the Precolonial
            Period.* Tervuren: Museé Royal de l'Afrique Centrale, Annales,
            Sciences Humaines.
Berger, P., and T. Luckman
1967   *The Social Construction of Reality.* New York: Anchor Books.
Bigirumwami, A.
1971   *Imigani Miremire.* Nyundo, Rwanda.
van Binsbergen, W.
1981   *Religious Change in Zambia.* London and Boston: Kegan
            Paul International.
Bissel, M.
1938   "Nyabingi." *Uganda Journal* 6, no. 2:73–86.
Bohannan, P., and P. Curtin
1964   *Africa and Africans.* Garden City, N.Y.: Natural History Press.
Bourgeois, R.
1956   *Banyarwanda et Barundi, tome IV: Religion et magie.* Brussels: Académie
            royale des sciences coloniales. Classe des sciences morales et politiques,
            vol. 4, fasc. 2.
Brain, R.
1970   "Child Witches." In *Witchcraft Confessions and Accusations,* edited by
            M. Douglas, 161–82. ASA monograph no. 9. London: Tavistock.
Caplow, T., et al.
1982   *Middletown Families: Fifty Years of Change and Continuity.* Minneapolis:
            University of Minnesota Press.
Chretien, J.-P.
1972   "La revolte de Ndungutse (1912): Forces traditionnelles et pression colo-
            niale au Ruanda allemand." *Revue d'histoire d'outre-mer,* 59, no.
            217:645–80.
de Clercq, A.
1982   "Problèmes en obstétrique et gynécologie." In *Santé et Maladies au
            Rwanda,* edited by A. Meheus et al., 627–56. Brussels: Administration
            Générale de la Coopération au Développement.
Comaroff, J.
1981   "Healing and Cultural Transformation Among the Tswana of Southern
            Africa." *Social Science and Medicine* 15B, no. 3:367–78.
Comaroff, J.
1985   *Body of Power, Spirit of Resistance.* Chicago: University of Chicago
            Press.

Comaroff, J., and J. L. Comaroff
1986   "Christianity and Colonialism in South Africa." *American Ethnologist* 13, no. 1:1–22.
Comaroff, J., and J. L. Comaroff
1990   "Goodly Beasts, Beastly Goods: Cattle and Commodities in a South African Context." *American Ethnologist* 17, no. 2:195–216.
Cooper, F.
1981   "Africa and the World Economy." *African Studies Review* 24, nos. 2–3:1–86.
Corin, E.
1979   "A Possession Psychotherapy in an Urban Setting: Zebola in Kinshasa." *Social Science and Medicine* 13B, no. 4:327–38.
Coupez, A., and T. Kamanzi
1962   *Récits historiques Rwanda*. Tervuren: Musée Royal de l'Afrique Centrale, Annales, Sciences Humaines, no. 43.
Darling, C., et al.
1990   "Female Ejaculation: Perceived Origins, the Grafenberg Spot/Area, and Sexual Responsiveness." *Archives of Sexual Behavior* 19, no. 1:29–47.
Darnaud, M.
1975   "Maladies mentales et dégradations sociales." *Cahiers internationaux de Sociologie* 58 (January–June): 161–65.
Devisch, R.
1984   *Se recréer femme*. Berlin: Dietrich Reimer Verlag.
Douglas, M.
1966   *Purity and Danger*. London: Routledge and Kegan Paul.
Dumont, L.
1965   "The Modern Conception of the Individual." *Contributions to Indian Sociology* 8:13–61.
Dumont, L.
1980   *Homo hierarchicus*. Chicago: University of Chicago Press.
Durkheim, E.
1902   *The Division of Labor in Society*. Reprint. Glencoe, Ill: Free Press, 1933.
Edel, M.
1957   *The Chiga of Western Uganda*. New York: International African Institute, Oxford University Press.
Etudes Rwandaises
1977   "Médecine traditionnelle et pharmacopée rwandaises." Vol. 10, numéro spécial (November). Butare: Université Nationale du Rwanda.
Evans-Pritchard, E.
1937   *Witchcraft, Oracles and Magic Among the Azande*. Oxford: Clarendon Press.
Fabian, J.
1971   *Jamaa: A Charismatic Movement in Katanga*. Evanston: Northwestern University Press.
Fabrega, H.
1974   *Disease and Social Behavior: An Interdisciplinary Perspective*, Cambridge: MIT Press.
Feierman, S.
1979   "Changes in African Therapeutic Systems." *Social Science and Medicine* 13B, no. 4:277–84.

Feierman, S.
1981   "Therapy as a System in Action in Northeastern Tanzania." *Social Science and Medicine* 15B, no. 3:353–60.

Feierman, S.
1985   "Struggles for Control: The Social Roots of Health and Healing in Modern Africa." *African Studies Review* 28, nos. 2–3:73–147.

Fernandez, J.
1982   *Bwiti*. Princeton: Princeton University Press.

Foster, G.
1976   "Disease Etiologies in Nonwestern Medical Systems." *American Anthropologist* 78, no. 4:773–82.

Foucault, M.
1980   *The History of Sexuality, Volume 1: Introduction*. Translated by Robert Hurley. New York: Vintage Books.

Frake, C.
1961   "The Diagnosis of Disease Among the Subanun of Mindanao." *American Anthropologist* 63, no. 1:113–32.

Freedman, J.
1974   "Ritual and History: The Case of Nyabingi." *Cahiers d'Etudes Africaines* 14, no. 53:170–80.

Freedman, J.
1975   "Principles of Relationship in Rwandan Kiga Society," Ph.D. diss., Princeton University.

Freedman, J.
1977   "Joking, Affinity, and the Exchange of Ritual Services among the Kiga of Northern Rwanda: An Essay on Joking Relationship Theory." *Man*, n.s., 12, no. 1:154–65.

Freedman, J.
1979   "East African Peasants and Capitalist Development: The Kiga of Northern Ruanda." In *Challenging Anthropology*, edited by D. Turner and G. Smith, 245–260. Toronto: McGraw-Hill Ryerson.

Freedman, J.
1984   *Nyabingi: The Social History of an African Divinity*. Butare, Rwanda: Institut National de Recherche Scientifique, publication 26.

Geertz, C.
1973   *The Interpretation of Cultures*. New York: Basic Books.

Gotanegre, J.-F.
1977   "Géographie médicale du Rwanda." *Etudes Rwandaises* 9, no. 3:17–31.

Gravel, P.
1968   *Remera: A Community in Eastern Rwanda*. Paris: Mouton.

Gregory, C.
1982   *Gifts and Commodities*. London: Academic Press.

Habimana, E.
1986   "Ibitega—Un trouble mental de l'Afrique centrale: Rwanda et région interlacustre." Manuscript, Montréal.

Habimana, E.
1988   "Envie comme cause d'attribution dans les maladies mentales *Ibitega*." Ph.D. diss., Université du Québec à Montréal.

Heritier, F.
1984   "Stérilité, aridité, sècheresse: Quelques invariants de la pensée symbol-
              ique." In *Le sens du mal*, edited by M. Augé and C. Herzlich, 123–54.
              Paris: Editions des Archives Contemporaines.
Heritier, F.
1985   "L'Humeur et son changement." *Nouvelle Revue de Psychanalyse* 32
              (Autumn): 111–22.
d'Hertefelt, M.
1971   *Les clans du Rwanda ancien*. Tervuren: Musée Royal de l'Afrique Cen-
              trale, Annales, Sciences Humaines, No. 70.
d'Hertefelt, M., and A. Coupez
1964   *La royauté sacrée de l'ancien Rwanda*. Tervuren: Musée Royal de l'Af-
              rique Centrale, Annales, Sciences Humaines, no. 52.
d'Hertefelt, M., et al.
1962   *Les anciens royaumes de la zone interlacustre méridionale: Rwanda, Bu-
              rundi, Buha*. Tervuren: Musée Royal de l'Afrique Centrale, Monographies
              ethnographiques, no. 6.
de Heusch, L.
1966   *Le Rwanda et la civilisation interlacustre*. Brussels: Université Libre de
              Bruxelles.
de Heusch, L.
1971   *Pourquoi l'épouser?* Paris: Gallimard.
de Heusch, L.
1972   *Le Roi ivre ou l'origine de l'état*. Paris: Gallimard.
de Heusch, L.
1982   *Rois nés d'un coeur de vache*. Paris: Gallimard.
de Heusch, L.
1985   *Sacrifice in Africa*. Manchester: Manchester University Press.
Hopkins, E.
1970   "The Nyabingi Cult of Southwestern Uganda." In *Protest and Power in
              Black Africa*, edited by R. Rotberg and A. Mazrui, 258–86. New York:
              Oxford University Press.
Horton, R.
1967   "African Traditional Thought and Western Science." *Africa* 37, no.
              50:50–71.
Jacob, I.
1984–87   *Dictionnaire Rwandais-Français*. 3 vols. Extrait du dictionnaire de
              l'Institut National de Recherche Scientifique. Kigali, Rwanda:
              Imprimerie Scolaire.
Janzen, J.
1977   *The Quest for Therapy in Lower Zaire*. Berkeley: University of
              California Press.
Janzen, J.
1982   *Lemba 1650–1930: A Drum of Affliction in Africa and the New World*.
              New York: Garland Publishing.
Johnson, M.
1987   *The Body in the Mind*. Chicago: University of Chicago Press.
Jules-Rosette, B. [et al.]
1979   *The New Religions of Africa*. Norwood, N.J.: Ablex Publishing.

Kagabo, J., and V. Mudandagizi
1974   "Complainte des gens de l'argile: Les Twa du Rwanda." *Cahiers d'Etudes Africaines* 14, no. 53:75–87.
Kagame, A.
1947   "Le code ésotérique de la dynastie du Rwanda." *Zaire* 1, no. 4:364–86.
Kagame, A.
1951   *La poésie dynastique du Rwanda*. Brussels: Mémoire de l'Institut Royal Colonial Belge, Section des sciences morales et poliques, vol. 22, no. 1.
Kagame, A.
1956   *La philosophie bantu-rwandaise de l'être*. Brussels: Académie royale des sciences coloniales, Classe des sciences morales et politiques, vol. 12, fasc. 1.
Kagame, A.
1972   *Un abrégé de l'ethno-histoire du Rwanda*. Université Nationale du Rwanda. Collection Muntu no. 3. Butare: Editions Universitaires du Rwanda.
Kagame, A.
1976   "L'historicité de Lyangombe, chef des Immandwa." *Cahiers des Religions Africaines* 10, no. 19: 5–18.
Kapferer, B.
1979   "Mind, Self, and Other in Demonic Illness: The Negation and Reconstruction of the Self." *American Ethnologist* 6, no. 1:110–33.
Kashamura, A.
1973   *Famille, sexualité et culture*. Paris: Payot.
Kileff, C., and M. Kileff
1979   "The Masowe Vapostori of Seki: Utopianism and Tradition in an African Church." In *The New Religions of Africa*, edited by B. Jules-Rosette, 151–167. Norwood, N.J.: Ablex Publishing.
Klein, M., ed.
1980   *Peasants in Africa*. Beverly Hills: Sage Publications.
Kleinman, A.
1980   *Patients and Healers in the Context of Culture*. Berkeley: University of California Press.
Kuper, A.
1982   *Wives for Cattle*. London: Routledge and Kegan Paul.
de Lacger, L.
1959   *Ruanda*. Kabgayi, Rwanda: Vicariat Apostolique.
Lemarchand, R.
1970   *Rwanda and Burundi*. New York: Praeger.
Lestrade, A.
1955   *La médecine indigène au Rwanda*. Brussels: Académie royale des sciences coloniales.
Lévi-Strauss, C.
1947   *Les structures élémentaires de la parenté*. Reprint. Paris: Mouton, 1971.
Lévi-Strauss, C.
1958   *Anthropogie structurale*. Paris: Plon.
Lévi-Strauss, C.
1962   *La pensée sauvage*. Paris: Plon.
Lévi-Strauss, C.
1976   *Structural Anthropology*. Vol. 2. New York: Basic Books.

Linden, I.
1977   *Church and Revolution in Rwanda*. New York: Manchester University
            Press and Africana Publishing.
Louis, R.
1963   *Ruanda-Urundi, 1884–1919*. Oxford: Clarendon Press.
Lugan, B.
1978   "L'église catholique au Rwanda., 1900–1976." *Etudes Rwandaises* 11,
            numéro spécial (March): 69–75.
Macfarlane, A.
1979   *The Origins of English Individualism*. New York: Cambridge Univer-
            sity Press.
MacGaffey, W.
1981   "African Ideology and Belief: A Survey." *African Studies Review* 24, nos.
            2–3:227–74.
MacGaffey, W.
1983   *Modern Kongo Prophets*. Bloomington: Indiana University Press.
de Mahieu, W.
1985   *Qui a obstrué la cascade*. Cambridge: Cambridge University Press.
Maindron, G.
1984   *Des apparitions à Kibeho*. Paris: O.E.I.L.
Maine, H.
1884   *Ancient Law*. Reprint of tenth edition. Gloucester, Mass.: Peter
            Smith, 1970.
Manning, P., and H. Fabrega
1973   "The Experience of Self and Body: Health and Illness in the Chiapas
            Highlands." In *Phenomenological Sociology*, edited by G. Psathas, 251–
            301. New York: John Wiley.
Maquet, J.
1954   *Le système des relations sociales dans le Ruanda ancien*. Tervuren: Musée
            Royal de l'Afrique Centrale.
Marwick, M.
1965   *Sorcery in Its Social Setting: A Study of Northern Rhodesia Cewa*.
            Manchester: Manchester University Press.
Marx, K.
1867   *Capital*, Vol. 1. Reprint. New York: Random House, 1977.
Mauss, M.
1925   *The Gift*. Reprint. New York: W. W. Norton, 1967.
Mbarutso, E.
1982   "Aspects socio-culturels en rapport de la santé et de la maladie." In *Santé
            et Maladies au Rwanda*, edited by A. Meheus et al., 85–93. Brussels: Ad-
            ministration Générale de la Coopération au Développement.
Morris, I.
1986   "Gift and Commodity in Archaic Greece," *Man*, n.s., 21, no. 1:1–17.
Muzungu, B.
1974   *Le Dieu de nos pères*. Bujumbura, Burundi: Presses Lavigerie.
Ndekezi, S.
n.d.   *Ubukwe bw'abanyarwanda*. Kigali: n.p.
Newbury, D.
1981   "The Clans of Rwanda: A Historical Hypothesis." In *La civilisation
            ancienne des peuples des Grands Lacs*, edited by L. Ndoricimpa et al.,

186–97. Colloque de Bujumbura, September 4–10, 1979. Paris: Karthala.

Newbury, M. C.
1974   "Deux lignages du Kinyaga." *Cahiers d'Etudes Africaines* 14, no. 53:26–38.

Newbury, M. C.
1978   "Ethnicity in Rwanda: The Case of Kinyaga." *Africa* 48, no. 1:17–29.

Newbury, M. C.
1988   *The Cohesion of Oppression: Clientship and Ethnicity in Rwanda, 1860–1960.* New York: Columbia University Press.

Van Noten, F., and J. Raymaekers
1988   "Early Iron Smelting in Central Africa." *Scientific American* (June): 104–11.

Nwafor, J.
1977   "Les problèmes de planification du développement agricole au Rwanda." *Environnement africain,* 2, no. 1:89–98.

Ortigues, M. C., and E. Ortigues
1973   *Oedipe africain.* Paris: Plon.

Packard, R.
1981   *Chiefship and Cosmology.* Bloomington: Indiana University Press.

Parry, J.
1986   "The Gift, the Indian Gift, and the 'Indian Gift.'" *Man,* n.s., 21, no. 3:453–73.

Pauwels, M.
1949   "La magie au Ruanda." *Grands Lacs* 1, no. 123 (October): 17–48.

Pauwels, M.
1951   "Le culte de Nyabingi (Ruanda)." *Anthropos* 46, nos. 3–4:337–57.

Polanyi, K.
1944   *The Great Transformation.* Boston: Beacon Press.

Roberts, A.
1984   "Religion and Political Economy among Colonized Tabwa." *Africa* 54, no. 2:49–70.

Rodegem, F.
1970   *Dictionnaire Rundi-Français.* Tervuren: Musée Royal de l'Afrique Centrale, Sciences Humaines, no. 69.

Rwabukumba, J., and V. Mudandagizi
1974   "Les formes historiques de la dépendance personnelle dans l'état rwandais." *Cahiers d'Etudes Africaines* 14, no. 53:6–25.

Sacks, K.
1979   "Causality and Chance on the Upper Nile." *American Ethnologist* 6, no. 3:437–48.

Sahlins, M.
1972   *Stone Age Economics.* Chicago: Aldine Publishing.

Sahlins, M.
1981   *Historical Metaphors and Mythical Realities.* Ann Arbor: ASAO Special Publications 1, University of Michigan Press.

Sahlins, M.
1985   *Islands of History.* Chicago: University of Chicago Press.

Sapir, D.
1977   "The Anatomy of Metaphor." In *The Social Use of Metaphor,* edited
                by D. Sapir and J. C. Crocker, 3–32. Philadelphia: University of Penn-
                sylvania Press.
Scarry, E.
1985   *The Body in Pain.* New York: Oxford University Press.
Schneider, D.
1968   *American Kinship.* Englewood Cliffs, N.J.: Prentice-Hall.
Silverman, M.
1979   "Dependency, Mediation and Class Formation in Rural Guyana." *Ameri-
                can Ethnologist* 6, no. 3:466–90.
Silvestre, V.
1974   "Différenciations socio-économiques dans une société à vocation égali-
                taire: Masaka dans le paysannat de l'Icyanya." *Cahiers d'Etudes Afric-
                aines* 14, no. 53:104–69.
Smith, A.
1776   *The Wealth of Nations.* Reprint. Chicago: University of Chicago Press,
                1976.
Smith, P.
1970   "La Forge de l'intelligence." *L'Homme* 10, no. 2:5–21.
Smith, P.
1975   *Le récit populaire au Rwanda.* Paris: Armand Colin.
Smith, P.
1979a   "Aspects de l'organisation des rites." In *La fonction symbolique,* edited by
                M. Izard and P. Smith, 103–28. Paris: Gallimard.
Smith, P.
1979b   "L'efficacité des interdits." *L'Homme* 19, no. 1:5–47.
Smith, P.
1985   "Aspects de l'esthétique au Rwanda." *L'Homme* 25, no. 4:7–21.
Tambiah, S.
1973   "Form and Meaning of Magical Acts: A Point of View." In *Modes of
                Thought,* edited by R. Horton and R. Finnegan, 199–229. London: Faber
                and Faber.
Taussig, M.
1977   "The Genesis of Capitalism Amongst a South American Peasantry: Devil's
                Labor and the Baptism of Money." *Comparative Studies in Society and
                History* 19, no. 2:130–50.
Taussig, M.
1980a   *The Devil and Commodity Fetishism in South America.* Chapel Hill: Uni-
                versity of North Carolina Press.
Taussig, M.
1980b   "Reification and the Consciousness of the Patient." *Social Science and
                Medicine* 14B, no. 1:3–13.
Thomas, K.
1971   *Religion and the Decline of Magic.* New York: Charles Scribner's Sons.
Turner, V.
1967   *The Forest of Symbols.* Ithaca, N.Y.: Cornell University Press.
Turner, V.
1969   *The Ritual Process.* Ithaca, N.Y.: Cornell University Press.

Vansina, J.
1962   "L'évolution du royaume Rwandais des origines à 1900." *Cahiers Interna-*
            tionaux de Sociologie 43:143–58.
Vansina, J.
1983   "Is Elegance Proof? Structuralism and African History." *History in Africa*
            10:307–48.
Vidal, C.
1969   "Le Rwanda des anthropologues ou le fétichisme de la vache." Excerpt
            from R. Botte et al., "Les relations personnelles de subordination dans les
            sociétés interlacustres de l'Afrique centrale." *Cahiers d'Etudes Africaines*
            9, no. 3:350–401.
Vidal, C.
1974   "De la contradiction sauvage." *L'Homme* 14, nos. 3–4:5–58.
Vidal, C.
1978   "Les anthropologues ne pensent pas tout seuls." *L'Homme* 18, no.
            3–4:111–122.
Wagner, R.
1975   *The Invention of Culture.* Chicago: University of Chicago Press.
Wagner, R.
1986   *Symbols That Stand for Themselves.* Chicago: University of Chicago Press.
Walker, S.
1979   "Women in the Harrist Movement." In *The New Religions of Africa,* ed-
            ited by B. Jules-Rosette, 87–97. Norwood N.J.: Ablex Publishing.
Wallerstein, I.
1976   *The Modern World System.* Text edition. New York: Academic Press.
West, M.
1975   *Bishops and Prophets in a Black City.* Cape Town: David Philip.
Zempleni, A.
1975   "De la persécution à la culpabilité." In *Prophétisme et thérapeutique,* ed-
            ited by J. Rouch et al., 153–218. Paris: Hermann.
Zempleni, A., and N. Sindzingre.
1981   "Modèles et pragmatique, activation et répétition: Reflexions sur la cau-
            salité de la maladie chez les Senoufo de Côte d'Ivoire." *Social Science and*
            Medicine 15B, no. 3:279–293.

Index